Communication in Health Organizations

Communication in Health Organizations

JULIE APKER

polity

The right of Julie Apker to be identified as Author of this Work has been
asserted in accordance with the UK Copyright, Designs and Patents Act 1988.

First published in 2012 by Polity Press

Polity Press
65 Bridge Street
Cambridge CB2 1UR, UK

Polity Press
350 Main Street
Malden, MA 02148, USA

ISBN-13: 978-0-7456-4754-8
ISBN-13: 978-0-7456-4755-5 (pb)

A catalogue record for this book is available from the British Library.

Typeset in 9.5 on 12.5 pt FF Scala
by Servis Filmsetting Ltd, Stockport, Cheshire
Printed and bound in Great Britain by MPG Books Group Limited, Bodmin,
Cornwall

The publisher has used its best endeavours to ensure that the URLs for
external websites referred to in this book are correct and active at the time of
going to press. However, the publisher has no responsibility for the websites
and can make no guarantee that a site will remain live or that the content is or
will remain appropriate.

Every effort has been made to trace all copyright holders, but if any have been
inadvertently overlooked the publisher will be pleased to include any necessary
credits in any subsequent reprint or edition.

For further information on Polity, visit our website: www.politybooks.com

Contents

Detailed Table of Contents

Figures and Tables

Acknowledgments

There are a number of people I wish to thank for their contributions to *Communication in Health Organizations*. The team at Polity for their assistance in the book development and production process: Lauren Mulholland, Clare Ansell, Tim Clark, and Susan Beer. I'm particularly grateful to Polity editor Andrea Drugan for her ongoing encouragement of the project and her helpful editorial feedback. My thanks also to Marianne Rutter and Breffni O'Connor for their promotional help.

Several scholars provided valuable commentary on the content and format of the book: Katherine Miller, Texas A&M University; Lisa Sparks, Chapman University; Shelly Rodgers, University of Missouri; Laura Ellingson, Santa Clara University; Kevin Real, University of Kentucky; Eileen Berlin Ray, Cleveland State University; Lynn Harter, Ohio University and Peter Northouse, Western Michigan University.

This book was made possible thanks to the time afforded by a sabbatical leave. I am grateful for the support of the School of Communication, College of Arts and Sciences, and Western Michigan University.

My thanks to research assistants Stephanie Ruhl and Caitlin Evans for researching literature, reviewing drafts, and providing ideas for the book's pedagogical features.

I am deeply grateful for the ongoing encouragement of my husband, Rod Phares, who was an important sounding board and source of social support as I wrote the book. I also thank our daughters, Margaret and Eliza, for their understanding of the many hours I needed to research and write. Their love of learning continues to inspire me.

Introduction

Students in the communication courses I teach often ask me, "Why study communication in health organizations?" While there are many answers to this question, the main reason is that the communication in these contexts influences human lives in profound ways, by affecting health and well-being. Perhaps the most visible example of this is the patient who turns to a health institution during a vulnerable moment. Patients depend on health professionals to display clear, timely, accurate, and responsive communication. A communication failure can have serious results and perhaps even life or death consequences.

The importance of communication in health organizations extends beyond the patient's bedside. For those who work in health professions, good communication builds cohesive, positive work environments. Bad communication creates barriers that reduce the quality of work life and job satisfaction. Negative communication experiences can ultimately affect healthcare delivery (e.g., turnover, staff shortage). For the public, communication in health organizations produces credible and reliable information that can be used to raise awareness of illness, disease, and wellness. This data can help consumers make more informed health decisions about treatment and prevention.

Communication in health organizations spans a wide range of topics and levels of interaction. Here are a few examples:

- A diverse yet cohesive hospital team communicates to solve a complicated medical problem.
- The use of an electronic medical record (EMR) allows a

physician to quickly access information from a specialist at another institution during a patient crisis.

- A health organization's leader struggles with communicating changes that will dramatically affect quality of work life for her employees.
- A social worker seeks mentorship and social support from supervisors and colleagues to ease the strain of job burnout.

After reading this book, you will know more about the communication principles, processes, and behaviors present in United States health organizations. Using the systems approach of organizational communication, you will gain greater familiarity with how health institutions function communicatively and why the people who work in health professions interact as they do. You will be able to analyze communication occurring in health organizations and apply communication skills to health organization experiences. This knowledge may enable you to improve your own communication as a patient, employee, or consumer and, ultimately, enhance communication in health organizations.

This introduction will define the characteristics of organizations, describe the role of communication, explain the systems approach, and preview chapter topics.

Definitional Issues

Organizations take many forms and have multiple purposes. Your personal experience with various types of organizations may include: a company that you work for, a non-profit organization where you volunteer, or an online organization from which you make regular purchases or that advocates for social issues you consider important. Despite their differences, these organizations share several common themes.

Organizational communication researcher Katherine Miller (2009) offers five defining features of organizations. First, organizations are **social** entities that consist of two or more people who are organizational members. Second, these individuals participate in activities that require **coordination** or synchronization. Third, organizational members' activities create and maintain **structure**, such as vertical hierarchies or flat, collaborative teams. Structure explicates who is in charge of particular responsibilities, who reports to whom, the priority of actions, etc. Fourth, organizational members work to achieve individual and organizational **goals**. Finally, organizations are situated within an **embedded environment** consisting of other organizations, and varied social, economic, and political forces.

Organizational communication consists of the dynamic interactions used to accomplish goals that satisfy individual and/or collective needs (Jablin and Putnam, 2001). **Health communication** is the "symbolic processes by which people, individually and collectively, understand, shape, and accommodate health and illness" (Geist-Martin, Ray, and Sharf, 2003, p. 3). Taken together, **organizational health communication** refers to the individual and collective communicative behaviors that constitute health organizations.

To summarize, organizations are complex, dynamic entities inextricably intertwined with the greater environment, and communication plays a central role in organizing healthcare processes. Next, you will learn more about the systems approach, including theoretical principles, evolution in organizational studies, and key concepts.

Systems Principles and Evolution

The systems approach is an enduring framework in organizational studies useful to understanding complex entities such as health organizations (Ray and Donohew, 1990; Wright, Sparks, and O'Hair, 2008). A **system** is a set of components, typically people, which interrelate with one another through sending and receiving messages. The interactions of these components form **subsystems**, such as work teams and departments, which form system structure. System components, and thus the system itself, form relationships with the embedded environment (Deetz, 2000).

Consider HealthWest, a large, comprehensive medical practice in the Southwest that has multiple components and subsystems:

clinical (physicians and nurses representing different medical specialties), administrative (finance workers, medical record clerks) and service (receptionists, customer service employees). Working together, the subsystems form an overarching structure that cares for patients. In addition to forming internal relationships, HealthWest employees develop connections with people from outside the organization. For instance, physicians and nurses provide care to patients; receptionists take external phone calls to book appointments and answer questions; and billing clerks talk with insurance representatives about medical claims. HealthWest's internal and external openness allows the organization to work effectively and, ultimately, promote its survival.

The systems approach originated in biology and engineering and was later used in other academic disciplines. Ludwig von Bertalanffy (1968) developed **general systems theory** to explore the interrelationships which constitute biological organisms (such as human beings) and to investigate the connections linking an organism to its environment. Bertalanffy argued that systems principles could also inform understandings of non-biological systems.

In the 1970s and 1980s, researchers in organizational studies used systems theory principles to better understand social relations and structures of organizations (Deetz, 2000). Scholars recognized its utility for describing how organizations function at multiple levels. At the broad interorganizational level or macro-level, systems principles explain how organizations interrelate with environmental contingencies. The systems approach also provides a micro-level perspective that examines how complex, interrelated components such as dyads and groups function in organizations. The range of ideas associated with systems theory also supplied scholars with a rich, conceptual vocabulary to more fully explain the intricacies of organizational life.

Systems Approach in Organizational Communication

The systems approach has been particularly influential on the study of organizational communication. Papa, Daniels, and Spiker

(2008) argue that a systems perspective sheds new light on the organizing role of communication. As they explain, "communication is not merely an activity that occurs "within" an organization, nor is it merely a tool for managerial control. Rather, all of the human processes that define an organization arise from communication . . . The linkages and connections among subsystems depend on communication and information flow" (p. 109).

Modaff, DeWine, and Butler (2008) take this argument a step further, identifying specific communication functions inherent to organizational systems:

- **Constitutive function**: Communication creates connections and acts as a binder that allows the system to coordinate activities and integrate components into a unified whole.
- **Adaptive function**: Feedback allows organizations to adapt to environmental change. Individuals who perform boundary spanning take center stage, giving and receiving information between the organizational system and the environment.
- **Maintenance function**: Communication provides information throughout organizational systems to ensure a dynamic steady state.

The systems approach has a substantial research history that informs our understanding of many different types of organizations. A systems approach to organizational communication theorizes that interactions form necessary components and relationships that promote organizations' existence. Let's take a closer look at specific systems concepts relevant to the study of organizational communication.

Systems Concepts

The systems perspective has a robust conceptual vocabulary designed to articulate the complexities of organizations. This section discusses relevant systems ideas and provides one extended health organization example. See Table 1 for a summary of systems concepts, definitions, and health organization examples.

Table I Systems Concepts, Definitions, and Health Organization Examples

Systems Term	Definition	Example
System and subsystems	A set of components, typically people, which interrelate with one another through sending and receiving messages. The interactions of these components create interrelationships that form subsystems.	A home healthcare organization's employees communicate to coordinate tasks and scheduling, with individuals who work in related areas (e.g., clinical care, administration) communicating with each other the most. These interactions reinforce departmental (subsystem) structure.
Openness	Component permeability allows messages and other sources of information to flow throughout and between the system and the embedded environment.	A community health clinic's leaders hold regular "town hall" meetings with the public to assess citizens' needs for health services.
Contingencies	Social, economic, and political forces present in the embedded environment that influence system functioning.	A community's rapidly growing elderly population creates heightened demand for gerontology care, causing a medical group to add several gerontologists to its roster of staff physicians.
Interdependence	The reliance that system components have with one another, creating interrelationships necessary to the system.	Data sharing between a public health institution's communication, research, and clinical departments in order to provide the public with accurate, timely, comprehensive health information.
Holism	System components work together to form a unified whole, forming complex reactions based on the interactions of components.	A hospital's provision of patient care typically involving multiple units (e.g., nursing services, various medical specialties, lab studies and testing).

Input-Throughput-Output	Messages and other sources of data enter the system from the embedded environment, are altered by components for system use, and leave the system as an end product.	Patients describe symptoms and communicate medical history during ED visits. ED staff uses this information to form a clinical impression and provide treatment. Patients leave the ED with improved health.
Feedback	Responses obtained internally (from system components) and/or externally (from the embedded environment) that enable a system to self-regulate.	A hospice conducts an employee satisfaction survey to assess employee perceptions about work (internal feedback). The hospice also surveys patients' families to gain impressions of care quality (external feedback). Both sets of feedback are used in organizational improvements.
Goals	The individual and collective aims of system components that tend to organize system activities.	A retail pharmacy's organizational mission is to "provide quality, affordable, and accessible care to patients." Employees' personal goals support this mission (e.g., achieving 100% patient satisfaction).
Order	The complex arrangement of components and subsystems within a system. Also refers to how a system fits into the greater supersystem of which it is a part.	A mental health clinic consisting of multiple therapeutic specializations. Workers report to unit middle-managers, who in turn report to the clinic's director. The clinic is one facility in the larger mental health industry.
Dynamic homeostasis	A system's ability to maintain a steady state while simultaneously adapting to change.	Several staff hygienists leave a dental practice simultaneously. To handle the immediate effects of the shortage, the dentists who own the practice add temporary hygienists while searching for long-term hires.

Openness refers to component permeability in which messages and other sources of information flow throughout the system and between the system and its embedded environment. Openness creates linkages that are vital to system functioning. To illustrate the concept of openness, let's consider the example of Jack, an elderly patient with a history of heart problems, who arrives in the Metro Hospital emergency department (ED) suffering from heart failure. Jack's family communicates his past medical history and current symptoms to physicians. After stabilizing Jack's condition, an ED physician contacts an internal medicine physician (hospitalist) to admit Jack for further testing and treatment. The open communication between the ED physician and hospitalist forms a critical link in Jack's care continuum as he transfers between different caregivers and hospital units.

Contingencies are the forces in the embedded environment that can influence system functioning. The systems perspective tells us that organizations must adapt and respond to contingencies in order to survive. For example, Jack went to Metro Hospital because of its reputation for quality cardiac care. Metro developed this specialization after determining that a gap in cardiac care existed in the community so that patients were being sent to hospitals many hours away. Metro doubled the size of its cardiac facilities, purchased state-of-the-art equipment, and hired a leading cardiac team to spearhead clinical care.

Interdependence refers to the system components that rely on each other, which creates interrelationships necessary for system functioning. The internal medicine physicians and nurses involved in Jack's care relied on ED clinical staff for information about Jack's condition. Conversely, the ED staff relied on the internal medicine caregivers to arrange for Jack's timely transfer to the inpatient floor in order to free up ED bed space for other patients with emergencies. The ED and inpatient staff coordinated care processes to achieve shared goals.

Holism occurs when system components work together interdependently to form a unified whole, forming complex reactions based on the interactions of components. Jack's heart failure required the ED staff to work together quickly and effectively.

Triage nurses and physicians received information from Jack's family and moved Jack immediately into an ED bed without wait time. Assistant personnel had prepared a clean and fully equipped bed space, which was ready with no delays. Nurses took Jack's vital signs, executed physician orders, and comforted his family while physicians determined a clinical diagnosis and began treatment.

Input-Throughput-Output is a process in which messages and other sources of data come into the system from the embedded environment as inputs, are altered by components for system use (throughput), and leave the system as an end product or output. Jack enters Metro Hospital with an emergency care need. ED staff use information provided in triage, along with data communicated in subsequent clinical assessment and workup, to sufficiently stabilize Jack's condition prior to inpatient admission. Days later, a much healthier Jack leaves the hospital with home nursing care.

Feedback refers to responses obtained internally (from system components) and/or externally (from the embedded environment) that enable a system to self-regulate. Feedback has a number of useful functions. First, feedback corrects a system when it deviates from the accepted status quo (**corrective feedback**). Second, feedback enhances a system by promoting efforts that further improve upon its current state (**amplifying feedback**). Finally, feedback provides opportunities for **sensemaking** about inputs brought into a system that can cause uncertainty (Weick, 1979). System components seek and give feedback to make sense of uncertain situations.

When he arrives in the ED, Jack's health status immediately conveys the message that his condition requires urgent medical attention. ED clinicians make sense of Jack's physical signs and communication, deciding to move him from the waiting room to an ED bed. Their ability to quickly secure an appropriate ED bed space is the result of housekeeping's efforts to "turn" or make a bed ready for a new patient. Housekeeping staff implemented this policy following negative feedback that ED room cleaning had become slower than was acceptable (corrective feedback). Positive reinforcement in the form of praise and appreciation by ED nurses has motivated housekeeping staff to continuously improve their work (amplifying feedback). For instance, they brainstorm ways to cut turn time without sacrificing quality (sensemaking).

Goals are the individual and collective aims of system components that organize system activities. System components use communication to achieve goals. The collective goal of Metro Hospital is to provide Jack with quality care. Each system component (nurses, physicians, and others) may have specific individual goals as well. For example, given the emergent nature of ED care, the ED physician may be oriented to short-term care that reduces or eliminates the health crisis. The hospitalist who admits Jack will most likely be concerned about Jack's long-term care on the inpatient floor, which is under internal medicine supervision.

Order is the complex arrangement of components and subsystems. Metro Hospital is able to deliver quality care to Jack through the collaboration of multiple subsystems such as the ED, inpatient care, cardiac care, laboratory and testing services, among others. Each subsystem has its own hierarchical reporting structure consisting of upper-level leaders, mid-level managers, and entry-level and/or front-line workers. The subsystems form clinical, support service, and administrative divisions that ultimately make up the hospital's overall system structure.

Dynamic homeostasis is the final systems concept, referring to a system's ability to maintain a steady state while simultaneously adapting to change. The resilience of a system can be found in its ability to respond and/or adapt to changes in the environment. Communication among components and subsystems provides information to ensure homeostasis. For instance, Metro Hospital faces an inpatient nursing shortage due to nurse turnover. Jack's floor lacks several permanent nurses, and in the short term, the hospital fills the gap with temporary staff and nurse floaters (staff who rotate to different units). Metro's leaders have also instituted long-term changes to improve nurse working conditions, such as enhancing nurse–physician communication and recognizing nurses' achievements throughout the hospital in formal and informal statements of appreciation. The hospital maintains a steady level of nurse staffing even during times of nurse shortage.

Thus far, you've gained a familiarity with systems' principles and concepts. These ideas provide the foundation for what you will learn about communication in health organizations.

Chapter-by-Chapter Summary

Chapter 1: Landscape of Healthcare Delivery

Chapter 1 begins by discussing the economic, social, and demographic contingencies influencing communication in health organizations. The chapter summarizes models of health and illness, healthcare contexts, as well as traditional forms (e.g., fee-for-service) and contemporary forms (e.g., managed care) of healthcare delivery. The chapter elaborates on communication in the managed care era, describing the different levels of communication in health organizations. Chapter 1 concludes by considering the different organizational contexts that comprise healthcare provision and public health in the U.S.

Chapter 2: Organizational Assimilation

Chapter 2 starts with an overview of health professions before examining the communication processes by which health professionals learn "the ropes" of their occupations and become familiar with institutional employers. After reviewing foundational issues pertaining to assimilation, you will consider the formal and informal processes and behaviors health workers use to transition into organizations. The chapter explores work roles in the assimilation experience, considering the individual behaviors and team dynamics that influence role enactment.

Chapter 3: Identity and Power

Chapter 3 begins by considering identity and identification from a systems perspective. Then, you will learn about key messages and important referent groups that develop and shape identity through the process of identification. The second half of the chapter focuses on power by first taking a systems approach. You will also learn about the intersecting dynamics of power, control, and ideology and how this influences communication in health organizations.

Chapter 4: Stress, Burnout, and Social Support

Professionals working in health organizations commonly experience multiple role and workplace stressors as part of performing their jobs. Chapter 4 considers major system contingencies that contribute to stress in health organizations. The chapter then overviews specific stressors and identifies the individual and organizational outcomes of chronic occupational strain, also known as burnout. Chapter 4 concludes by examining supportive communication processes in the healthcare professions.

Chapter 5: Change and Leadership

Health organizations are constantly transforming as they anticipate and respond to shifting contingences. Chapter 5 explores major changes affecting health organizations, responses to change, and the communication processes that enhance change adoption. Health system change creates a need for people who can lead successfully during organizational transformation. As such, this chapter examines the challenges facing health leaders, foundational leadership theories that inform their leadership behaviors, and attributes of effective leader communication.

Chapter 6: Health Teams

Health teams play an important role in healthcare delivery and public health. Today's health teams vary in size, professional composition, goals, and structure, features that add to the health organizations' complexity. Understanding teams requires exploring their defining qualities and health communication activities. Chapter 6 also considers team synergy and conflict before taking a closer look at health team diversity. You will learn about cultural variables that affect teamwork and culturally competent communication.

Chapter 7: Health Organization Quality

Even though patients expect safe, high-quality care, and health organizations and professionals work hard to meet these expectations, quality problems do exist throughout the nation's health system. Chapter 7 explores the role of communication in quality-improvement efforts and considers quality as an important part of organizational culture. The chapter focuses on safety and patient-centeredness, two areas in which communication figures prominently.

Chapter 8: Health Communication Technologies

Advances in communication have dramatically altered communication in health organizations. Chapter 8 describes the major forms of health communication technologies and discusses how these innovations have affected health communication contexts, processes, and relationships. The chapter explores how communication technologies have been a factor in health globalization, especially in efforts to promote public health efforts worldwide.

Pedagogical Features

Each chapter presents two types of applications that encourage you to analyze, discuss, and relate concepts and skills to health organization experiences. First, "Communication in Practice" provides applied principles and strategies for enhancing communication skills in health organizations. Second, "Ripped from the Headlines" describes real media accounts of selected chapter topics and poses questions for reflection and discussion.

Summary

Health organizations play an important and unique role in our lives, as patients, as employees or members, and as consumers of health information. Health organizations share the defining characteristics of organizations: they are social, goal-oriented, structured, coordinated, and function in an embedded environ-ment. Communication constitutes these characteristics and makes health organizing possible.

This book takes a systems approach to understanding commu-nication in health organizations. The systems approach provides multiple views of organizational life, examining micro-processes occurring within internal organizational relationships as well as investigating the macro-processes taking place in relationships between a health organization and its embedded environment. Communication is central to these internal and external connec-tions. Communication creates organizational linkages to form a unified whole as well as enables organizations to adapt to change while maintaining a dynamic steady state. Using the systems principles and concepts presented in this Introduction, you will learn more about the complexities of communication in health organizations in subsequent chapters. To begin your investigation, in Chapter 1 you will explore the contingencies and contexts that make up the health system landscape.

1

Landscape of Healthcare Delivery

As I write this chapter, the United States is revisiting healthcare reform, a policy debate that has arisen in each of the past six decades. The current national discussion is perhaps best characterized as intense and contentious, with members of the public and elected officials arguing passionately about the goals, structures, and processes of healthcare delivery. Everyone seems to have an opinion on healthcare reform—from the political pundits who dominate talk shows and virtual spaces to the citizens who actively participate in town halls and public meetings occurring nationwide.

As an organizational health communication researcher, I'm fascinated by the discourse of healthcare reform and accompanying civic engagement. Most people agree that the current health system does not work well enough to achieve affordable, quality, and accessible healthcare. The agreement ends when discussion of how to accomplish these goals begins. Messages such as "moral obligation," "universal coverage," "socialized medicine," and "rationing," grab public attention and stimulate difficult conversations at all levels of American society. Talk about how to reform the health system inherently involves examination of our cultural values and brings to the surface deep-seeded assumptions about how the world works. While lawmakers continue to hash out the legislative details, the debate over healthcare reform is far from over. The U.S. will continue to face challenging decisions with no easy answers.

This chapter addresses the complex landscape of the U.S. health system—the contingencies, delivery forms, and contexts—which are in constant transformation. Ongoing change requires structural and communication adaptations by health organizations and their members which ultimately affects patients and consumers. By understanding the environment of healthcare delivery and the role of communication within health organizing, health professionals, patients, and consumers may be better able to communicate in the health system.

This chapter focuses on the complicated environment in which U.S. health organizations are embedded. Chapter 1 begins by exploring major economic, social, and demographic contingencies that influence communication in health organizations. The chapter then examines models of health and illness, health organization contexts, and forms of health organizing.

A Systems Perspective on the Healthcare Environment

This book takes a systems approach to understanding health organizations and uses systems concepts throughout its chapters to explore key issues and processes in health organizational communication. In this chapter, you will learn more about **system contingences**, which are forces in the embedded environment that influence system functioning (Table 1.1). Health institutions must remain open to these forces and respond with dynamic changes in communication structures and processes.

Economic Contingencies

Cost and **access** to healthcare are two major priorities of the health system. Regarding cost, the U.S. has the most expensive health system in the world and its health expenditures continue to skyrocket. The following trends demonstrate the problem's magnitude:

- Health spending has exceeded $2 trillion since 2007 and is projected to reach $4.4 trillion by 2018 (more than 20% of GDP) (Centers for Medicare and Medicaid, 2008; Kaiser Family Foundation 2009).

Table 1.1 Health System Contingencies

Contingency	Description and Communication Interdependencies
Economic affordability	Care costs escalate and consume higher percentages of overall spending for governments, employers, and individuals. Demands for cost containment force health organizations to do more with less, resulting in altered communication due to speed ups, staff reductions, and changing roles.
access	Millions of Americans lack access to care because they are uninsured or can't pay out-of-pocket. Lacking ability to pay causes more patients to seek care from safety-net organizations, often putting stress on resources and staff. These pressures exacerbate poor communication.
social consumerism	Trends include demands for greater flexibility and convenience as well as for communication behaviors that improve patient satisfaction. Health organizations have altered their communication to meet these needs (e.g., varied care locations, interactions that heighten patient satisfaction).
prevention	Preventative medicine is less costly than curative approaches yet can require more complex, multi-level communication responses from health organizations. Prevention necessitates heightened teamwork among caregivers as well as consistent and long-term communication with patients.
demographic aging population	Americans are living longer and, as they age, they require more health services. Heightened demand means that members of health organizations will need to adapt their communication to meet the needs of those over 65 and emphasize communication about prevention.
racial and ethnic changes	Rising numbers of health workers and patients come from diverse racial and ethnic groups. Health organizations will need to bolster employees' cultural communication competence and increase diversity initiatives and programs.

- From 2005 to 2009, healthcare costs for a family of four rose from $12,214 to $16,771 (37%) (U.S. News and World Report, 2009).
- Annual healthcare spending per person increased from $6,687 in 2005 to $7,420 in 2009, an 11% increase (Centers for Medicare and Medicaid, 2008).

Several factors contribute to rapidly escalating costs: 1) advancements in medical technology; 2) the population growth of those over 65 years of age and subsequent increase in chronic and/or intensive care needs; 3) rising rates of uninsured and underinsured patients whose healthcare costs are passed along in the form of higher insurance premiums; 4) emphasis on medical specialization, which fragments care and adds to unnecessary duplication of services across multiple caregivers and; 5) reimbursement system incentives that reward curative medicine rather than prevention (Sultz and Young, 2009).

Cost is an economic contingency that profoundly affects communication in health organizations. Cost contingencies place heightened pressures on caregivers to do more with less and even speed up care. Faced with an increased workload and reduced institutional support, those working in health organizations may reduce or even stop all nonessential communication. Apker (2001) found that hospital changes brought about by cost containment efforts reduce nurse–patient communication as well as decrease the nurse–team communication that leads to group cohesion.

The next economic contingency to explore is access, a topic that closely relates to cost. Health insurance coverage is an important determinant of access to healthcare (Institute of Medicine [IOM], 2001). An estimated 47 million Americans either lack insurance or have inadequate insurance, with a disproportionate number represented by the poor and people of color (Sultz and Young, 2009). According to the National Center for Health Statistics (2008), major disparities exist by socioeconomic status, race/ethnicity, and insurance status. Such as:

- People of color make up more than two-thirds of the uninsured population.
- Individuals with incomes less than twice the poverty level are likely to have no health insurance coverage.
- Uninsured children and adults under 65 years of age are substantially less likely to have a primary source of healthcare than those insured.
- Persons living in poverty are considerably less likely to use healthcare services, conditions which can result in reduced quality of life and shorter life spans.

Lack of access to care is a contingency that affects communication in health organizations. Consider the dilemma faced by health safety-net organizations (e.g., public hospitals, federally funded community health centers) that are "legally obligated to provide care to persons who cannot afford it" and, consequently, are common sources of care for people without health insurance (Gresenz, Rogowski, and Escarce, 2007, p. 240). The needs of millions of uninsured Americans have increased stress on safety-net organizations in ways that affect care quality, caregiver communication, and resource availability (IOM, 2006; 2009).

The circumstances experienced by many public hospital EDs provide an exemplar of these problems. Rising numbers of patients use EDs for their care needs, a phenomenon often attributed to poor access. Elevated patient demand often creates overcrowded ED conditions and an environment known for increasing communication barriers such as multitasking, interruptions, and distractions (Solet, Norvell, Rutan, and Frankel, 2005). These barriers hinder communication among caregivers in the form of information omissions, rushed interactions, etc. Ultimately, these problems exacerbate medical mistakes, treatment delays, and reduced care continuity.

Social and Demographic Contingencies

Multiple social and demographic contingencies have also altered the healthcare landscape. One notable social contingency is consumerism. **Consumerism** refers to attitudes, beliefs, and behaviors that commodify healthcare. This means that healthcare is sold in a competitive marketplace influenced by consumer expectations and supply and demand. For example, more and more health consumers demand flexibility and immediacy in care delivery (Wright, Sparks, and O'Hair, 2008). Health organizations have responded by providing patients with a wide range of options to receive health services. Patients receive medical care in traditional settings such as hospitals and physician offices as well as alternative contexts such as retail outlets and urgent care facilities. While the range of care outlets meets patient needs for convenience, it also complicates communication by increasing the number and variety of health encounters. Fragmented and inconsistent communication may result. To overcome such difficulties, patients and health professionals must display a wider repertoire of interaction skills and adapt to increasingly varied relationships (Miller and Ryan, 2001).

Consumerism has also encouraged health organizations to address patient satisfaction (Scalise, 2006). It is common practice for health organizations to survey patients about their satisfaction with care. Patients provide feedback about wait time, the physical environment, and caregiver communication, among many other factors. Health organizations use patient responses to identify institutional strengths and weaknesses and to make improvements. For example, a home health agency may implement communication training for clinicians whom patients identify as having a poor bedside manner. Or, a clinic may make changes to improve communication efficiency in response to patient dissatisfaction with long wait times.

The second social contingency is the heightened focus on prevention rather than curative medical care. **Prevention** typically involves holistic care that addresses behaviors, attitudes, beliefs, culture, and environmental conditions. It is now generally accepted that prevention improves patient quality of life and costs less than curative medical care. Thus, more organizations are implementing prevention as key parts of their health services. Prevention requires coordinated, consistent, and clear organizational communication.

Because prevention involves myriad factors, health professionals must work together to develop an approach that educates and empowers patients. Messages must be communicated by multiple caregivers throughout patients' encounters in the health system to maximize prevention effectiveness. Furthermore, prevention demands that clinicians communicate with patients on an ongoing basis, using targeted messages designed to meet patients' unique health circumstances (Office of Disease Prevention and Health Promotion, 2003).

The final contingency pertains to demographic shifts in the U.S. population. Societal changes affect national health needs and influence the demands made on health organizations. In regard to the **aging** population, the U.S. Census Bureau (2008) provides compelling projections. By the year 2030, nearly one in five U.S. residents is expected to be 65 or older, with persons over 85 years representing the fastest-growing sector. As people age they experience chronic physical ailments and long-term cognitive problems that require greater and more intensive health resources. Thus, the increase in the aging population means greater rates of care use.

Institutions and their employees have to make structural and process changes to meet priorities commensurate with the aging population (IOM, 2003a; 2003b), with communication figuring prominently in health system transformation. For instance, health professionals will need to become more knowledgeable about communicating with people over 65 years of age. Generational differences present in patient-caregiver interactions will require understanding and negotiation. In addition, health organizations must use more institutional resources to educate and support aging patients about avoiding illness and disease. Greater prevention efforts will demand open lines of communication as well as improved collaboration among health professionals throughout the health system and in healthcare teams.

The health system will also need to adapt to **racial and ethnic** changes in the U.S. population. Projections indicate that American society that will become increasingly diverse, with racial and ethnic minorities becoming the majority by 2050 (U.S. Census Bureau,

Box 1.1 Communication in Practice

Adapting Successfully to Health System Contingencies
The economic, social, and demographic contingencies presented in this chapter profoundly affect health organizations. Rather than viewing factors such as cost, access, and racial/ethnic disparities as overwhelming obstacles, members of health organizations could more usefully perceive these contingencies as continuous opportunities for innovation. Health services researcher Paul Plsek (2003) argues that health organizations can successfully adapt to system contingences by following principles such as:

Learning and adjusting on an ongoing basis.
Recognizing that innovations can come from anyone in the healthcare organization.
Taking local context conditions into account when executing innovation.
Avoiding a "one-size-fits-all" approach because organizational contexts differ; what works for one organization may not work for another.

According to Plsek, communication is a key factor in determining how successfully health institutions respond to contingencies. He underscores the importance of interactions occurring in organizational social networks and offers the following recommendations:

Identify natural social networks existing in organizations and the key opinion leaders within them.
Create and support mechanisms that encourage social networking.
Develop structures that reinforce creative thinking at all levels.

> Use communication technologies that encourage interaction within and across organizations so that people can easily engage in problem-solving with others.

2008). This trend will have implications for health organizations and their communication. First, it means that more patients will represent racial and ethnic groups. Second, there will be a greater pool of racial and ethnic minorities that may enter the health professions and work for health organizations. Patient and employee diversity requires health organizations to develop heightened cultural competence (see Chapter 6). Health organizations must show an ongoing commitment to practices and policies that support diverse groups. Initiatives include recruitment and retention programs for diverse employee populations, cultural communication competence training, and policies that reward diversity efforts (Moore and Thurston, 2008).

To summarize, the U.S. health system is undergoing a fundamental transformation due to economic, social, and demographic contingencies. While the ultimate outcome of these forces is unknown, health organizations will need to constantly anticipate and adapt to system change. In the next section, you will gain familiarity with another aspect of the health landscape: health models that influence perceptions of health and illness and guide care delivery.

Models of Health and Illness

Three models of health and illness—biomedical, biopsychosocial, and relationship-centered care—have been particularly influential in the health system. The models explain cultural beliefs about health and illness in ways that help ascertain the importance of symptoms and resulting use of medical resources (Wade and Halligan, 2004). This section describes each model and explores how they shape health organization communication.

Biomedical and Biopsychosocial Models

The biomedical and biopsychosocial models are traditional approaches that remain prominent in modern healthcare delivery. The **biomedical model** has provided a practical and philosophical framework for Westernized medicine for more than 100 years (Starr, 2004). Biomedicine asserts that ill health can be accounted for in terms of purely biological causes. Social, psychological, and behavioral reasons for illness are considered extraneous, confusing variables. Any behavioral deviations displayed by patients must be explained by biologic variables. Health professionals, usually physicians, employ principles of scientific method (e.g., objectivity, prediction, experimentation) to identify and treat illness (Engle, 1977).

For much of the twentieth century, biomedical principles were used not only in clinical decision-making and research, but to guide health policy, develop professional standards for occupations such as medicine, and maintain distinctions between care providers and recipients (Hafferty and Light, 1995). In health organizations, communication that is influenced by the biomedical model is concise and concentrates on biomedical information (Sarangi, 2004) as well as privileges caregivers who have high status and authority, such as physicians (Roter et al., 1997).

In the 1970s, health researchers and practitioners became dissatisfied with the biomedical model. There was a growing recognition that ill health may have social, psychological, and behavioral origins. Further, it was reasoned that involving patients' verbal accounts during medical encounters would provide information useful to diagnoses and treatment (Epstein et al., 2003). Soliciting such accounts requires changes in health organization communication, particularly on the part of physicians, to heighten rapport-building and increase give-and-take in patient-caregiver interactions.

The **biopsychosocial model** integrates mind and body in order to better identify, explain, and treat illness (Frankel and Quill, 2005). Rather than reducing ill health to biological causes, biopsychosocial medicine recognized that "illness is not solely a physical phenomenon but is also influenced by people's feelings, their ideas about health, and the events of their lives" (du Pre, 2005,

p. 11). Scientific method principles remain important, but other ways of knowing, such as patient narratives, also play an integral role in care. The biopsychosocial approach also encourages clinicians to explore alternatives for illness and treatment with patient participation. Like its predecessor, the biopsychosocial model has affected interactions occurring in health organizations, and particularly physician communication. Talk is considered central to patient care and involves discussion of social and psychological issues along with biological factors as contributors to illness (Sarangi, 2004). In biopsychosocial medicine, clinicians use the voice of the lifeworld—that is, discourse regarding patients' contextually based experiences of life events and problems (Mishler, 1984). This discourse fosters a greater understanding of how patients experience illness and establishes relational connections. Further, biopsychosocial communication allows for more give-and-take among healthcare professionals, active listening, and equitable distribution of talk time.

The biopsychosocial model addresses mind-body connections but does not sufficiently account for contextual factors present in the wider health environment that affect patient care. The relationship-centered model was developed to meet this need.

Relationship-Centered Care Model

The **relationship-centered care (RCC) model** is predicated on the belief that illness, health, and care occur in relational contexts. The health system's functions and activities are carried out and mediated by interdependent relationships between patient, clinician, team, organizations, and community. RCC is based on the following four principles (Cooper et al., 2006):

1. Relationships in healthcare should include the personhood of all participants.
2. Emotions and their expression are salient aspects of these relationships.
3. All relationships happen in the context of mutual, reciprocal influence.

4. The creation and maintenance of genuine relationships is morally valuable.

Rather than focusing on clinician-patient dyads like the biomedicine and biopsychosocial approaches, the RCC model applies to multiple forms of health relationships and interactions. For example, RCC proponents argue that caregiver relationships contribute in meaningful ways to caregiver well-being as well as patient health. The RCC model emphasizes that relationships between clinicians and key constituencies (e.g., patients, their families, members of the local community) are important to forming partnerships necessary for effective care (Safran, Miller and Beckman, 2006).

Effective RCC begins with what Epstein (1999; 2003) calls mindful practice, a reflexive process by which a person intentionally attends to personal thoughts and actions occurring in daily life events or tasks. He argues that mindfulness enables clinicians to become more self aware, to listen with greater attentiveness, show flexibility, recognize personal bias, and act with more compassion toward others. For instance, an ultrasound technician engages in mindful practice when he routinely monitors his thoughts and work practices rather than mindlessly performing procedures. Safran, Miller, and Beckman (2006) take the RCC model further, beyond dyad interactions (e.g., clinician-colleague, clinician-patient), by proposing a framework of relationship-centered organizations (Figure 1.1). These authors argue that health organizations consist of a web of communication relationships. Seven dimensions form the hub of relationship-centered organizing, helping to create collaborative and supportive cultures. Positive outcomes of relationship-centered care include heightened patient safety, reduced patient mortality, decreased worker turnover, and improved employee morale.

These models of health and illness are prototypes that provide general understandings of how people think and behave in health organizations. They influence how health professionals and patients interpret and talk about disease, symptoms, and treatment. With this knowledge, you have a greater sense of the fundamental influences that shape communication in health organizations. The

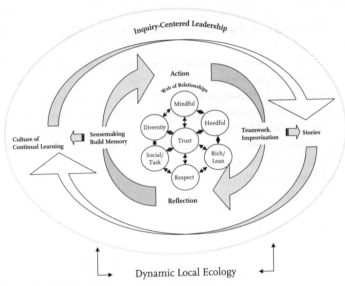

Figure 1.1   *A model of relationship-centered organizations.*
With kind permission from Springer Science and Business Media: *Journal of General Internal Medicine* Organizational dimension relationship-centered care 21, 2006, Safran, D.G., Miller, W., and Beckman, H.

remainder of this chapter builds on this foundation by addressing specific health organization contexts and forms of health delivery.

Health Organization Contexts

The health system consists of a vast and complex array of organizations. This section addresses two major areas that represent the majority of health organizations: healthcare providers and public health organizations.

Healthcare Provider Organizations

Healthcare provider organizations are entities that provide care to patients. Traditional examples include but are not limited to health professionals working in individual or group practices, hospitals,

Box 1.2   Communication in Practice

Improving Communication Using a Relationship-Centered Approach

According to Safran et al. (2006), collaborative, supportive communication promotes relationship-centered care (RCC). Relationship-centered environments contribute to high-performing organizations and yield a number of positive health outcomes. The seven RCC dimensions show that health professionals need a wide repertoire of communication skills, including:

Mindfulness

- Reflexive communication that simultaneously recognizes thoughts, beliefs, and the actions of self and others.
- Conveying an openness to alternative ideas and viewpoints.

Diversity of mental models

- Encouraging multiple perspectives.
- Using different viewpoints in decision-making and problem-solving.

Heedful interrelating

- Showing awareness of individual and group efforts.
- Displaying understanding of how combined efforts contribute to goals.

Rich and lean communication

- Selecting rich channels (e.g., face-to-face) for situations that are ambiguous, complex, and/or sensitive.

- Choosing lean channels (e.g., written forms) for clear, simple situations.

Social and task interactions

- Using task and/or formal messages for less personal or work situations.
- Communicating social and/or informal messages for non-work relationships or friendships.

Mutual respect

- Interacting in ways that display truthfulness, diplomacy, and esteem for others.

Trust

- Showing competence, consistency, and vulnerability in interactions.

pharmacies, outpatient clinics, and nursing homes. More recently, alternative healers such as herbalists and therapeutic masseurs have been added to this category (Goldsmith, 2005). Although healthcare organizations provide a range of services, they tend to share the following characteristics: 1) supplying clinical medicine that is primarily curative and 2) providing services to relatively small numbers of patients rather than large populations (Sultz and Young, 2009). Table 1.2 provides examples.

Hospitals, ambulatory care, and long-term care are three major healthcare providers. **Hospitals** supply a comprehensive array of services, 24-hours-a-day, seven-days-a-week, for patients requiring overnight hospitalization. These institutions bring together multiple professions and specializations in centralized locations to care for patients with a wide range of urgent, acute, and chronic health needs. Hospitals have advanced technology, equipment, and facilities necessary for all aspects of patient diagnosis and

Table 1.2 Examples of Healthcare Provider Organizations

Hospitals	Ambulatory Care	Long-Term Care
• Community hospitals located in rural, urban, and suburban locations • Teaching hospitals or academic medical centers • Federal hospitals (e.g., Veterans administration hospitals) • Specialty hospitals (e.g., psychiatric, children's)	• Physician offices • Medical groups • Outpatient clinics • Retail clinics • Hospital emergency care • Urgent care facilities • Community health centers • Alternative caregivers	• Nursing Homes • Assisted Living Centers • Home Care • Hospices/End-of-Life Facilities • Adult Daycare

(Adapted from American Hospital Association, 2009; Goldsmith, 2005; Longtermcareeducation.com, 2007)

treatment. Patients must be admitted under the supervision of physicians and teams of healthcare workers who monitor their care until discharge. Individual hospitals may be a part of larger health networks—a group of hospitals, physicians, other providers, insurers and/or community agencies—that deliver a broad spectrum of health services to communities (American Hospital Association, 2009). Factors such as specialized personnel, medical technology, and facility operations make hospital care expensive. Cost containment pressures have moved many of the services once provided only in hospitals to **ambulatory care organizations** where patients receive short-term or emergent care services but not overnight hospitalization. Ambulatory care organizations may also house multiple professionals and specializations, such as multi-physician practices or medical groups, but not to the extent provided by hospitals. Some institutions are affiliated with hospitals whereas others operate independently. The majority of healthcare in the U.S. is delivered in ambulatory care contexts (Goldsmith, 2005).

Recall that a major demographic variable affecting the health system is the increase of the aging patient population. This contingency has heightened demand for **long-term care organizations.** These institutions provide care to patients who have long-term health needs due to factors such as age, chronic illness, and disability (Longtermcareeducation.com 2007). Long-term care may last several months or even years, as in the cases of assisted living and nursing homes, or could be required for a few days or weeks, as in the case of hospice care.

Care given by healthcare provider organizations is financed by another set of institutions, called **payers.** Prominent sources of payment are insurance companies, Medicare and Medicaid, federal, state, and local government funds, and out-of-pocket expenditures made by individuals (Agency for Healthcare Research and Quality [AHRQ], 2007). You will learn more about payers later when we discuss forms of health organizing.

Public Health Organizations

Public health generally focuses on organized community efforts to prevent disease and promote health (Rowitz, 2006). Public health efforts also center on the health needs of large populations rather than smaller groups of individuals. Organizations that offer public health services include government institutions at local, state, and federal levels as well as voluntary and private organizations (Table 1.3). They focus primarily on preventing disease and promoting healthy living as well as developing policies and researching issues affecting populations such as infant mortality and chronic disease (American Association of Public Health, n.d.):

Public health has significantly contributed to the health and well-being of Americans. Consider the emergency response efforts in the aftermath of the September 11, 2001 attacks and Hurricane Katrina's devastation. Public health activities helped ensure the health and safety of survivors as well as the emergency responders who worked the crisis sites. Public health organizations contribute to quality of life conditions that many of us take

Table 1.3   Examples of Public Health Organizations

- Colleges and universities
- Public and private secondary schools
- Consumer advocacy organizations
- International organizations
- Consulting firms
- State legislative committees
- Health service delivery organizations
- Community organizations
- Federal and state health agencies
- Voluntary health agencies

(Source: whatispublichealth.org/careers/careers.html)

for granted, such as the provision of clean, safe drinking water, basic standards of hygiene, secure, accessible workplaces, and health screenings. Local, state, and federal government funds drawn from taxes pay for public health programs and personnel. The preventative nature of public health helps save human and financial costs but, historically, public health organizations have lacked the funding of health providers. This disparity may change in the years to come.

Both healthcare provider organizations and public health institutions are shaped by the ways in which the health system is organized in the U.S., namely, in fee-for-service and managed care forms. Next, you will learn more about fee-for-service, managed care, and how people in health organizations communicate in the managed care era.

Forms of Health Organizing

The experiences of patients, consumers, and health workers are largely influenced by how the health system is organized to provide and pay for care. Below, you will consider the alternative payment and organization structures which dominate the American health landscape. Following this discussion, you will learn about the implications of managed care for communication in health organizations.

Fee-for-Service and Managed Care

The vast majority of healthcare organizations use **fee-for-service** and managed care structures simultaneously to provide and finance patient care. That is, medical services are performed for which healthcare providers receive payment but the fees are the product of contracted agreements with payers (Geist and Hardesty, 1992). The fee-for-service structure pays healthcare providers, typically physicians for each medical service they perform. For example, a routine well-child visit with a pediatrician may include multiple services such as immunizations, physical exams, hearing and vision tests, etc. Each service has a separate fee. The pediatrician can earn more money by providing more services and seeing more patients. In the past, physicians have had considerable autonomy—deciding on the nature, price, setting, and timing of the care—and patients, insurers, employers, and government entities paid the bills (Freidson,1975; Starr, 2004). Now, insurance companies and other payers influence these decisions through administrative and contractual controls in an effort to contain costs and reduce care consumption.

Managed care is a philosophy and a system that refers to "a financial and organizational arrangement for the provision of healthcare services (almost always but not exclusively medical services)" (Lammers, Barbour, and Duggan, 2003, p. 332). Managed care tries to balance the often contradictory concerns of cost containment, access, and quality through the interaction of patients, providers, and payers. Payers carry the primary financial risk of care and thus are dominant forces in determining what services are provided and how care is delivered.

While specific managed care plans vary with each payer, they share several principles (Hacker and Marmour, 1999a; 1999b; Shi and Singh, 2000):

- Healthcare providers and payers share the risks of care, such as costs.
- Administrative oversight, usually from payers, constrains clinical decisions regarding fees, medical services performed, length of care, and care settings.

Box 1.3   A Patient's Experience in the Healthcare Landscape

Unable to find a corporate communication job, Gabrielle starts her own consulting business. Since she is self-employed, Gabrielle purchases individual indemnity insurance (non-network based) through a private company, Big Blue Insurance. She pays a monthly $1,000 premium to Big Blue and in return, Big Blue agrees to pay 80% of her health costs after she pays a $500 deductible. This means that Gabrielle pays $12,000 annually in premiums plus a $500 deductible in addition to 20% of her care costs *after* reaching her deductible. Her physicians and other care providers set customary fees which are paid for retrospectively. Gabrielle or her physicians select her care providers; there are no restrictions from Big Blue.

Gabrielle continues her job search while running her own business. After a year, she is hired by a rapidly growing internet marketing firm. She is enrolled in the company's Health Maintenance Organization (HMO) and pays a flat-rate, $100 co-pay for her healthcare with no deductible. Gabrielle selects Dr. Fox, an internal medicine physician, as her primary care provider whom she sees for all of her medical needs. Gabrielle has suffered from migraine headaches for years, which have worsened over the past few months. Dr. Fox first counsels her on prevention efforts such as reducing work stress and avoiding foods that trigger the problem.

Gabrielle's migraines don't improve so Dr. Fox refers her to a specialist that is also in the HMO network. The specialist orders tests from a local hospital, some of which must be pre-approved by the HMO prior to Gabrielle receiving care.

Although she enjoys her job at the internet firm, after three years Gabrielle tires of the long hours working nights and weekends. She decides to seek a job with more regular hours and is quickly hired by a large health organization in their corporate communication unit.

Her new employer's health plan is a Preferred Provider Organization (PPO). Now, Gabrielle has a wider range of choices regarding care providers than her previous HMO plan and she's able to see specialists of her choosing. Gabrielle stays in-network for most of her healthcare needs and she pays a small co-insurance fee. When she goes out-of-network, her co-insurance is much higher and sometimes Gabrielle must pay the entire cost up front and get reimbursed from the PPO. Gabrielle pays monthly $150 co-pays, a rate that is higher than the HMO plan, and the PPO has a higher overall premium than the HMO.

- A defined population of enrollees receives care from a network of providers.
- Payers receive a fixed or regular payment in return for assuming the risk of care; providers are paid a preset amount in advance of services.

Table 1.4 summarizes major concepts and terms associated with a managed care system.

Health Maintenance Organizations (HMOs) and Preferred Provider Organizations (PPOs) are the most widely used types of managed care structures. Health Maintenance Organizations (HMOs) coordinate and finance healthcare to a set patient population in return for a prepaid, fixed fee, providing profit incentives for prevention and wellness (Jonas, Goldsteen and Goldsteen, 2007). Patients usually have co-payments rather than deductibles and must choose their providers from a defined network. Primary care physicians assume the main responsibility for patient care and provide referrals to specialists as needed (AHRQ, 2007).

Table 1.4 Glossary of Managed Care Organizing*

Term	Definition
Parties	
Provider	A person or organization that gives healthcare to patients, such as an individual healthcare professional, hospital, or pharmacy.
Patient	The person enrolled in the health plan (or an approved dependent) who receives care from the provider.
Payer	The financing organization, typically a third party, that pays for healthcare (e.g., Medicare, Medicaid, private health insurance company).
Payment	
Out-of-pocket costs	Health expenses paid by patients' personal funds. This includes co-insurance, co-pays, and deductibles.
Deductible	The amount insured patients have to pay annually before the health plan begins to pay benefits.
Premium	The amount patients pay to belong to a health plan usually paid monthly. Enrollees of employer-sponsored plans pay through paycheck deductions.
Co-payment	A flat rate patients pay each time they receive care (e.g., $30 per physician office visit; $15 for each drug prescription).
Co-insurance	A percentage of the cost paid by the patient for particular healthcare services post-deductible (e.g., 20% of inpatient hospitalization).
Rules	
Diagnostic Related Groups (DRGs)	A classification system used in payment that relates kinds of patients treated to the resources they use. DRGs determine how much a hospital is paid for a patient's care.
Capitation	Providers receive a fixed payment from a health plan for each enrollee assigned to them.
Prospective payment	Healthcare plan payments made in advance of care delivery.
Network	A group of care providers who participate in a particular managed care plan. Enrollees pay less if they see in-network providers rather than those who don't participate in their plan (out-of-network).

Table 1.4   (continued)

Term	Definition
Precertification	Preapproval given by an insurance plan for a particular service.

(Adapted from Agency for Healthcare Research and Quality, 2007)

*Note: Terms may be missing and/or will change with managed care's evolution. The goal is to provide you with a general guide to enhance your understanding of the current health system.

Procedures, hospitalization, and other services may require precertification before care is provided.

Preferred Provider Organizations (PPOs) function similarly to HMOs with co-payments and in-network provider requirements. The key difference is that patients have greater flexibility in their choice of care providers, although they should stay in-network to avoid paying deductibles and/or higher premiums (Shi and Singh, 2000). PPOs typically reimburse a portion of out-of-network services and patients make up the difference out-of-pocket. This difference is called co-insurance and in some plans it pertains to in-network care as well. PPOs use primary care physicians, but patients may not need referrals to see specialists (AHRQ, 2007)

The pervasiveness of managed care has changed how care is provided and financed in the U.S. These changes have transformed how patients, consumers, and health workers understand and participate in the health system. Next, you will learn about how managed care has fundamentally altered, and will continue to influence, communication in health organizations.

Communication in the Managed Care Era

Miller and Ryan (2001) argue that "institutions and human relationships are both changing as a result of the influx of managed care in our health care system, and communication plays an ever-increasing role in these developments" (p. 92). A review of the research literature shows that managed care has shaped multiple levels of communication in health organizations.

At the level of **interpersonal communication**, managed care has placed boundaries on interactions between patients, providers and payers, thereby altering relationships between these parties. Scholars generally agree that managed care has changed **patient-caregiver dynamics.** Lammers and Duggan (2002) argue that managed care has transformed patients from unique individuals into health plan population members whose healthcare needs are balanced against costs incurred to the plan. This change creates perceptions among patients that to earn incentives, caregivers will prioritize health plan objectives above care. Such perceptions foster distrust in caregiver-patient relationships and possibly place patients at odds with their clinicians.

It has also been argued that managed care has influenced the quantity and quality of patient-caregiver communication because of health plan constraints on the frequency, duration, and content of interactions (Barbour and Lammers, 2007). For instance, plan requirements regarding specialists and drug formularies may limit communication to only what is "covered by the plan." Some plans limit the number of patient visits thereby reducing the frequency of patient-caregiver communication. Patients may seek out alternative and less costly forms of care (e.g., phone nurses) as a result of such constraints. Consequently, alternative care sources may encounter heightened patient communication and must be prepared to communicate with timely, accurate, useful, and sufficient information (Ledlow, O'Hair, and Moore, 2003). Regarding patient-caregiver talk time, the research is more mixed, with studies reporting that managed care has both increased and decreased contact time (Hayes, 2007; Mechanic, 2001).

Managed care has shaped **caregivers' administrative communication.** Mechanic (2003) argues that managed care transforms caregivers, particularly physicians, into bureaucrats who must increasingly deal with the financial and administrative aspects of care. These activities take caregivers away from the patient bedside. In addition, research shows that caregivers perceive managed care to have influenced the content of their communication. For example, some managed care plans require precertification for hospitals, specialists, and other forms of care—rules that may

Box 1.4   Ripped from the Headlines

Practicing Medicine in the Managed Care Era
Managed care has shaped how care is delivered in health organizations and how providers communicate. Perhaps nowhere are these changes more visible than in the medical profession. Physicians once were afforded considerable professional autonomy but this sovereignty has been eroded in the wake of managed care pressures and policies (Dorsey and Berwick, 2008). Now, health plans have substantial control over how care is provided and paid for, and over who receives it. News accounts depict a range of situations in which managed care has shaped physicians' work practices and communication, such as the following:

Seeing more patients—to counter lower reimbursement rates from insurers, some physicians boost revenues by increasing patient volume. Greater numbers can reduce the quality and quantity of medical encounters (O'Connell, 2004).
More time spent navigating gatekeepers—physicians increasingly have to call the insurance companies or their designated representatives for approval on referrals and tests. Doing so can mean less time spent with patients and colleagues (Norbut, 2006).
Resolving disagreements with patients—physicians face disgruntled patients who believe that their care is influenced by financial incentives and restrictions. Physicians explain why tests and procedures are medically unnecessary, potentially creating conflicts that reduce patient trust and satisfaction (Spiegel, 2009).

How do physicians manage managed care? A broad spectrum of strategies may help, from hiring additional staff to handle managed-care-related administration tasks to developing communication tools that allow physicians to quickly update themselves on health plan rule changes so interactions with insurers are more efficient (Berry, 2008). Physicians can also change their communication with patients to reduce the possibility of contentious conversations about managed care.

A *JAMA* article authored by communication and medical scholars and practitioners suggests some useful guidelines (Levinson et al., 1999). The authors offer two general principles: 1) physicians must believe they are on firm ethical ground in their recommendations so they can discuss medical decisions without embarrassment, and; 2) physicians need to show empathy, encourage patients to discuss care options, and respectfully discuss differences in opinion.

Discussion Questions

1. Think about a time when you or a family member visited a physician's office for medical care. How would you describe the experience? What satisfied you about the visit? What made you dissatisfied?
2. Given what you know now about managed care, how do you think the experience at the physician's office was shaped by managed care constraints?
3. Based on your overall experiences in the health system, what suggestions can you offer which might improve managed care for patients, or for care providers?

impose limits on caregivers' professional autonomy and decision-making (Gittel, 2008). Research suggests that as administrative tasks go up, satisfaction and commitment go down, and vice versa (Barbour and Lammers, 2007; Hoff, 2000). Dissatisfaction and lack of commitment affect patient care by reducing openness and responsiveness in caregiver-patient relationships as well as leading to higher caregiver turnover and diminished productivity (Hayes, 2007).

At the **group/team** level, the research literature presents communication in the managed care era in a more positive light. Scholarship indicates that managed care has fostered **professional collaboration** within health teams. Today's health teams are made up of direct caregivers as well as administrative staff who collectively have managed care functions (Poole and Real, 2003). Despite their different specializations and job tasks, team members share a common goal of working together for the good of the patient. The interdisciplinary nature of teams has been found to increase understanding of managed care functions and roles among direct caregivers, an awareness that has helped them deal with managed care changes (Apker, 2004). Managed care has also heightened the importance of non-clinical professionals to the health team. For example, Keigher (2000) argues that managed care prioritizes case management and thus emphasizes social workers' team contributions to linking patients with community services.

Managed care appears to also contribute to collaboration at a larger **organizational level**, fostering improved relationships between once disparate units within health institutions. Gittell (2008) found that in response to perceived managed care threats, caregivers across multiple hospital departments engaged in relational coordination—communicating and relating for the purpose of task integration. Gittel concluded that this relational work system not only improves organizational performance but also promotes resilience in the face of managed care pressures. Managed care influences have also generated new interdependencies between health organizations' administrative and direct care structures (Miller, 2003). For example, medical and nursing administrators must work alongside financial executives to help their institutions meet health plan expectations for quality care at lower costs. Rundall, Davies, and Hodges (2004) argue that transparency and communication between clinicians and health administrators are processes critical to establishing strong, participatory organizational structures that can flourish in a managed care health system.

Managed care will continue to dominate healthcare delivery in the years to come and communication in health organizations will evolve along with it. For health professionals, patients, and others, communication will remain a key process in navigating the health system.

Chapter Summary

This chapter presents an overview of the major environmental factors shaping communication in health organizations. Economic, social, and demographic contingences require ongoing organizational adaptation, particularly in communication. Models of health and illness and different organizational forms influence perceptions and communication activities pertaining to health delivery. The healthcare landscape is vast and complex, made up of varied providers and public health agencies, among others. These settings are the specific contexts which you will read about in subsequent chapters. You will begin this investigation with Chapter 2's consideration of organizational assimilation.

2

Organizational Assimilation

Toni is a registered nurse specializing in wound and burn care. After working for several major metropolitan hospitals in the Southeast in clinical and education roles, she began a new job as a regional sales representative for Healing Skin, Inc., a small, but rapidly growing medical device company. The company manufactures and distributes products used to help patients with pressure ulcers, severe burns, and other forms of skin trauma. Toni was hired for her nursing expertise, years of clinical experience, and outstanding people skills, all of which will be used to educate clinicians about Healing Skin's product line and increase the company's sales. At first, Toni was excited about her career change and, after a few weeks of work, she still loves challenge of learning a new role. It has been a relief to leave the scrubs, long hours, and pressure-filled work of bedside nursing behind.

The transition has not been entirely smooth, however. Healing Skin is so small that it has no formal orientation program for employees. Toni's introduction to her new job and employer consists of reviewing product marketing materials and shadowing other sales representatives for a week. Then, she's on her own with a designated sales territory, prospect list, and samples. Toni faces many challenges in her first few weeks in the field as she attempts to establish her territory. She encounters busy, stressed-out clinicians who have little time to meet with her. Some sales prospects criticize Healing Skin's products while others just take the free samples (and the bagels and coffee she brings) with no intention of making purchases. There's little, if any, socialization effort by Healing Skin coworkers and bosses to help Toni get off to a positive start. She feels disconnected and wishes for friendships with colleagues like those she had at previous employers. Unless things turn around for the better, Toni is seriously considering quitting Healing Skin and going back to bedside nursing.

Toni's story exemplifies the highs and lows of assimilating in a new organization. Like Toni, you may have encountered the excitement of a new role and employer as well as the disappointment when reality doesn't meet your expectations. These experiences can have an important influence on how you communicate with others on the job, the degree to which you enjoy your work role and, ultimately, even your tenure with an organization. This chapter explores how health professionals experience organizational assimilation with a focus on the roles they perform once they are organizational members.

Learning about assimilation and roles requires knowing more about health occupations. Thus, the chapter begins with an overview of trends and types of healthcare and public health professions. Next, you will consider assimilation from a systems perspective and learn about the communication processes by which health professionals "learn the ropes." Finally, you will become more familiar with roles using the systems approach and examine the communication behaviors and processes accompanying role enactment in health organizations. This chapter uses the terms **health profession(s)** and **health professional(s)** in a general sense to encompass anyone who provides care for the well-being of others, either directly or indirectly, using specific skills, knowledge and/or expertise (Miller and Considine, 2009).

Professions Overview: Trends and Occupations

The healthcare industry is one of our nation's largest employment sectors, comprising more than 200 occupations (Sultz and Young, 2009). Estimates indicate that it will supply 17 million jobs by 2016 (Lacey and Wright, 2009). Seven of the 20 fastest-growing occupations are healthcare related. Health industry expansion will continue to outpace employment in all other sectors of the economy. While total job growth is estimated to increase by 10% by 2016, jobs for health practitioners and technicians will rise by

20%, and health support positions will increase by 27% (Lacey and Wright, 2009).

Two trends accompany this demand. The first is the **personnel shortage** in key health professions. According to the U.S. Health Resources and Services Administration (HRSA), there is a significant lack of primary care physicians in some parts of the country and fewer medical students are selecting primary care as a medical specialty (HRSA 2008a). Moreover, the majority of the physician population is nearing retirement age at the same time as demand for medical services is increasing. The nursing shortage has been reported for decades and projections indicate it could reach one million by 2020 (HRSA, 2006a). For pharmacists, an 11% shortfall is projected by 2030 (HRSA, 2008b).

The second trend pertains to **lack of racial and ethnic diversity**. The current health workforce does not reflect the diversity of the overall U.S. population and projections indicate that the diversity gap will not be adequately filled in the near future (HRSA, 2006b). Caregiver shortfalls exist in several racial and ethnic groups, most notably for African-Americans, Latinos, and Native Americans. This under-representation poses problems for health organizations and healthcare delivery, especially in light of the health disparities described in Chapter 1. A lack of health professional diversity has a host of negative outcomes for racial and minority patients such as reduced access and care quality, lower satisfaction and adherence to treatment, and ineffective physician-patient communication (Smedley, Stith, and Nelson, 2003).

Most health occupations fall into two major categories, healthcare professions and public health professions. **Healthcare professionals** are individuals who directly care for patients or who provide support services for direct caregivers. These people supply clinical medicine or treatment to small patient populations, such as the enrollees of particular health plans. There are three major categories that comprise most healthcare professions:

- **Health diagnosis and treatment professionals** give direct care to patients and/or conduct research. Their roles are defined by complex tasks, a high degree of autonomy and responsibility, and supervision of others. They have the most advanced training and specialization, usually requiring a minimum of a baccalaureate degree in a specific health area. (American Medical Association, 2009).

- **Health technologists and technicians** assist diagnosing and treating providers typically by operating specialized equipment. These occupations require post-high school education, usually in the form of one- to two-year training programs (Bureau of Labor Statistics, 2008).
- **Support service professionals** support the other two groups. Jobs can range from those caring for patients to performing administrative/managerial responsibilities. Depending on the nature of the job, these roles may require post-high school education or may require little or no specialized education or training. (ExploreHealthCareers.org, 2009).

Table 2.1 provides a list of sample professions from these categories.

Public health focuses on health promotion and disease/injury prevention in populations. **Public health professionals** focus their work activities on education, research, and promotion of healthy lifestyles (American Association of Public Health, n.d.). There are several core areas of public health careers (Association of Schools of Public Health, 2010):

- **Biostatisticians and epidemiologists** use statistical methods to analyze health information, and to study the dissemination and causal factors of disease and disability.
- **Health services administrators** study issues pertaining to health management operations (e.g., leadership, finance, and policy analysis).
- **Health educators/behavioral scientists** choose, use, and monitor appropriate change strategies to improve public health.
- **Environmental health professionals** study issues associated with environmental conditions that negatively affect human health.

Table 2.1   Examples of Healthcare Professions

Health Diagnosis and Treatment Professionals	Health Technologists and Technicians	Support Service Professionals
• Physicians and surgeons • Physician assistants • Dentists • Registered nurses • Social workers • Physical therapists • Mental health counselors • Pharmacists • Dieticians and nutritionists	• Medical records and health information workers • Dental hygienists • Pharmacy technicians • Licensed practical and vocational nurses • Emergency medical technicians and paramedics	• Nursing aides • Dental assistants • Medical assistants • Medical and health services managers • Medical transcriptionists • Occupational therapy assistants and aides • Physical therapy assistants and aides

(Adapted from Lacey and Wright, 2009)

Table 2.2 lists sample public health professions from these areas.

Some occupations within public health involve activities similar to healthcare professions, as for example with public health physicians and nurses who provide direct care to patients through efforts such as community health screenings and immunizations. Other occupations center on wider population-based activities that occur as public health organizations research, plan, implement and assess prevention programs. Public health training and specialization requirements vary by occupation. Typically, jobs demand a minimum of a bachelor's degree in a field of specialty and many require post-baccalaureate education (ExploreHealthCareers.org, 2009).

The health professions span a broad spectrum and this variety contributes to the overall complexity of the health system. With this background in mind, let's turn our attention to understanding organizational assimilation in health organizations from a systems perspective.

Table 2.2   Examples of Public Health Professions

Biostatistics and Epidemiology	Health Services Administration	Health Education/ Behavioral Science	Environmental Health
• Biostatistician • Epidemiologist • Scientist • Researcher	• Community planner • Policymaker • Writer • Medical and health services manager	• Health educator • Nutritionist • Nurse • Physician	• Environmental health specialist • Occupational health and safety professional • Emergency responder • Food safety specialist

(*Source: American Association of Public Health, n.d.; Association of Schools of Public Health 2010*)

A Systems Perspective on Organizational Assimilation

Organizational assimilation is the ongoing process of individualization and socialization by which people, typically newcomers, undergo integration in an organization (Jablin, 1987; 2001). **Individualization** refers to individuals' attempts to adjust by actively modifying their roles and contexts in order to meet personal needs. **Socialization** involves attempts by organizations to help members make the transition from outsider to insider.

Assimilation can perhaps be best understood through the systems concepts of input-throughput-output and feedback. **Input-throughput-output** refers to how messages and other sources of data enter a system from the embedded environment, are altered by the system components (usually people) for use, and leave the system as a final product. **Feedback** is a primary tool of assimilation. Newcomers receive reactions to their behaviors from other members of their organization which tell them whether those behaviors match organizational expectations. Feedback promotes self-regulation which helps newcomers fit in.

Graduate medical education (residency) provides an illustrative example of input-throughput-output and feedback. While residents hold medical degrees and are considered physicians when they begin their residency programs, they are not licensed to practice medicine. They spend the first year rotating among medical specialties before specializing in a particular area for the second and third years of residency. As inputs, these physicians-in-training bring information gained in medical school to their residency experiences. Through a variety of communication-based activities—rounding, morning report meetings, classroom instruction, etc.—residency programs alter residents' skills, abilities, and knowledge (throughput). Residents receive ongoing feedback from senior physicians, peers, and patients about their role performance. Residents provide feedback to the residency program in the form of their quality and quantity of work and their communication with others. Ultimately, residents leave graduate medical education transformed as outputs with enhanced clinical competencies and expertise.

Next, you will review how the research literature conceptualizes assimilation. You will also learn about the role of communication in the transition process, especially with regard to newcomer information-seeking and organizational socialization.

Conceptualizations of Organizational Assimilation

The body of literature in organizational communication, largely influenced by the work of the scholar Fredric Jablin, has traditionally conceptualized assimilation as a process made up of four stages (see Jablin, 2001, for a review):

- **Anticipatory socialization** occurs prior to entry into an organization. Individuals attempt to learn more about occupations/professions and organizations try to manage impressions among potential recruits.

- **Entry** refers to the first days, weeks, and months of organizational membership. These are often characterized by "reality shock," where previously held expectations confront the reality of organizational life. Newcomers transition into roles, relationships and cultures.
- **Metamorphosis** occurs with the evolution from outsider to insider, characterized by heightened familiarity with organizational tasks, norms, and values. Individuals and organizations no longer have to exert considerable effort to help incumbents fit in.
- **Disengagement/exit** occurs as individuals either leave one organization for another or transfer from one role/work group to another in the same institution.

For instance: Leroy is a new lab technician working at radiology clinic. He has several years of technical experience so is familiar with his work role tasks, but he's unfamiliar with the personalities of his coworkers and organizational norms. Leroy is an insider because of his job expertise, but he's an outsider when it comes to his coworkers' expectations about communication, teamwork, and other work relationship behaviors. Leroy will gain more familiarity with these aspects of his job over time as he seeks information and clinic employees communicate their expectations to him. Eventually Leroy will learn the ropes of the clinic and feel comfortable with his tasks and relationships there.

Recent understandings of assimilation tend to focus on key communication processes occurring throughout a person's tenure in an organization, regardless of specific time period or stage. Researchers have primarily explored how newcomers use **information-seeking tactics** (Table 2.3) to learn more about their work roles, relationships, and organizational environment as well as how organizations use **socialization tactics** to ease newcomers' integration (Table 2.4). These tactics and techniques occur throughout assimilation, forming a dynamic interplay of giving and receiving information between newcomer and institutional employer.

Table 2.3   Newcomer Information-Seeking Tactics

Tactic	Description	Health Organization Example
Overt question	A question that directly seeks information.	"Would you show me how to process this patient's claim for medical reimbursement?"
Indirect question	A query that implies information-seeking.	"I'm so busy that I'll have to work late today to complete all my patient charting" (Implied: "Will you help me with my work?")
Third parties	Soliciting information from a secondary source (peer) rather than a primary source (supervisor).	(To a student peer) "Does the attending mind if you ask a lot of questions during rounds?"
Testing limits	Purposefully breaking or bending rules and/or deviating from group norms and watching to see the effects of such behaviors.	Wearing business casual clothes while working at an insurance company with a strict, formal dress code.
Disguising conversations	Masking information-seeking attempts through natural conversation.	"I'm so stressed out from work. I wonder if people ever go out to have a little fun and deal with the pressure" (Gauge reactions to see if invited to socialize outside of work).
Observing	Seeking information by observing others in relevant situations.	An intern watching senior medical residents receive praise and encouragement for giving a successful case presentation in order to duplicate their successful behaviors.
Surveillance	Soliciting information by understanding previous observed behaviors.	A novice nurse recalling how an experienced nurse calmed an anxious child during a medical exam as a guideline for future experiences with pediatric patients.

(Adapted from Miller and Jablin, 1991)

Table 2.4   Organizational Socialization Tactics

Tactic	Description	Health Organization Example
Collective	Activities that occur for a group of newcomers.	A multi-center health system conducts a monthly new employee orientation.
Individual	Newcomer is provided with a unique set of learning experiences from a designated organization representative.	A nursing student works with a nurse preceptor (instructor) during clinical rotations.
Formal	Newcomers are separated from other organizational members for officially sanctioned training.	HMO customer service workers take courses in how to answer patient questions and respond to complaints.
Informal	Newcomers learn their roles while on the job; no separation from others.	A receptionist at a cancer center job shadows another receptionist before doing the job on his own.
Sequential	Newcomers get step-by-step job procedures which they are expected to follow to meet job requirements.	A technician learns how to perform the repetitive steps of dialysis treatment.
Random	Newcomers receive role information in a random manner and/or in a way that allows for multiple interpretations.	A physician takes on varied administrative responsibilities for his group practice with little, if any, mentoring.
Fixed	Organization enforces exact timing for completion of each phase of a job before a transition can take place.	A nursing home requires a 90-day probationary work period for all new employees before job benefits begin.
Variable	Little, if any, data is given to newcomers about the timing of transition to the next stage of a role.	A retail pharmacy transfers a new pharmacist to another store without telling her in advance of hire.
Serial	Newcomers learn the ropes from mentors, role models, or other experienced organizational members.	Medical students learn to perform physical exams on patients by watching faculty attendings, residents.

Table 2.4   (continued)

Tactic	Description	Health Organization Example
Dis-junctive	Newcomers "sink or swim," learning the job on their own without assistance.	A dental hygienist working at a private practice must learn group norms on her own, with no formal training.
Investiture	Organization does not want to change newcomers and strives to maximize their unique skills and abilities.	A pharmaceutical company's new human resources manager is asked to develop a new online training program for sales representatives.
Divestiture	Newcomers must change previous behaviors, beliefs, and attitudes and acquire those desired by the organization.	Residency programs "break" interns of old behaviors and beliefs so they learn approved ways of doing things.

(Adapted from Van Maanen and Schein, 1979)

As in many occupations, organizational assimilation in the health professions often begins with formal instruction offered by higher education institutions (e.g., academic medical centers, universities, community colleges). Health professionals learn the knowledge, skills, and identities of their chosen careers as well as gain insights into what it would be like to work for particular institutional employers. Assimilation continues when health professionals exit these educational settings and make the transition into jobs at health institutions where they learn and enact specific roles commensurate with profession and organization expectations. You will learn more about role experiences and communication later in this chapter.

Assimilation of Health Professionals

Much of the literature examining assimilation in health organizations focuses on medicine, one of the largest and perhaps most influential health professions in the U.S. This research shows a unique assimilation experience unlike that of any other health profession and one that exerts long-term influence on physician communication behaviors.

Assimilation of Medical Professionals

Medical education in the United States is a highly selective and competitive process that consists of several years of formal course-work and on-the-job training. Physicians-in-training work long, exhausting hours, immerse themselves in medical culture, and may struggle to balance the many responsibilities of their work and personal lives (Hirschmann, 1999; Zorn and Gregory, 2005). It is perhaps not all that surprising, then, that physician training has been described as "the longest rite of passage in the Western world" (Bonsteel, 1997, p. 15). It consists of distinctive norms, beliefs, and values that shape how physicians view their occupational identities and their roles in health organizations (see Hughes, 1956; Becker, Greer, Hughes and Strauss, 1961). The professional worldviews developed during medical education ultimately affect how physicians communicate with patients and professional associates.

It is generally agreed that medical education consists of: 1) the stated, formal curriculum that builds medical expertise and 2) the informal and hidden curriculum that teaches physicians-in-training about organizational structure and professional culture. The **formal curriculum**—what is intended, officially offered, and endorsed by the medical profession—occurs when students enter medical school following the completion of pre-medical baccalaureate degrees (Conrad, 1988). Medical school typically involves the following:

- **Years 1–2 (preclinical)**: The first two years are commonly devoted to mastering basic science and principles of human body functioning, with limited clinical time.
- **Years 3–4**: In their third year students are immersed in clinical training and rotate through different medical specialties under the supervisor of medical residents and attendings. Their final year is spent taking electives and becoming more immersed in patient care. Students also decide their residency specialization.

Students who complete medical school are officially physicians with the title of "Doctor," but they are not fully qualified to practice medicine. The next step is graduate medical education or residency—usually another three to eight years of medical training—followed by professional licensing exams. Residency mainly consists of clinical work and residents care for patients under the supervision of senior physicians.

While communication training has always been a part of medical education, through activities such as case presentations and direct patient care, students mostly learned communication and interpersonal skills informally through role modeling/apprenticeship. With growing evidence that communication has an impact on patient care and correlates with improved health outcomes and care quality (Rider and Keefer, 2006), communication was formally recognized as a core clinical skill by the Accreditation Council on Graduate Medical Education (ACGME) in the late 1990s. ACGME requirements now mandate that physicians demonstrate proficiency in their interactions with patients through behaviors such as listening, questioning, and information-giving as well as show aptitude in team collaboration and leadership (Cegala and Broz, 2003).

Formal instruction constitutes an important component of medical socialization, yet scholars argue that an even more powerful socializing force exists in the informal and hidden curricula (Inui, 2003). The **informal curriculum** consists of unscripted, impromptu, and interpersonal instructional communication that takes place among and between faculty and students (Hafferty, 1994). For instance, important teaching moments can occur in spur-of-the moment hallway interactions or in casual conversations happening over meals as medical students and residents talk with more experienced coworkers. The **hidden curriculum** refers to structural and cultural influences that function beneath the surface of formal teaching and learning (Hafferty, 1988). An intern, for example, may learn to always answer questions posed by senior physicians and to allow those with greater experience and authority to control conversations. These behaviors are not officially sanctioned; rather they are learned implicitly through direct and vicarious communication with others.

Box 2.1   Communication in Practice

Building Communication Competence in the Formal Medical Curriculum
Effective communication is so important in medicine that it is one of six core clinical competencies identified by the ACGME (2006). This means that communication and interpersonal skills must be taught and evaluated at all levels of medical training in a formal effort to improve physicians' interactions with others. For medical educators, the ACGME competencies provide general principles useful for physician training, but specific instructional techniques are often at the discretion of the specific health institution. A group of leading medical educators desired to fill this gap by giving specific advice and instructional techniques to enhance physician communication skills training. They expanded the ACGME communication and interpersonal skills competency and developed the following strategies for use across different medical settings and specialties (Rider and Keefer, 2006):

1. **Create and sustain a relationship that is therapeutic for patients and supportive of their families.**

   - Pay attention to the patient; accept and investigate the patient's feelings.
   - Talk with the patient's family truthfully and supportively.
   - Acknowledge when mistakes are made, showing honesty and sorrow.
   - Use communication that is preferred or currently used by the patient and/or best meets the needs of the situation.
   - Show mutual respect and collaboration by involving the patient in decision-making.

2. Work effectively with others as a member or leader of the healthcare team or other professional group. In all areas of communication and interaction, show respect and empathy toward colleagues and learners.

- Collaborate with other team members by asking and answering questions specifically, taking steps to be understood and to understand others.
- Settle conflict and give useful critiques on errors.
- Communicate to identify team member expectations and participate in helpful feedback processes.

3. Use effective listening skills to establish relationships. Elicit and provide information using effective non-verbal, explanatory, and questioning skills.

- Display listening behaviors so that the patient feels heard and understood (e.g., nodding, maintaining eye contact, paraphrasing).

The hidden and informal curricula play a major role in teaching medical values. One such value is **insider status** (Harter and Krone, 2001; Harter and Kirby, 2004). Physicians-in-training begin their education as relative outsiders to medicine, but over time their assimilation gives them insider status. They spend most of their training participating in collective, highly structured activities that separate them from the lay, nonmedical world. In this distinct clinical environment they learn espoused medical values such as competence, effectiveness, and good judgment. Students and residents also learn that departing from accepted values (e.g., through poor performance, not following group behavior norms) will invite unwanted marginalization and embarrassment (Smith and Kleinman, 1989). For example, studies by Harter and Kirby (2004) and Scheibel (1996) show that medical

students and residents learn to talk quickly and follow a structured pattern of interaction when speaking with patients. They
also learn to speak concisely and smoothly with no hesitations or
uncertainties when interacting with senior physicians. Following
these accepted communication norms shows confidence, clinical
proficiency, and expertise, and those who perform such behaviors
are rewarded with insider status. However, those who deviate
from or avoid these norms may experience mocking, criticism,
and even ostracism. Such interactions reproduce power roles and
hierarchical structures that influence physicians' communication
with patients and other health professionals (see Chapter 3).

Physicians-in-training also learn to value **emotion management** primarily as a way to deal with medical education's
emotional, intellectual, and physical rigors (Harter and Krone,
2001; Harter and Kirby, 2004). The concept of **affective neutrality**, also known as detached concern, is critical to emotion
management. Medical students and residents learn to separate
themselves from the personal and emotional dimensions of caregiving and rely on the principles of objectivity, rationality, and
logic inherent to medical culture (Radcliffe and Lester, 2003).
Through their education experiences, students and residents
manage their emotions as a way not only to display competence
and professionalism, but also to deal with the stresses and pressures accompanying caregiving. For instance, Jacob, a resident
treating a patient with HIV, may distance himself from the
patient's fear and anxiety as a way of avoiding getting too emotionally involved, a circumstance which he has been taught may
cloud his medical judgment. Further, managing his emotions
through detachment allows Jacob to "leave work at work" so
he can focus on his family and personal life. While managing
emotions has significant practical value, it has been found to
decrease physicians' empathy, increase their cynicism, and negatively affect their communication and relationships with others
(McCue and Beach, 1994).

Box 2.2   Ripped from the Headlines

Lessons Learned from the Hidden Curriculum
A large amount of what is taught and learned in medical school occurs behind the scenes of formal course offerings and within medicine's hidden curriculum (Hafferty, 1988). According to an article in the *American Medical News*, a newspaper published by the American Medical Association, medical students arrive "fresh as the driven snow" but the hidden curriculum "chews up idealistic students and spits out cynical doctors" (Croasdale, 2006, paras 1 and 4). Students learn lessons about how to fit into medical culture, but, ultimately, their assimilation experiences may reduce their empathy for others.

The following story is an excerpt from a blog titled "How I learned to stop asking questions during medical school" (http://oldmdgirl.blogspot.com, 2009). Written by a medical student, the account describes a conversation in which the values of medicine are conveyed in ways that influence the communication behaviors of a physician-in-training.

Allow me to introduce you to the hidden curriculum of medical school. The one in which we become brainwashed into thinking that questions, sleep, intellectual curiosity, and anything other than helping your patients at all times are evil Evil EVIL. Questions are evil because they waste other people's time. You should just look it up yourself you lazy med student!

I was on rounds one day, and the attending was talking about sick euthyroid syndrome. I couldn't hear something she said, so I said, "What?"

And she said, "YOU," (She didn't know my name even though I'd been on her service over a week at that point.)

"You're doing a presentation on this for tomorrow before rounds."

"I didn't say 'what' because I didn't understand what you were talking about. I DIDN'T HEAR YOU," I said.

Didn't matter. From that point on I never uttered a word during rounds.

Let this be a lesson to you. Medical students are to be seen and not heard. And apparently, attendings are not to be heard either

Elsewhere in the blog, the author explains that she used to be a question-asker but not so much after medical school. Now, she answers rather poses questions. This pattern of behavior is pervasive among her peers even when student participation is solicited by instructors as part of formal classroom instruction.

This blog provides insights into medicine's hidden curriculum and draws attention to how, in their desire to become "insiders," students conform to the accepted values of their chosen profession. Such actions reinforce traditional power roles and status hierarchies in health organizations that ultimately influence physician relationships with patients and professional associates (Scheibel, 1996; Goldberg, 2008).

Discussion Questions
1. What are your reactions to the hidden curriculum of medicine? How do other professions, including your own as a student, have their own versions of the hidden curriculum? Identify examples.
2. Why did the attending demand a presentation from the medical student in response to her question? Why do you think the author conformed to the attending's

demands? What does the conversation say about medical culture?
3. How might the hidden curriculum influence physician communication with other members of health organizations and the patients they serve?

Assimilation of Nonmedical Professionals

This line of research emphasizes the reality shock health workers encounter when they exit formal education and begin jobs in health organizations. Two major themes dominate the literature: mastery of clinical competence and mastery of professional relationships.

Mastery of clinical competence involves efforts to fulfill organizational role expectations, particularly the task or technical aspects of occupational roles. Several separate studies in nursing demonstrate that newcomers struggle to feel comfortable and confident in patient care responsibilities (Boswell, Lowery, and Wilhoit, 2004; Casey et al., 2004; Valdes-Pierce, 2004). Perceptions of skill and knowledge deficits exist as novice nurses encounter a learning curve between their experiences as supervised students and that of full-fledged nurses dealing with significant healthcare pressures. Not only must new nurses develop clinical expertise without extensive experience, they must achieve this mastery within environments characterized by heightened patient acuity, high nurse-patient ratios, personnel shortage, and demanding length-of-stay requirements. Given such challenges, new nurses report dissatisfaction with working conditions and patient care, factors that contribute to turnover.

Mastery of professional relationships consists of actions meant to manage role expectations and assert professional expertise with those in authority. For instance, Abramson (1993) argues that a key part of social worker socialization is working in an interdisciplinary setting where coworkers may not understand or value social work. Research into nurse practitioner (NP) assimilation shows that after years of constructing a professional identity and developing unique skills in formal education, NPs may face having their roles questioned or discounted by others (Casey et al., 2004; Kelly and Mathews, 2001). Difficulties communicating with physicians appear particularly problematic. Nurses and social workers must adjust to power differences as displayed during their interactions with physicians (Boswell, Lowery, and Wilhoit, 2004; Etheridge, 2007). Consider Curlita, an oncology nurse who has a master's degree and years of clinical experience. Despite her impressive credentials, Curlita finds that she must continually establish her professional expertise when talking with oncologists at the cancer center where she works. Curlita makes an effort to speak with physicians as a peer rather than as a subordinate and she encourages other center nurses to do the same as a way to gain respect and improve teamwork.

What eases assimilation in health organizations? Mentoring appears frequently as a critical factor (Jaskyte, 2005; Jaskyte and Lee, 2009) and may be implemented formally by health organizations or emerge informally as newcomers and veterans work together. Mentoring helps novice professionals learn their jobs and organizational cultures more quickly and effectively. Brown and Olshansky (1998) argue that "Mentors can provide crucial information about appropriate expectations and create key structures to facilitate new practitioners' needs for consultation and advice" (p. 46). Among nurses and social workers, establishing mentoring relationships has been found to foster job satisfaction, commitment, and retention (Bowles and Candela, 2005; Miller et al., 2008). Such findings are particularly noteworthy given the shortage of qualified personnel in these health professions.

To summarize what you have learned so far, assimilation consists of multiple phases of transition in which newcomer information-seeking and institutional socialization techniques figure prominently. Context matters as formal education and on-the-job settings influence how health professionals think and communicate. Learning tasks and relational roles is a central part of assimilation and a primary means by which people make the transition from outsider to insider. Thus, the next section considers the communication by which health professionals create, shape, and maintain their occupational roles in health organizations.

Role Communication

Roles refer to "specific forms of behavior associated with given positions that originally develop from task requirements" (Katz and Kahn, 1978, p. 43). By interacting with **role set members** (e.g., professional associates, patients, and their families), health workers perform specific roles. Role theorists explain that individuals tend to behave consistently with assigned or chosen roles, yet the dynamic nature of communication promotes role flexibility and change. The fluid nature of roles is very useful in health organizations, where workers must constantly respond and adapt to environmental contingencies (Chapter 1). Further, the rising use of teams has transformed the jobs of many of health professionals and required them to redefine their roles and communication. Teams are contexts in which issues surrounding role clarity, overlap, conflict, and ambiguity take center stage, influencing the effectiveness of team communication and patient care quality (Makary et al., 2006).

Next, you will learn about traditional and contemporary perspectives on roles as well as how this theorizing informs role communication in health organizations. Table 2.5 summarizes four research domains: role development, role negotiation, role performances, and role dialectics.

Role Development and Negotiation

Early role theorizing considered the communication processes by which individuals define and change their roles in organizations (Katz and Kahn, 1978). Scholars argued that individuals create and recreate roles based on their self-concept and through interactions with others (Graen; 1976; Nicholson, 1984). People define and/or change their roles on an ongoing basis and members of their role set respond to those behaviors, thereby creating role communication patterns.

Role development—also known as leader-member exchange—is a three-part process that occurs during unstructured task accomplishment (Graen and Scandura, 1987). **Role taking** happens

Table 2.5 Research Conceptualizations of Roles

Concept	Description
Role development	A three-part process enacted by role incumbents as they interact with other members of their role set. Consists of role taking (receiving role definitions), role making (modifying role definitions) and role routinization (maintenance of existing role definitions).
Role negotiation	Conscious interactions between role incumbent and role set members which change expectations about how a role should be executed and evaluated. Primarily occurs in the developmental stage of role making.
Role performances	Communication and other behaviors produced by a role incumbent during frontstage (formal, public) and backstage (informal, private) activities which influence role set members. The presentation of pre-established patterns of action, such as in a routine.
Role dialectics	The dynamic interplay of contradictions or tensions that create, shape, and maintain behaviors connected with a particular role. Role tensions emerge from varying, and potentially conflicting, expectations held by members of a social group. Role incumbents negotiate contradictions communicatively with others.

when a person, typically a newcomer, receives role definitions from role set members, usually an incumbent such as a boss. Newcomers and incumbents send and receive role messages through formal and informal channels (e.g., job procedures, routine conversations). **Role making** refers to when newcomers become incumbents and modify their roles based on personal and organizational needs. They "make" their roles, usually in situations that are unstructured and after they have begun to trust others. In **role routinization**, changes made during role making are now a natural part of the incumbent's role. Individuals may cycle through role development phases multiple times or skip phases entirely, depending on circumstances.

Organizational communication researchers first focused on supervisor-subordinate relationships to understand role development. More recent studies recognize that although worker-boss communication is important, a person's interactions with other role set members can also affect role development. This newer understanding is particularly useful in health settings, where members of healthcare teams may not formally report to other team members, but their roles are greatly influenced by team interactions (Miller, Joseph, and Apker, 2000). For example, research by Apker et al. (2006) into nurse-team communication found that team members hold differing communication expectations of nurses, often related to team member position and occupation, and that nurses adapted their communication to meet varying role expectations. Box 2.3 takes a closer look at what constitutes "best" nurse role communication with healthcare teams.

Role negotiation is behavior that "occurs when two or more persons consciously interact with the express purpose of altering the others' expectations about how a role should be enacted and evaluated" (Miller et al., 1996, p. 296). Negotiations involve relational and task requirements (what to do in a role, how to do it) and they are influenced by predefined role expectations, shifting organizational needs, individual interests, and ongoing interactions among role set members. Overall, studies show that participation in role negotiation enhances employees' role satisfaction, job success and organizational tenure (Jablin and Miller, 1993; Meiners and Miller, 2004). In her study of nursing roles, Apker (2002) found that mid-level nurse managers who successfully altered their roles to meet personal and organizational needs were satisfied with their workplace relationships and interested in long-term careers with their hospital employers.

Role negotiation skills are especially useful in organizations—such as those found in the health system—that are constantly in a state of flux due to greater, shifting contingencies in the embedded environment. In separate studies of nurse role ambiguity, Miller, Joseph, and Apker (2000) and Apker (2001) found that nurses make sense of system ambiguity (in these instances brought about by managed care) and its effects on their individual roles by interacting with coworkers and supervisors. Study results suggested that nurses who are able to negotiate their roles in light of

Box 2.3   Communication in Practice

"Best Practice" Role Communication in Health Organizations
Members of health organizations take on a variety of roles as they work together to care for the patient. While individual circumstances and contextual factors may influence communication practices, Apker et al. (2006) argue that the following four "best" role communication skill sets contribute to an optimal work environment in health organizations:

Collaboration—working together for the collective good

- Seek information from others and analyze data accuracy and completeness
- Organize, prioritize, and provide pertinent information to others
- Engage in give-and-take to identify solutions and participate in decisions

Credibility—showing proficiency and expertise

- Speak credibly, without jargon or unclear terminology/phrasing
- Adjust communication to the needs of others and the situational dynamics
- Display assertiveness and address conflict directly, yet respectfully

Compassion—displaying empathy to build relationships

- Demonstrate consideration and regard for individuals' concerns

- Advocate for others' needs when warranted
- Show respect and affiliation in verbal and nonverbal interactions

Coordination—leading or managing work processes

- Designate responsibilities to others and follow up
- Mentor less experienced individuals in work tasks and relationships
- Promote feedback from others and value their input

uncertainty are better able to adapt to organizational change and cope with its accompanying stressors (e.g., role ambiguity, role transformation).

Role Performances and Role Dialectics

In his classic work, *The Presentation of Self in Everyday Life*, Goffman (1959) defines a **role performance** as "all the activity of a given participant on a given occasion which serves to influence, in any way, any of the other participants" (p. 15). He argues that individuals play one or more roles, typically within a group performance that occurs "frontstage" (in front of the audience) and "backstage" (away from the audience). For example, a physician's medical office consists of multiple performance sites and types of interactions. The clinical frontstage consists of reception area/waiting room, office hallways, and examination rooms whereas the clinical backstage refers to personal office space, testing or lab rooms, and staff break/lunch areas. There are clear domains where patients and their families are allowed and conversely, prevented from accessing. Frontstage communication is typically more formal and consists of task messages such as those pertaining to diagnoses, physical examinations, treatment options, etc. Backstage communication is usually informal: physicians, nurses, and administrative staff exchange work and personal information. Messages may include joking, slang, etc., that may not be appropriate in frontstage communication.

The theorizing of performance is evident in studies of roles and socialization in health organizations. In their examination of medical education, Haas and Shaffir (1982) argue that the medical school and residency programs are replete with symbols (jargon), stage fright (new scripts, unfamiliar settings), dress rehearsals (residency), and reciting lines (displays of expertise). By performing the doctor role, students and residents transform into full-fledged physicians and learn a great deal about their professional identities. Work by Ellingson (2003; 2005) and Morgan and Krone (2001) highlights how role performances in health teams function as importance sources of newcomer socialization. These authors contend that team members' role communication creates dominant scripts, such as what behaviors represent professionalism, that reinforce team norms and institutional values. For instance, Morgan and Krone's study of communication in a cardiac care center found that team members followed scripted performances that show calmness, confidence, and a polite demeanor, regardless of the complexity of the case, in order to reduce patient anxieties. Crying or showing other types of "negative" emotions was discouraged and those who stepped out of sanctioned role performances were disparaged, mocked, or had their competence questioned by other team members.

The final role perspective considered is **role dialectics**, defined by Apker et al. (2005) as: "[T]he ongoing interplay of contradictions that produce, shape, and maintain behaviors associated with a particular role. Role contradictions are constructed and reconstructed by the dynamic and interdependent expectations for behavior of the self and other in multiple relationships. Role tensions are negotiated communicatively within the varied relationships which comprise social units" (p. 97). Drawing upon relational dialectics theory (Baxter and Montgomery, 1996; Montgomery and Baxter, 1998), Apker et al. investigated the role contradictions that emerge in team communication and the discursive processes by which nurses manage role tensions. Hierarchy and status was identified as a key source of role contradiction that nurses must negotiate in their communication with team members.

For example, traditional views of teams consider physicians as the leaders and decision-makers with nurses and other health professionals functioning as subordinates. Changes in multi-disciplinary teams and more collaborative relationships have empowered nurses to participate in decision-making as well as assert their professional autonomy and judgment. Nurses experience role contradiction when they encounter these two diverging views in team interactions (e.g., physicians expecting deference, allied health workers and other nurses expecting assertiveness and collaboration). Apker et al. (2005) concluded that nurses navigate the tension by accommodating and/or denying the hierarchy. Accommodating involves working within the status hierarchy by using indirect forms of communication when speaking with physicians (e.g., asking questions to guide conversation rather than asserting knowledge). Denying the hierarchy entails that nurses refuse to act deferentially to physicians in order to be treated like equals (e.g., confronting conflict directly).

Individuals occupy roles or positions in an organization, but how they perform their roles is largely communicative in nature and, as such, subject to change. Conceptualizations of role communication show that creating, shaping, and maintaining roles is a highly contextual process, based largely on the needs and expectations of role incumbents and role set members.

Chapter Summary

The health system is made up of a wide range of professions that work together to contribute to healthcare delivery and public health. Assimilation in health organizations depends on communication, as newcomers learn the ropes of their jobs and organizations through their interactions with others. Education institutions and organizational employers are key contexts in which assimilation occurs and shapes how health professionals communicate with professional associates and patients. Role communication figures prominently in assimilation as newcomers attempt to master their roles and ease the transition into new tasks and relationships. The dynamic, fluid nature of role enactment enables health professionals to adjust to changes in health teams and organizations as well as respond to shifting contingences in the health system environment. In Chapter 3, you will learn about identity development and power dynamics in health organizations, two topics that are intimately connected to how health professionals learn and make the transition into those organizations.

3

Identity and Power

Take a moment to think about how you introduce yourself to others. How do you identify yourself? Do you, like many people, begin with what you "do," such as your current occupation and employer? Or do you lead off talking about your hometown and family background? Perhaps you take an entirely different approach and describe your aspirations and hopes for the future. How you introduce yourself gives others some insights into your identity. It tells them about what makes you distinct as well as how you might share similarities. What you say in an introduction can also explain how you view yourself as a member of organizations.

For example, a physician's assistant (PA) working in a family medicine practice introduces herself to others by title and credentials. Since some patients may be unfamiliar with this role, the PA may also explain what she does in her job as well as the similarities and differences between PAs and medical doctors. Some informal chitchat may prompt her to talk about her background as a former nurse, her decision to switch careers, and how much she has learned by assisting the physicians in the practice. This brief encounter provides some cursory insights into her identity as it is influenced by her professional and organizational experiences.

Identity ties in nicely with assimilation (Chapter 2) because people develop their identities as they learn about the work they need to accomplish and their organizational roles. In the landscape of healthcare delivery, health organizations provide important communication contexts in which individuals understand what it means to be health professionals. Interactions with other organizational members such as teachers, supervisors, and coworkers establish attachments between individuals and organizations. As you will learn, these kind of affiliations inform health professionals' identity development.

Power dynamics can play a key role in how individuals develop, understand, and perform their identities in health organizations. For example, health professionals who have a great deal of expertise and specialized knowledge and also hold positions of authority and status are often perceived as powerful institutional leaders. This identity is reinforced in their communication with those in subordinate positions (e.g., giving orders or directives, dispensing rewards and punishments) and in the reactions of lower-status personnel (e.g., following institutional norms and avoiding challenging power and authority). Further, the identity attachments that people develop toward groups, a concept known as identification, can influence how individuals communicate and make decisions in health contexts.

Identity and power matter because they influence how health professionals interact with colleagues, coworkers, and patients. Developing one's identity and engaging in power dynamics provides individuals with a sense of self, affects their institutional relationships, and facilitates sensemaking critical to organizational assimilation. This chapter begins by considering identity and identification from a systems perspective. Then, you will learn about key messages and important referent groups that develop and shape identity through the process of identification. The second half of the chapter focuses on power by first taking a systems approach. Then, you will learn about the intersecting dynamics of power, control, and ideology and how it influences communication in health organizations.

A Systems Perspective on Identity and Identification

Personal identity was once understood to be a fixed, singular entity consisting of personal traits such as personality, physical appearance, and communication style which remain largely unchanged over a person's life span. More recent conceptualizations view identity as a dynamic process that evolves as people communicate in their memberships in social collectives such as families, organizational employers, educational institutions, work teams, etc. (Eisenberg, 2006). While a person may have distinctive, enduring identity characteristics, personal identity can be altered over time and through experiences with various social groups.

Social identity is closely connected to contemporary understandings of personal identity. It refers to the part of a person's self-concept derived from participating in social collectives and the value significance of group membership (Ashforth, Harrison, and Corley, 2008). For instance, statements such as "I am an inspector for the U.S. Occupational Safety and Health Administration. I feel proud to work for OHSA and value its mission to protect American workers' safety" visibly demonstrate social identity. Social identity attachments are known as **identifications**. Identifications teach people the norms, values, and behaviors of key referent groups in ways that ultimately produce social identity (Scott, Corman, and Cheney, 1998). People develop identifications as they communicate with members of these referent groups. In health organizations it has been found that workers develop identifications or attachments with referent groups such as professions, employers, and teams.

Insights from systems concepts of **dynamic homeostasis** and **interdependencies** add to our understanding of identity and identification. Recall that dynamic homeostasis refers to maintaining a steady state while simultaneously adapting to environmental contingencies. System components (typically people) alter their self concepts or identities as they interact with others within a system (a social collective). Such transformation allows them to grow and change to meet the needs of the system and its embedded environment. A submissive, introverted lab technician, for example, may become more extroverted and assertive at work when she is promoted to a management position.

Identifications help create interdependencies between system components in ways that promote system survival. For instance, a cancer center team identifies strongly with salient group values (e.g., professional collaboration, mutual respect). Their attachment helps team members rely on one another to achieve shared goals and make decisions aligned with team values. Through their team identification, these health professionals support the mission of the cancer center in ways that contribute to the organization's track record of quality care.

With these concepts in mind, let's turn our attention to notions of identity and identification as they have been portrayed in the research literature. The next section takes a closer look at the referent groups that have profoundly affected, and will continue to influence, how members of health organizations perform their identities and develop group attachments.

Identification

Through communication, individuals develop affiliations with various identification referent groups or targets and incorporate those identifications into their construction of personal and social identity (Larson and Pepper, 2003). This section first discusses the messages and targets of identification before addressing the complexities of negotiating competing identifications.

Identification Messages and Targets

How do referent groups or targets encourage identification? In the search for answers, organizational communication scholars have identified a range of techniques that can build and reinforce attachments to collectives such as institutional employers, professions, and work teams (Cheney 1983; Cheney and Tompkins, 1987). Table 3.1 offers a sample of tactics identified in the research literature and provides health organization examples.

These messages tell others, particularly newcomers, about group membership such as how to behave and what is important (Tracy, Meyers, and Scott, 2006). Group interactions also reinforce shared values and emphasize distinctions between groups. Consider Ashley, a certified nursing assistant (CNA) who works at a daycare center for senior citizens. The CNAs pride themselves on developing close relationships with the center's clientele, many of whom have health problems. As a relative

Table 3.1   Identification Messages and Examples

Technique	Description	Health Organization Example
Common ground tactic	Explicitly connect with others through strategies such as boasting about task accomplishment and inviting members to become or stay involved in collective activities.	"We worked the crisis 24-hours, seven-days-a-week until every survivor received medical care and was given food and shelter." "We need you to keep giving your time and talent by encouraging students to consider medicine as a profession."
Expression of concern for the individual	Display concern for others as essential parts of the social collective (e.g., profession, organization, team).	"You are an important member of this medical group and I'm concerned that you might be burned out. What can I do to help?"
Recognition of individuals' contributions	Commend people by name for their efforts to help the social collective.	"Thank you, ____, for your willingness to mentor new nursing assistants so they feel a part of the team."
Espousal of shared values	Overt talk of communal values held by membership.	"Excellent patient care is our number one priority."
Advocacy of benefits	Expression of benefits provided to individuals by the social collective.	"This nursing home rewards employees' hard work and dedication."
Identification by antithesis	Persuading members to unite against a mutual adversary.	"Our independent pharmacy offers better customer service than chain pharmacies. It's up to all of us to compete with them on service and win."
The assumed "we"	Using pronouns such as "we" and "us" in reference to all members of a social collective.	"We are regarded as the best unit in the hospital because we go above and beyond to help patients and their families."

(Adapted from Disanza and Bullis, 1999)

newcomer, Ashley routinely hears from other CNAs "We care for patients like family members. We are the only employees here who treat them as human beings. Everyone else just sees them as a paycheck." These statements are reinforced when Ashley is encouraged by her coworkers to take extra time to listen to patients and develop friendships with them so the center feels like a caring, nurturing home rather than an impersonal clinical environment.

Professions have figured prominently in the research literature as popular targets of health professionals' identification. Attachments to health occupations are usually made in young adulthood as individuals view themselves as having a "calling" to help others. They seek careers that represent personal values of caring, compassion, and service for those in need (Nosse and Sagiv, 2005). Attachments to such values often grow stronger over time, as individuals experience years of formal education in their chosen health profession (Harter and Krone, 2001; Harter and Kirby, 2004). Novice health professionals are typically immersed in the culture of their profession where they receive ongoing messages of what it means to be a physician, nurse, social worker, etc. In medicine, a study of identity development found that residents relied on professional principles first learned in medical school to guide their work behaviors during residency (Pratt, Rockmann, and Kaufmann, 2006).

Feelings of professional identification typically become stronger once health workers embark on their chosen careers in full-time jobs. Factors such as the type of work performed, the time spent doing a job, and the kind of people workers communicate with play influential roles. For instance, in separate studies of nurses and nursing assistants, researchers found that professional identification positively correlates with time devoted to job-related activities and frequency of role communication with professional associates (Apker and Fox, 2002; Pfefferle and Weinberg, 2008). These findings suggest that health professionals will feel more attached to their profession over time and with more interactions that require the enactment of a particular occupational role. The converse is also true.

Box 3.1   Ripped from the Headlines

Identifying with Profession and Team in Health Social Work
Social workers employed in medical, public health, mental and substance abuse services have jobs that are simultaneously rewarding and demanding. Social workers have the opportunity to change patients' lives for the better, but often their work consists of long hours, large caseloads, and understaffing that can result in emotional exhaustion and burnout. Given these highs and lows of their occupation, how do social workers stay motivated and remain in their challenging yet satisfying roles? For some, the answer to this question lies in their identification with the principles of the social work profession as well as with the values espoused in their health teams.

The video "This Could be You: The Many Faces of Social Work" (available at www.youtube.com) provides a useful commentary on the importance of professional and team attachments. It specifically highlights the experiences of Jennifer, a medical social worker employed by the Children's Hospital in Boston, who works in the young parents program. She helps provide teenage parents with medical care, supports their social and mental health needs, and offers services that promote healthy families.

Jennifer's reflections on the nature of her work demonstrate a strong identification with her occupation's values such as service, social justice, and the importance of human relationships (National Association of Social Workers [NASW], n.d.). For instance, when explaining what attracts her to the social work profession, Jennifer talks about "caring for others," and "working with families to find solutions to problems." She likes the fact that social work allows her "look at the whole picture . . . the families . . . the schools . . . the whole system" which contributes to the health of patients. Her comments align closely with the profession's focus on "the individual well being in a social context" (NASW, n.d., para 1).

Jennifer's responses also provide insight into the salience of her attachments to the value of collaboration espoused by her social work team. Here, she talks about "the awesome team of people" who come from different backgrounds and do different things, but work together for the good of the patient. Her views are reinforced by her coworkers (also in the video), Paul and Anu, who assert that teamwork is vital to making an immediate and long-term positive difference in patients' lives.

This video's depiction of Jennifer and other social workers provides a compelling portrayal of what health social workers do in their jobs and why they remain in the social work profession. Their insights are exemplars of findings from the research literature, which suggest that professional and team attachments contribute to employee retention in health organizations (Apker, Ford, and Fox, 2003).

Discussion Questions
1. With whom or what do you identify? Think about the professions, organizations, and/or work teams for which you feel strong attachments.
2. What types of messages should professional associations and health organization employers communicate to foster identification among health professionals?
3. What advice would you give Jennifer and her coworkers to help them maintain their identifications with their profession and team?

Organizations and **teams** are other visible sources of identification for health professionals. Organizational or team identification happens when individuals consider the interests and values of the organization and/or their work group as relevant in the process of making decisions (Cheney and Christensen, 2001). For instance, community health educators working in rural areas may travel long distances and use personal funds to help needy clients even if those efforts are not compensated or publicly recognized. They perform these extra role duties and go above and beyond formal job expectations to support the public health mission of their state-run, institutional employer.

Similar to professional identification, health workers develop identifications with organizations and teams by receiving messages of affiliation and communicating with other members of referent groups. For example, novice nurses working at a home health agency hear how much they are valued and appreciated when they go through new employee orientation. These messages of affiliation and support are reinforced during routine interactions with supervisors and coworkers and, over time, the novices feel strongly attached to the agency and their health teams. Their identification improves teamwork and creates a work environment that reduces staff turnover.

In the search for answers to better understand the complexities of identification with multiple targets, researchers have turned to the Organizational Identification Questionnaire (for one example, see Figure 3.1—try taking the survey yourself now, using different targets or referent groups that comprise your life, e.g., employer, work team, occupation).

Studying identification offers insights into health organization performance, with the research suggesting mixed effects. Hodges, Keeley, and Grier (2005) argue that professional identification promotes nurses' career longevity. However, professional identification may contribute to profession-centrism—"a constructed and preferred view of the world held by a particular professional group developed and reinforced through their training experiences" (Pecukonis, Doyle, and Bliss, 2008, p. 420), the results of which can include heightened occupational isolation, reduced

Appendix—Identification Questionnaires

Please indicate how strongly you agree or disagree with each of the statements below using the following scale. Please note that area refers to the geographical extension area of which you may be a part. Circle one number per question:

1 = strongly disagree
2 = somewhat disagree
3 = neither disagree nor agree
4 = somewhat agree
5 = strongly agree

1.	I'm very concerned about the success of my county office.	1	2	3	4	5
2.	I'm very concerned about the success of my area office.	1	2	3	4	5
3.	I don't feel much loyalty to my profession/occupation.	1	2	3	4	5
4.	I am willing to put in extra effort in order to help the Colorado Cooperative Extension be successful.	1	2	3	4	5
5.	I don't like working with my county office.	1	2	3	4	5
6.	I am willing to put in extra effort in order to help my profession/occupation be successful.	1	2	3	4	5
7.	I don't like working with my area office.	1	2	3	4	5
8.	I'm very concerned about the success of my employer, Colorado Cooperative Extension.	1	2	3	4	5
9.	I'm very concerned about the well-being of my profession/occupation area.	1	2	3	4	5
10.	I don't like working for Colorado Cooperative Extension.	1	2	3	4	5
11.	I don't like to hear others criticize Colorado Cooperative Extension.	1	2	3	4	5
12.	I don't like to hear others criticize my county office.	1	2	3	4	5
13.	I don't like to hear others criticize my profession.	1	2	3	4	5
14.	When I make job-related decisions, I think about how my decisions will affect my area office.	1	2	3	4	5
15.	I don't like working with others in my profession.	1	2	3	4	5
16.	When I make job-related decisions, I think about how my decisions will affect my profession's success.	1	2	3	4	5
17.	When I make job-related decisions, I think about how my decisions will affect the success of Colorado Cooperative Extension.	1	2	3	4	5
18.	I am proud to be a member of Colorado Cooperative Extension.	1	2	3	4	5
19.	I am proud to be a member of this county office.	1	2	3	4	5
20.	I am proud to be a member of this area office.	1	2	3	4	5
21.	Colorado Cooperative Extension is like a family to me.	1	2	3	4	5
22.	My profession is like a family to me.	1	2	3	4	5
23.	I don't feel much loyalty to Colorado Cooperative Extension.	1	2	3	4	5
24.	My county office is like a family to me.	1	2	3	4	5
25.	I don't like to hear others criticize my area office.	1	2	3	4	5
26.	I identify closely with my area office.	1	2	3	4	5
27.	I don't feel much loyalty to my area office.	1	2	3	4	5
28.	I identify closely with my occupation/profession.	1	2	3	4	5
29.	When I make job-related decisions, I think about how my decisions will affect my county office.	1	2	3	4	5
30.	I am willing to put in extra effort in order to help my county office be successful.	1	2	3	4	5
31.	I am willing to put in extra effort in order to help my area office be successful.	1	2	3	4	5
32.	I identify closely with my county office.	1	2	3	4	5
33.	My area office is like a family to me.	1	2	3	4	5
34.	I don't feel much loyalty to my county office.	1	2	3	4	5
35.	I am proud to be a member of this profession.	1	2	3	4	5
36.	I identify closely with Colorado Cooperative Extension.	1	2	3	4	5

Figure 3.1

(Source: Scott, C. R. Identification with multiple targets in a geographically dispersed organization. *Management Communication Quarterly*, 10, 1997, 491–522. Reprinted by permission of SAGE publications.)

interdisciplinary collaboration, and limited professional communication competence (Goldberg, 2008; Makary et al., 2006).

Scholarship investigating organizational and team identification also shows a range of pros and cons. For instance, organizational attachments have been found to reduce nurses' intent to leave institutional employers (Apker, Ford, and Fox, 2003) and to foster cooperation and extra-role behaviors among physicians (Dukerich, Golden, and Shortell, 2002). However, strong organizational affiliations may also hinder innovation because change can threaten deeply held health institution values (Apker, 2004). Team identification has been found to promote intragroup cohesion (Apker, Propp, and Ford, 2009) but may also contribute to team dynamics that prevent potentially useful conflict from occurring (Callan et al., 2007).

So far you have learned that messages communicated during interpersonal and group interactions are important factors in the degree to which health workers develop attachments to their professions, organizations, and teams. Let's take a closer look at how health professionals negotiate multiple identifications occurring simultaneously.

Negotiating Identifications

The work of health professionals can be incredibly complex, demanding a wide repertoire of role behaviors to meet the needs of varying constituencies such as patients and their families, supervisors, colleagues, and subordinates. Multiple groups attempt to induce identifications, creating exigencies where various attachments converge and/or contradict one another. For instance, Susan is a travelling physical therapist (PT) who works in a new location every three to four months within the same multi-state health system. She loves the variety of her work and the opportunity to see different parts of the country, but she often develops deep attachments to the workplaces and health teams where she works. Each time Susan is due to move on to a new location, her coworkers try to persuade her stay and become a permanent PT at their location. While she feels attached to her professional associates and enjoys her working relationships, Susan feels most identified with her profession. As long as she can provide therapy she's happy to do the work anywhere. So, she says fond goodbyes to each team and looks forward to the new challenges of another clinic, office, or hospital. Susan has been able to prioritize her identifications and understand how targets such as team and organization are subordinate to her professional identity.

While resolving such competing identifications may be easy for a person like Susan, it may not be as straightforward for other health professionals. For instance, research by Harter and colleagues (Harter and Krone, 2001; Harter and Kirby, 2004) found that osteopathy medical students receive contradictory messages of identification that contribute to role tension and stress. Their findings showed that medical students desired to identify with the principles of osteopathy (an holistic approach to healing; an emphasis on the role of the musculoskeletal system in health and disease), but pursuing those identifications was contradicted by working in health organizations which emphasized traditional biomedicine. Students coped through a variety of strategies, with many seeking a middle ground that incorporated both osteopathic and biomedical principles in their work activities. Similarly, Apker et al. (2009) discovered that nurses working in multidisciplinary teams cope with conflicting team and professional attachments by segmenting their communication to meet the expectations of various team member constituencies. Nurses maintained team attachments with subordinates and coworkers by talking in a nurturing, supportive, and upbeat manner whereas they affiliated with their profession when speaking with physicians in a direct and assertive manner which demonstrated their nursing expertise.

Health organizations can influence the degree to which negotiating identification is a process of convergence or contradiction (Ashforth, Harrison, and Corley, 2008). For example, Pratt and Rafaeli (1997) found that a hospital supported nurses' professional identity by allowing them to choose work attire aligned with their nursing values. Acute care nurses wore scrubs to symbolize their efforts to help patients gain medical health and/or stability whereas rehabilitation nurses wore street clothes to symbolize their role in

Box 3.2   Communication in Practice

Constructing Professional Identity in Healthcare
Health organizations are contexts in which health professionals learn and perform their professional identities on a daily basis, often by working with members of multiple health occupations. Through their interactions with key referent or role model groups, health workers construct self concepts commensurate with professional expectations.

What occurs when the work health professionals do in their jobs doesn't match who they are as professionals? A longitudinal study conducted by Pratt, Rockmann, and Kaufmann (2006) addresses this question by exploring how medical residents construct their professional selves in response to identity violations. Pratt et al. interviewed and observed primary care, surgery, and radiology residents as they experienced various stages of "Boot Camp" at a highly ranked medical education center.

The researchers found that each group "struggled to reconcile their professional self-conceptualizations with the work that they did" (p. 245) when faced with identity violations such as performing menial tasks and doing paperwork. Residents resolved these violations by using the following identity customization strategies:

- **Enriching**: recognizing the scope of physician responsibility toward patients and showing greater understanding of how physician activities contribute to care.
- **Patching**: drawing upon preexisting ideas of what it means to be a physician, as exhibited by current role models, to patch the holes in the self concept.
- **Splinting**: temporarily strengthening a weak sense of professional self by relying on prior

medical student identity (discarded after gaining self-confidence).

Communication with senior physicians, peers, and role models provided important social validation for these identity customization techniques. Residents received feedback which told them how well they were doing in two major ways: 1) "bites" or explicit corrections from senior physicians when mistakes were made, and 2) performance comparisons between self and others made through gossiping or grapevine communication. This feedback affected residents' professional identities by shaping their workplace behavior.

Pratt et al. argue that "By learning what they, and others, were doing wrong and consequently how the work should be performed, [residents] changed how they viewed themselves as physicians" (p. 251). At the end of their Boot Camp experiences, residents reported a higher level of perceived competence as physicians and stronger work identities than when they started their residency training.

helping patients make the transition to self-care at home. For both sets of nurses, attachment to the hospital increased when they had the freedom to wear what they wished. In contrast, Real, Bramson, and Poole (2009) conclude that physicians experience different—and potentially conflicting—identification discourses which play out in their medical encounters. These authors argue that physicians receive messages communicating classic notions of serving patients and making sacrifices for others while at the same time receiving messages that reinforce rules set by third-party payer goals and structures. Physicians negotiate the contradiction in their interactions with patients by attempting to establish a rapport and solicit patient participation while heeding time and resource restrictions.

To summarize what you've learned so far, health professionals construct and negotiate important identity attachments through their communication with members of key referent groups. The process of identification is complex, involving multiple messages, targets, and communication processes that work together to develop a self concept. Ultimately, identifications shape health professionals' personal and social identities, guide their workplace behaviors, and influence their organizational relationships.

Identification contributes to power dynamics that play out in health organization contexts, in the interactions that health professionals have with patients, peers, leaders, and subordinates. Individuals who strongly identify with the values of their profession, for instance, are likely to behave, communicate, and make decisions consistent with those occupational principles. The next section explores the concept of power by understanding it from a systems perspective. Then, you will learn about different sources of power and control in health organizations as well as the salience of medical ideology in power dynamics.

A Systems Perspective on Power

Generally speaking, **power** is an effort to influence others' behavior in order to generate desired results (Papa, Daniels, and Spiker, 2008). French and Raven (1959) provide a classic consideration of organizational power which explains that power comes from many different sources. The more a person has access to and uses these sources of power, the more powerful he or she is perceived to be by other organizational members. Table 3.2 identifies these power sources and provides illustrative examples of them in health organizations.

A system approach focuses our attention on the concept of **interdependencies**. The team-based nature of most health organizations creates conditions where health professionals must depend upon one another in order to fulfill individual and collective goals. This mutual reliance may be affected by power differences due to factors such as position and knowledge/expertise.

For example, pharmacists depend on physicians to write appropriate prescriptions while physicians need pharmacists to fill

Table 3.2   Sources of Power and Examples

Concept	Description	Health Organization Example
Reward	The power to provide compensation such as money, promotions, and awards for compliance.	Dentists working in a group practice receive bonuses for increases in new patient visits.
Coercive	The power to punish in the form of public criticism, demotions, poor work assignments, etc., in response to lack of compliance.	A nursing school dean is fired by her university president for failing to meet goals for faculty and student recruitment.
Referent	The power of affiliation and charisma which motivates others in their efforts to comply with organizational values.	A nursing aide goes above and beyond his job requirements in order to feel a part of his healthcare team.
Expert	The power of specialized knowledge, where compliance occurs out of respect for expertise.	The board of a not-for-profit organ donor organization makes investment decisions after hearing recommendations from financial experts.
Legitimate	The power of position or status, where compliance occurs because of a person's status hierarchy.	A physician writes orders for treatment, medications, lab studies, and tests which are carried out by other health team members.

prescriptions accurately. Physicians have the more visible power role in this relationship because they have the authority to order prescriptions (an authority given in medical credentialing and licensure). A pharmacist can question or even challenge the order, but physicians have the ultimate decision-making role. However, even though it appears that pharmacists are in a subordinate position, they too can assert power. For instance, a pharmacist could refuse to fill a prescription or could persuade a physician (or their patients) to consider alternative drugs.

The systems concept of **order** also figures prominently in understandings of power. Despite some attempts to reduce hierarchies and decentralize decision-making in healthcare, many health organizations remain highly bureaucratic. Bureaucracies are typically composed of structures such as vertical chains of command, clear lines of reporting, and fixed rules that govern member behaviors. These structures provide certain people with power—typically those with high rank and in leadership positions—as well as bring order or organization to how work gets accomplished, when it gets done, and by whom. Individuals such as leaders demonstrate their power by establishing order in an organization (e.g., creating rules that reward and punish, giving directives, developing group norms that guide who gets to talk and when).

As you will learn in the rest of this chapter, power drives much of what gets done in health organizations by influencing how health professionals make sense of organizational life, make decisions, and behave toward others. The next section considers power and the associated concepts of control and ideology as they are understood and exhibited in health organizations.

Power in Health Organizations

Research regarding power in health organizations has been greatly influenced by French social theorist Michel Foucault (1973; 1980), who established important connections between knowledge, power, and control as revealed in social interactions. Foucault specifically explored health organizations as sites of institutional power, and two core elements of his theorizing—knowledge power and disciplinary power—are particularly salient here.

Knowledge Power and Disciplinary Power

Foucault (1980) considers power and knowledge to be intertwined and to reside in individuals' communication behaviors. He argues that **knowledge power** is produced through regular and identifiable interaction patterns that determine what can be said and by whom. Those in powerful and/or high status positions are able to assert their versions of truth and knowledge as reality while those in subordinate roles largely accept those versions when they follow organizational rules and norms. Murphy et al. (2008) state that "For Foucault, power relations between institutions, people, groups, and individuals are both accomplished and realized through discourse, with privilege afforded to those who claim specialized knowledge, such as lawyers and physicians" (p. 276).

The biomedical model's influence in physician-patient interactions provides an illustrative example of communicating knowledge power. Recall from Chapter 1 that the biomedical model is based on the premise that illness is a purely physical phenomenon that can be identified, explained, and treated through physical interventions. Physicians have a great deal of knowledge power in this approach thanks largely to their years of training during which they absorb vast amounts of data not generally available to patients and consumers. Physicians trained in this approach may consider that their perspectives are "the best" and that the accounts given by patients—most of whom who lack medical knowledge and training—should be discounted or ignored. Knowledge power plays out in a medical encounter when physicians display their authority by managing information exchange with patients. For instance, a physician might attempt to intimidate a patient with her knowledge and expertise as a way of silencing questions and ensuring compliance with medical recommendations.

Disciplinary power is a concept closely related to knowledge power. It refers to the standardization of behaviors that discipline or regulate individuals to act in accordance with the social norms desired by their referent groups (Foucault, 1980). Institutions, such as healthcare and higher education organizations, are comprised of people who represent different disciplines in the form of professions or occupations. Each discipline has its own standardized behaviors, values, and worldviews that differentiate members from nonmembers. For example, the *Essentials of Baccalaureate Education for Professional Nursing Practice* (2008) is an influential set of disciplinary standards authored by the American Association of Colleges of Nursing, a health organization that governs the undergraduate preparation of professional nurses in U.S. nursing schools, and such programs must demonstrate actions (e.g., classroom instruction, clinical experiences, research) supporting these standards in order to obtain and keep professional accreditation. The *Essentials* directly communicates the scope of nursing practice and what activities differentiate nurses from other health professionals. Those standards are reinforced in formal and informal instruction where nurses learn certain ways of behaving "like a nurse."

According to Foucault (1973; 1980), disciplinary power is reinforced by **discursive formations**—social norms, developed in communication within a group, about who can talk with authority and who has credibility and why. Group members reward behavior that supports established customs and, conversely, punish individuals who dispute norms. Apker and Eggly's (2004) study of morning report case presentations provides a vivid example of discursive formations in action. A cornerstone of medical education, morning report requires medical residents to publicly discuss patient cases, answer questions, and explain and/or defend their medical decisions in front of their peers and supervising physicians. In a case study conducted at an urban teaching hospital, senior physicians established powerful behavioral norms for speaking in morning report. Residents who focused on biomedical factors as causes for ill health were affirmed by senior physicians whereas residents who considered social issues (e.g., a patient's occupation or living conditions) as illness contributors were often ridiculed and attacked. Apker and Eggly conclude that this type of discourse served as a form of social punishment and discouraged residents from bringing up social concerns during case presentations.

Power and Control

Control refers to how people exercise power through formal and informal means. Rules, regulations, and policies are common means of formal control. Social punishments such as mocking and verbally attacking others and social rewards such as including and complimenting others function as informal ways of control. Organizational communication scholars pay particular attention to how individuals assert control over others through formal and informal interactions in institutional settings. Table 3.3

Box 3.3 Communication in Practice

Communicating Powerfully with Others

Healthcare organizations present unique contexts for power dynamics. Factors such as disciplinary and knowledge power, authority, status, and hierarchy influence relational power dynamics. Paul Preston (2005), a professor of management and healthcare administration, provides advice for "power players" in health organizations such as:

1. Remain calm when faced with negativity. While responding with surprise or anger is a common initial reaction, doing so may make people reluctant to share bad news. Strive to remain calm. You will appear more approachable to others.

2. Share information. Having information and knowing how to use it increases others' perceptions of your power. Sharing information tells others that you are knowledgeable, trustworthy, and equitable.

3. Deliberate carefully, and stand by your position. Carefully evaluate information before making a decision and seek out others for opinions. You may change your mind when considering options, but stick to your decision once it is made. Doing so demonstrates decisiveness, prevents "waffling," and reduces overly quick decisions.

4. Accept praise. Gracious acceptance of praise from subordinates, peers, and bosses shows others that you are comfortable, not cocky when receiving accolades. Honesty and conciseness appeal to others more than superficial modesty.

5. Know when to remain silent. Stay silent and allow others to express their views. Silence may prompt others to talk and provide information that improves your decision-making. Remaining silent may also provide you with more time to reflect.

6. Learn how to say no. Saying no all the time creates the impression that you don't consider other perspectives and/or that you are hard to please. Say no after thoughtful deliberation and make sure you explain your reasons specifically.

7. Do not apologize for saying no. Avoid apologizing because doing so reduces your power image. Say no with calmness and professionalism. Listen to the other party, but keeping opposing remarks short and to the point.

8. Build your networks. Cultivate relationships with a variety of people with whom you can share information, build alliances, and talk about options and opportunities. Such a network also expands your reputation and ability to manage others' impressions.

identifies major forms of control considered influential to understanding power in organizations and provides examples unique to healthcare.

Eliot Freidson's (1975) concept of **professional control** represents an important addition to understanding control in health organizations. This form of control is gained from formal education, training, and restrictive licensing. Those who embody the standards, principles, and behaviors of certain professions, such as are found in healthcare, education, and legal systems, are allowed to perform and control certain types of work. For instance, physicians' education, training, and licensing requirements give them legal and clinical control over patients' medical care. In light of

Table 3.3   Forms of Organizational Control and Examples

Concept	Description	Health Organization Example
Simple	Direct and authoritative control through use of incentives to reward and measures to punish.	A midwife at a women's health clinic receives a promotion to nurse manager following several positive performance evaluations about her management style.
Technological	Control asserted through familiarity with and use of technology (equipment, technical processes).	Hospital information technology staff control the design, implementation, and clinical staff training of a new electronic medical record system.
Bureaucratic	Control stemming from bureaucratic rules and structures.	Nursing home aides punch in and out on a timeclock because the rules of the organization require them to do so in order to get paid.
Concertive	Control emanating from affiliation with shared values and identity.	Nurses regularly work overtime in order to meet team expectations and values for quality patient care.

(Adapted from Miller, 2009)

their unique roles, physicians display considerable professional control in medical encounters (e.g., they ask highly personal questions, perform physical exams) and patients willingly cede control because of physicians' professional authority. Freidson argues that such allowances have both pros and cons. On the plus side, the display of such professional control enables patients to get the care they need. However, emphasizing professional control can be problematic when it undermines or devalues patients' perspectives and/or experiences about their health and illness.

Professional control is a popular topic in medical education, where power, status hierarchy, and authority intersect in physician communication. According to Graham (2009), the talk of medical "rounding" provides an illustrative example of how attending physicians assert their control over subordinates. Rounding is a formalized, routine practice found in most U.S. teaching hospitals. Medical students and residents join an attending physician to see patients collectively on a particular medical service. The rounding group enters a patient's room and the resident assigned to treating the patient briefly summarizes the case. The presentation updates the group about the patient's history, presenting condition, diagnosis, treatment, etc. A "good" presentation means that the resident has addressed all important issues and no additional questions are asked. Omissions and/or inaccuracies invite questions from the attending. On the surface, the use of questions solicits necessary information. At a deeper level, however, these queries can tell the rest of the rounding group that expectations in knowledge were not met. By using questions or silence, the attending defines good and poor case presentations.

The extant literature has primarily focused on exploring power and control in medical settings and professions. Scholars argue that the institution of medicine—and by extension healthcare—remains predominately bureaucratic, consisting of "top-down" communication in which physicians control conversations with other caregivers (Ellingson, 2008; Lupton, 1994). DiPalma (2004) observes that when speaking with physicians, other caregivers tend to show deference and obey physicians' oral directives. She concludes that these compliance behaviors make physicians' power and authority unmistakable. While professions such as nursing have made concerted efforts to "level the playing field" there remains an asymmetry in physician-caregiver relationships (Foley and Faircloth, 2003; Geist and Dreyer, 1993).

A more limited set of the research literature examines power and control in non-physician professions or settings. Jervis' (2002) study of an urban nursing home revealed a clear "pecking order" or chain of command among nursing staff. Staff nurses with higher prestige (RNs, LPNs) distanced themselves from lower-status nursing assistants through various communication behaviors (e.g., avoiding personal talk, speaking to the nursing aides in an authoritarian manner). Nurse administrators demonstrated similar patterns of communication when they talked with staff nurses, indicating cultural assumptions about power and authority. These findings are echoed by Apker, Propp, and Ford (2005) who found that power imbalances due to status and authority complicate communication between nursing aides and staff nurses. Even though nursing aides were nurses' subordinates, the aides disliked communication that reinforced status and authority distinctions (e.g., being ordered rather than asked to do tasks). Ellingson's (2007) exploration of team communication indicates that asserting power may have more to do with the ability to solve problems rather than formal authority and status. She argues that caregivers with more training, education, and professional prestige are powerful because they are highly valued team members.

Power and Ideology

Ideology—the often unstated assumptions and beliefs that constitute a system of thought—is intimately connected to power and control in organizations (Papa, Daniels, and Spiker, 2008). Ideology shapes how individuals understand and participate in organizational life so that current perceptions of the status quo are unquestioned. The phrase "this is the way we do things around here" to explain a rule, procedure, or action is an illustrative example of ideology. Ideological assumptions also limit awareness and acceptance of other worldviews and ways of doing things. By influencing what is considered normal in an organization, ideology enables traditional power and control structures to remain in place without being challenged (Mumby, 1987).

Consider Tameka, a wellness coach who works at LifeHealth, a wellness consulting firm which provides services for major corporate employers in the Northeast. Tameka works directly with LifeHealth clients' employees to help them adopt healthier lifestyles. For years, Tameka has advocated for innovations to expand LifeHealth's client services on the internet. She has proposed online health assessments and virtual wellness coaching, but her bosses ignore or dismiss her ideas. They worry that an online presence will make their "bread and butter" services of face-to-face, personalized coaching obsolete. They tell Tameka, "This firm has successfully relied on tailored, face-to-face wellness coaching and that's the way we will continue to do business." Realizing that she is "hitting her head against a wall" to advocate change, Tameka accepts their decision and continues to advise clients in face-to-face visits. In this example Tameka's supervisors asserted their power by promoting LifeHealth's current way of doing business as the best model of success. They displayed their control by refusing to approve Tameka's ideas for organizational improvements. While Tameka disagrees with their decision, she also realizes that change is futile and keeps doing her job as is.

The concept of medical ideology has been particularly influential in understanding power in health organizations, particularly as it is made visible in physician communication with patients and with professional associates. **Medical ideology** is conceptualized as a worldview that espouses objectivity, value neutrality, authority, and social control through technical expertise (Geist and Dreyer, 1993; Waitzkin, 1979). This ideology reflects the tenets of the biomedical model and traditional principles of medical education which teach physicians to identify, predict, and control illness as well as display authority in medical decision-making.

In his book, *The Politics of Medical Encounters*, Waitzkin (1991) argues that through what physicians say and do in medical encounters they convey to patients ideological notions about what constitutes desirable behavior. For instance, physicians might keep medical encounters brief and to the point, focusing on biomedical issues, and block patient attempts to introduce psycho-social information (e.g., domestic problems, emotional displays). Other behaviors such as using a condescending tone, medical jargon, and an assertive, dominating communication style may encourage patients to show deference to authority and comply with medical advice/treatment without question. Waitzkin (1979) argues that physician behaviors reinforce traditional medical ideology and promote medical authority and control over patients.

Researchers have also explored the presence of medical ideology in physician-physician discourse. Here, findings also show that physician discourse reproduces medical ideology in ways similar to physician-patient communication. Apker and Eggly (2004) argue that talk between physicians predominantly articulates the voice of medicine (Mishler, 1984), a perspective that mirrors scientific interests and removes events from personal and social contexts. They further argue that physician talk reflects biomedical principles such as a concern for accuracy, an emphasis on medical terminology, and a focus on the purely physical details. In their study of teaching techniques in residency training, Kennedy and Lingard (2007) found that attending physicians judge residents' medical competence by the degree to which residents produce case-related knowledge and assert authority. These authors argue that defining "good" physician behaviors reflected ideological principles of physician expertise and control.

The final area of research examines the influence of medical ideology regarding physician communication with other members of healthcare teams. Ellingson (2005) argues that problems in physician-team communication may be a function of the different health professions' varying ideological worldviews. For instance, the holistic approach to healthcare that emphasizes the interconnections between mind, body, and spirit espoused by alternative healers may conflict with traditional biomedical principles advanced by mainstream health occupations such as medicine and nursing. Studies have also shown that communicative displays of physician power and control play an influential role in collaboration among health professionals. Thomson (2007) argues that medical ideology enables physicians to retain authority over nurses, but this dominance reduces the professional collaboration necessary to quality care. She concludes that new, nurse-physician work relationships need to be based on principles of partnership and mutual respect rather than traditional medical authority.

Chapter Summary

Identity and power are concepts that have an enduring importance to communication in health organizations. Identity is directly and indirectly shaped by attachments to or identifications with salient referent groups. The process of identification involves multiple messages, targets, and communication processes. Health professionals negotiate competing identifications through a variety of discursive behaviors with patients, professional associates, and the public. Power, control, and ideology are intertwined concepts that play a significant role in the lives of health workers. Power comes from multiple sources and is exercised through organizational control. Ideological assumptions figure prominently in the ways in which power and control are enacted in health organizations. As you will discover in Chapter 4, identity and power contribute to dynamics that influence how health professionals experience stress and burnout.

4

Stress, Burnout, and Social Support

As a graduate student working on my Ph.D. in communication studies, I became intrigued that dedicated, caring, and skilled health workers, particularly those working at the patient bedside, were leaving their jobs and professions because of stress and burnout. I recall job-shadowing Rob, a self-described "supernurse" as part of my dissertation research. A general medical floor RN (registered nurse), Rob constantly went above and beyond his required job tasks to provide excellent care—working long hours, volunteering to help coworkers, and generally making himself available to anyone who needed assistance. Rob confided to me that he was on the edge of burnout and often contemplated leaving his job. He was so stressed that periodically during his shift we would walk to the floor's nursing station so he could "silently scream" in frustration away from patients! It was not all that surprising when I learned later that Rob had left his position for an administrative job at another facility.

While many of us might identify our jobs as stressful, stress and burnout are more prevalent among health service workers than in other professions (Health Resources and Services Administration, 2007). By understanding the nature and outcomes of occupational stress from a communication perspective, we might be better able to explain why and how health workers communicate (du Pre, 2005). Such knowledge can also help health organizations attract and retain qualified employees as well as enhance working conditions and patient care.

Chapter 3 outlined communication processes pertaining to organizational culture, power dynamics, and roles. Delving deeper into the organizational contexts of healthcare delivery, the present chapter first considers major contingencies that contribute to stress in health organizations. The chapter then overviews specific stressors and identifies the individual and organizational outcomes of chronic occupational strain, also known as burnout. Next, you will learn about different types and sources of social support that help health professionals cope with job stress.

A Systems Perspective on Stress and Burnout

Stress is a biological reaction to any internal or external stimulus that can disturb an organism's **homeostasis**, also known as a steady state (Rada and Johnson-Leong, 2004). In the health system, when homeostasis is disrupted, the outcome can have serious negative consequences for health organizations, caregivers, and even patients and their families (Ray and Miller, 1990). System **contingencies** inherent to healthcare delivery are inextricably intertwined with the stressors considered later in this chapter. The contingencies presented below place individuals working in health organizations at risk of stress and burnout.

First, **work structure** in health organizations differs from many other types of institutions. Work in the health professions is typically shift-based and non-routine, especially in settings requiring 24-hour, seven-days-a-week care delivery (e.g., hospitals, nursing homes, hospices). A significant staff shortage exists in many health professions, including but not limited to nurses, nursing aides/assistants, and physicians, thus reducing staff resources and productivity. Technological advancements speed up work and require health professionals to constantly update their technical skills.

Second, **workload,** or work overload, is a common complaint in the fast-paced environment of today's health organizations. Direct caregivers and those who support them must multi-task continually as they make decisions and perform job responsibilities, often with urgent consequences. Further, health workers must interact with many different stakeholders on a routine basis (e.g., patients, their families, subordinates, coworkers from different medical specialties, managers), each with different needs and expectations that must be met. This variety demands that health professionals

Table 4.1 Major Sources of Health Workplace Stress

Role Stressors	Emotional Labor Stressors	Organizational Stressors
Role Overload	Emotional Contagion	Work-life Overlap
Role Conflict	Constant and/or intense	Spillover
Role Ambiguity	emotional interactions	Conflict
Lack of Role	Emotional Dissonance	Managed Care
Control	Emotional Display Rules	

display a wide repertoire of communication skills and respond to each stakeholder group appropriately (Apker, Propp, and Ford, 2005).

Third, health work is inherently emotional, as caregivers bear witness to the complex array of feelings that patients and their families experience in times of illness (Myerson, 2000). Health professionals routinely come into contact with patients' joys, sorrows, frustrations, and fears as a part of their job and experiencing emotions can cause stress.

Contingencies and job stressors ultimately play out in the experience of caregiver job strain and burnout. In order to better understand this interdependent relationship, let's explore the specific sources of stress commonly found in health organizations.

Sources of Stress in Health Organizations

A review of the research literature suggests three major areas that contribute to stress: role stressors, emotional labor stressors, and organizational stressors. Table 4.1 identifies these stressors, which are discussed in detail below.

Role Stressors

When individuals perform their roles in health organizations, the performance of those roles may be characterized by several different stressors. **Role overload** refers to having too many and/or too difficult work responsibilities within a given role. Overload has been identified as a leading cause of stress and burnout among health workers (Kennedy, 2005; Layne, Hohenshil, and Singh, 2004; Steiger, 2006). For example, Rod is a nurse shift manager at a busy community hospital. His role combines personnel responsibilities (e.g., managing dozens of nursing and assistive staff on day shift, hiring and firing employees) and traditional bedside care (e.g., nursing care for patients and families, discharge and admission duties). There are not enough hours in the day to complete all of his job obligations and Rod gets stressed out constantly. To cope, he often calls in sick, creating a shortage of managers on his shift. Other nurses must cover for his absence, which creates a ripple effect of role overload for nursing staff.

Role conflict refers to a clash between two or more competing and/or divergent roles. Role conflict figures prominently as a source of stress for health workers in today's healthcare system, where increasing demands for streamlined processes and cost efficiency have led to more tasks or roles being added to caregivers' scope of responsibilities (Apker and Ray, 2003). Role conflict may occur *within* one organizational role (e.g., in addition to treating patients, a physical therapist must order and stock all her supplies as well as perform tasks once completed by an aide). Conflict may also occur *between* the different roles held by the same individual (e.g., a quality control worker is assigned an additional role as emergency/crisis coordinator, requiring him to manage completely separate responsibilities that compete for his time on the job). The stress created by balancing competing roles results in healthcare workers spending less time communicating with patients and peers as well as heightened burnout (Apker and Ray, 2003).

Role ambiguity refers to the uncertainty that exists about specific role requirements and expectations. Factors creating ambiguity can range from the particular tasks associated with a role to how a role fits into a larger organizational system to future role security/longevity. In a study of nurses working in newly created positions called "care coordinators," Miller, Joseph, and Apker (2000) found that participants experienced role ambiguity in various ways. Lacking a specific job description (a purposeful decision by their hospital employer), the care coordinators were forced to develop their roles for themselves, often using the expectations of others (i.e., physicians, other nurses, administrators) as guidelines for how to perform the new role. Some nurses enjoyed the flexibility and empowerment granted by role ambiguity. Others reported feeling "stressed out" by constantly attempting to meet others' competing role expectations and communicating to coworkers about what the care coordinator role entailed.

Lack of role control can create stress when individuals perceive a deficiency in freedom and/or power over their work. Numerous studies report important findings regarding this role stressor across health professions. In nursing, Apker, Ford, and Fox (2003) found that high levels of professional autonomy improved nurses' identification (attachment) with their organizational employer, a factor linked to reduced burnout and increased nurse retention. In medicine, Harms et al. (2005) identified practice changes mandated by an organizational employer as a major stressor for surgeons. Research by Keeton et al. (2007) indicates that control over work predicts perceptions of career satisfaction and burnout among obstetricians-gynecologists. A case study of public hospital employees by Park, Wilson, and Lee (2004) shows that caregivers who perceived greater control over work experienced less job strain.

Participation in decision making appears to influence stress and burnout by giving individuals a sense of control over work roles. Apker's (2002) study of nurse managers found that lack of participation is a major job stressor. In their study of nurse participation, personal control, assertiveness, and nurse burnout, Ellis and Miller (1993) found that nurse participation predicts burnout, with evidence suggesting involvement reduces the burnout dimension of emotional exhaustion. Among social workers, upward participation (from subordinate to supervisor) minimizes subordinate role stress and burnout (Kim and Lee, 2009). Morgan and Krone (2001) argue that healthcare team participation in decision-making creates a supportive, less stressful work environment. Such research suggests that participative work environments, in which health professionals have an input into their work roles, help reduce stress and burnout (Angermeier et al., 2009).

Box 4.1   Ripped from the Headlines

"Good Grief:" Stress and Social Support in Nursing
Work in health organizations can be incredibly stressful, routinely requiring health professionals to respond to stressors such as role overload, role ambiguity, and role conflict. Further, the emotional nature of caregiving demands that health professionals display appropriate feelings (e.g., joy, sadness, frustration, concern) to meet the needs of numerous constituencies (patients and their families, coworkers, etc.). Fortunately, many forms of supportive communication exist in health organizations, ranging from formal support groups to informal hallway conversations with peers.

In a *New York Times* blog, Theresa Brown, RN, highlights her own experience with stress and social support on the front lines of nursing (Brown, 2009). Brown's role as a hospital oncology nurse requires her to care for cancer patients, many of whom are in the final stages of dying. In addition to the emotional strain of caring for terminally ill patients, Brown's job involves long work hours, high-ratio, high-acute patient loads, and conflicting role expectations. Brown laments that such a stressful work environment leaves little time for mourning patients' deaths.

Enter the Good Grief Center, an organization dedicated to helping people express healthy grief and recognize the importance of making time for themselves. The Good Grief Center hosts lunchtime workshops for nurses, providing a support group where they can openly communicate their thoughts and feelings about work. For Brown, the Good Grief meetings serve two important functions: 1) to model healthy grieving, and 2) to convey job frustrations—as in "Good grief, Charlie Brown" (para. 4). Nurses may attend the support groups as time allows or meet individually with Good Grief counselors.

Brown's blog also discusses how peer interaction helps nurses make sense of their work stressors. She writes: "The most helpful thing we do on the floor to process our grief is talk to each other. Out of the blue the nurse working next to me might tell me, with disbelief, that a patient has died. 'He was just here; it seemed like he was doing so well.' Word spreads in whispers, 'So-and-so is going home on hospice,' 'Mrs. X is "comfort measures only".' We sit around the conference table at the start of shift getting report. As one nurse says, 'Oh, he died,' everyone briefly stops to listen, to ask, 'Who died?' and to leave a small moment of silence" (para. 14).

Recalling images of the "Peanuts" comic strip, Brown compares oncology nursing to Charlie Brown's failed attempts to kick a football held by his nemesis Lucy. She encourages fellow nurses to "get into position and run their hearts out toward the football" (para. 16), knowing that their efforts to preserve patients' time on earth are worth overcoming significant job stressors.

Discussion Questions
1. How does stress and burnout in the health professions affect health organizations?
2. How does stress and burnout in the health professions affect the United States' health system?
3. In addition to the ideas in Theresa Brown's blog, what can individual caregivers do to cope with and/ or avoid stress and burnout? What can organizations do?

Caregivers are expected to present a public face or front when performing their jobs. Meeting these expectations, through emotional labor, may, in fact, act as an additional stressor. The next section reviews the strain placed on care providers by emotional labor demands.

Emotional Labor Stressors

The concept of **emotional labor** provides a useful lens through which to understand how feelings can produce significant stress in a health organization. Arlie Hochschild's (1983) work in this area provided the foundation for emotional labor scholarship in numerous disciplines. Hochschild argues that performing emotion is "work" and individuals labor emotionally in their jobs just as they do mentally or physically. She contends that organizational life is not neutral, rational, or logical. Rather, it is laden with positive and negative emotions that create strain.

Miller, Stiff, and Ellis (1988) assert that human service providers, such as health professionals, may be predisposed to experiencing emotional labor. These individuals want to help others and view caregiving as a "calling" to serve society. Such predispositions can lead caregivers to engage in emotional labor, thus heightening their risk of burnout. Miller et al. differentiate between **emotional contagion** (feeling *with* others) and **empathic concern** (feeling *for* others), concluding that individuals who display empathic concern for others are best able to handle the emotional stress of caregiving. Caregivers who experience emotional contagion are prone to burnout.

[handwritten margin note: emotional contagion]

Consider the example of Hannah, a first-year medical resident, who must tell Phil, a cancer patient, that he is dying. Hannah has developed a close friendship with the patient during his stay at the hospital and, while giving the bad news, both Hannah and Phil become noticeably upset. Hannah cries so hard that she is unable to convey the information about Phil's prognosis and a senior resident must finish the delicate conversation. Later, the senior resident calls Hannah's behavior "unprofessional" and he warns her that "she won't last long in medicine" if she continues to vicariously experience patients' feelings. Hannah learns over time to detach herself from patients' emotional highs and lows yet still show concern.

[handwritten margin note: discussion?]

According to Ashforth and Tomiuk (2000), health professionals must enact a "certain range, intensity and frequency of emotions for a given situation" (p. 184) regardless of their personal, internal feelings. Thus, a health worker's role may be considered emotionally laborious because of **constant and/or intense emotional displays** (positive and/or negative), and **emotional dissonance** (disconnect between actual and felt emotions). For example, Melissa, a community health nurse, provides infant care education for at-risk mothers and their babies. She feels compelled to display maternal-like qualities of concern, nurturing, and encouragement every time she visits her clients even though she may not authentically feel those emotions. Her job also involves constant client contact, caring for individuals who frequently show the intense emotions that accompany new motherhood (joy, frustration, etc.). In her current role, Melissa experiences intense, dissonant, and frequent emotional labor, a combination that places her at risk of burnout. Melissa feels "stressed out" and emotionally exhausted at the end of each day. She doesn't know how she can serve her clients without feeling "wrung out" and wonders whether it is time to leave public health for a less emotional work environment.

Caregivers must manage their emotions not only with patients and their families, but also when interacting with supervisors, subordinates, and coworkers. These **non-patient relationships** involve emotional labor in ways that can cause stress. Consider Jon, a dentist who owns his own practice. He cares for patients while at the same time managing a staff of hygienists, clerical workers, and administrators. Further, Jon must communicate as a peer with the dentist from whom he purchased the practice (and who still works there part-time). All these relationships require Jon to display a range of communication behaviors to meet the needs of different constituencies (e.g., comforting an anxious patient, mediating a conflict between two employees, soliciting feedback from the other dentist regarding recent equipment purchases). Never having had formal leadership or management training, Jon frequently feels overwhelmed at the variety and complexity of relational communication in his role and he identifies learning to manage others by trial and error as a major source of stress.

Emotional labor behavior adheres to **display rules**, which are produced and enforced by occupational, organizational, and larger societal expectations. Display rules guide individuals' work behaviors, particularly their communication, and provide the basis for which their work is evaluated by others (Ashforth and Tomiuk, 2000). For example, health insurers routinely survey their customers' satisfaction with the service they provide. A survey may ask a customer to rate the friendliness, responsiveness, and thoroughness of information provided by customer service representatives. These categories indicate the display rules valued and expected by the insurer for worker-customer communication. Feedback from the survey may be used by the insurance company's managers to train employees on appropriate customer service skills, to evaluate high-achieving employees for promotion, and to fire underperforming workers.

Display rules can powerfully influence organizational culture beliefs, values, and assumptions about stress and burnout. Myerson (2000) describes this connection in a study of social workers in two different health organizations. In one setting, the language of "control and treatment" prevailed and social workers considered stress a disease to be managed and burnout a form of personal weakness. As such, stress and burnout were normalized and rarely discussed openly. At the other organization, stress and burnout were understood as a natural component of health work, and caregivers sought and provided social support for one another.

Display rules appear to be a double-edged sword that can either exacerbate job stressors and burnout or help caregivers handle work stressors more effectively. For example, de Castro, Agnew, and Fitzgerald (2004) argue that in high-replacement health professions (e.g., nurses, medical technicians, assistant personnel), workers frequently and directly hear about organizational expectations for appropriate emotional behaviors. They must abide by those rules or risk negative repercussions. Lacking control over the emotional components of their jobs, these workers face heightened risk of stress and burnout. On a more positive note, Morgan and Krone (2001) found that organizational display rules (e.g., the need to display rationality, objectivity, and technical expertise) can usefully guide caregivers' communication when dealing with stressors such as emotionally charged situations and uncooperative patients.

This chapter has addressed stressors occurring *within* roles and in relational contexts requiring emotional labor (micro-level approach). Stressors also come from the larger organization level (macro-level perspective), spanning across individuals in a health organization. The next section takes a look at two such stressors: work-life overlap and managed care.

Organizational Stressors

The first organizational stressor examined here is **work-life overlap**. The advent of the "sandwich" generation (individuals, typically working mothers, who take care of their own children as well as aging parents simultaneously) and the continued dominance of women in the health professions make stress brought about by work-life overlap particularly notable in health organizations (Apker and Ray, 2003). This stressor is even more salient when viewed in light of research suggesting that those employed in the health professions show predispositions to engage in emotional labor (Miller, Stiff, and Ellis, 1988). The overlap of emotionally laborious roles in domestic and professional spheres of life can heighten healthcare workers' risk to stress and burnout.

Work-life overlap research in the health professions has been mainly concerned with work-life spillover and work-life conflict. **Work-life spillover** occurs when aspects of a person's personal life overflow into work life and vice versa. **Work-life conflict** happens when personal and work interests compete, leading an individual to attempt to balance work and home life responsibilities (Ray and Miller, 1994). An example of both phenomena can be identified in the experiences of Kathy, a single mother who works as a discharge planner at an urban hospital. She is primary caregiver for her 76-year-old mother, Ava, who has been suffering with dementia for several years. Kathy suspects that Ava will soon have to move to an assisted living facility due to her worsening condition, an option Ava vocally resists. Kathy's domestic responsibilities spill over into her job when she spends her "free" time at work interviewing caregivers on the phone, checking assisted living organizations' websites, and arguing with her mother about the decision. She doesn't have enough time in the day to fulfill all her home and work duties, thus she routinely works evenings and weekends from home to catch up. The stress caused by home-life conflict causes Kathy to communicate negatively with coworkers, patients, and her own family. She answers questions abruptly, acts distracted, and argues with others constantly.

Some research suggests that the intersection of home and work responsibilities can exacerbate an individual's stress level, while other studies point to the benefits of work-life overlap. In a study of physicians, Keeton et al. (2007) discovered that non-routine work hours combined with work-family balance problems contributed to occupational stress and turnover. Studies also show that a life outside of work can buffer a person from stressful conditions. Woodside et al. (2008) found that female medical residents who had children were less prone to burnout than their male counterparts. The authors argued that domestic responsibilities buffered female physicians from taking work stressors too seriously as well as fostered empathy that reduces the effects of occupational stress. Such resilience helps prevent burnout.

Control over work is a particularly salient factor in work-life conflict. For example, volunteer caregivers in a not-for-profit health organization who also cared for elderly relatives at home reported significant stress due to competing work-home demands (Beitman et al., 2004). Unsuccessful attempts to reduce or manage work-life conflict resulted in caregivers feeling overloaded and inadequate in both domestic and professional spheres. In contrast, physicians who have more control over work-life responsibilities appear to be more satisfied with their careers and less apt to burnout, particularly those doctors who work non-routine hours (e.g., obstetrician-gynecologists). Keeton et al. (2007) found that reducing work hours in order to spend more time with family is a popular alternative for such physicians, especially females. According to McNeely, it is up to health organization leaders to create flexible and supportive environments that help caregivers manage dual work and domestic responsibilities. Doing so will "fundamentally alter stress reactions" (McNeely, 2005, p. 292), ultimately benefiting health workers, their employing organizations, and patient care.

The second organization stressor considered in the research literature is **managed care**, a restructuring of healthcare delivery that has fundamentally transformed the U.S. health system (see Chapter 1). Changes brought about by managed care have created new work stressors (e.g., heightening health professionals' clinical and administrative workload, downsizing staff, and redefining caregiver roles). In turn, these stressors affect communication among and between healthcare workers. In a study conducted by Apker (2001), nurses reported that they felt overwhelmed by the complexity of their patient caseloads because managed care directives only approved highly acute (severely ill) patients for hospitalization. Such a complicated patient mix, combined with increased workload and reduced institutional support, stressed nurses on a daily basis to the point that they had little, if any, time to establish empathetic relationships with patients or fully educate patients about post-discharge care. Moreover, lack of information about managed care creates uncertainty among health workers that contributes to role ambiguity, with Lammers and Duggan (2002) and Miller, Joseph, and Apker (2000) finding that caregivers desired more and better quality information about managed care changes from leaders in their employing organizations.

Like any bureaucratic system of organizing, managed care consists of rules that guide organizational processes and behaviors. Rules designed to contain costs (e.g., mandated patient length-of-stay requirements, reduced use of medical tests) also constrain caregivers in ways that can result in stress. For example, Shirey (2006) concludes that managed care has reduced the extent of caregivers' job control. When combined with reduced time, resources, and motivation, lack of job control creates stressful conditions that lead to burnout. The trend to codify professional decisions in order to respond to the needs of managed care mandates has lessened professional autonomy, once considered a defining characteristic of health professions such as medicine (Lammers, Barbour, and Duggan, 2003). McNeely (2005) argues that for nurses, the relinquishment of professional control in light of managed care structures undermines nursing practice and makes health organizations uncertain and stressful places to work.

The burden of managed care stress has affected communication in health organizations. As mentioned above, the demand to meet or beat managed care patient length-of-stay requirements has led healthcare workers to care for more patients in less time. Such pressure reduces the time caregivers can spend communicating with patients and their families as well as collaborating with colleagues and peers. When faced with stressors such as managed care rules, caregivers who adhere to rules adopt more formal communication behaviors whereas those who attempt to work around or bypass regulations engage in conspiratorial communication.

The research reviewed thus far indicates that there's no definitive source of job strain in health organizations. Rather, stress arises from multiple sources—roles, emotional labor, relationships, and organizations—which all take a toll on personal well-being. The more a health worker encounters multiple (and different) stressors, the more likely he or she is to experience chronic occupational stress, also known as burnout. The next section describes burnout and explores how it has profound, harmful implications for caregivers and health organizations.

good conclusion

Burnout in the Health Professions

Burnout is perhaps best described as the "wearing out" or "gradual erosion" experienced by a person suffering from long-term and often chronic occupational stress. Following work by Maslach and colleagues, scholars typically conceptualize burnout in three dimensions: reduced personal accomplishment, depersonalization of others, and emotional exhaustion (Maslach and Jackson, 1981; Maslach and Leiter, 1997).

Burnout Dimensions

Reduced personal accomplishment occurs when people believe they cannot make progress in or achieve job responsibilities. They may leave their jobs at the end of the day feeling worthless or unproductive, which contributes to role stress as the individuals feel incapable of meeting role expectations reinforced in their communication with others. Over time, reduced personal accomplishment can translate into negative self-esteem, poor morale/motivation, and lack of quality job performance (Maslach and Leiter, 1997). For example, Faith, a social worker employed at a free public health clinic, is so consumed by "putting out fires" or dealing with immediate crises every day that she cannot advance on long-term projects central to her sense of accomplishment. Faith perceives her lack of performance as evidence that she is not an effective professional and she becomes frustrated that her personal work goals are neither achievable nor valued.

Depersonalization occurs when an organizational member marginalizes others by stripping them of unique, humanizing characteristics in favor of generalized and often negative stereotypes (Maslach and Jackson, 1981). Depersonalization results in problematic communication behaviors. For instance, Scott, an emergency room physician working in an overcrowded, understaffed hospital may label unnecessarily needy patients as "whiners" and call patients who come back again and again to receive ED care "frequent flyers." Such perceptions lead him to communicate with those patients with less compassion and empathy. Over time, Scott starts to view all of his patients as "whiners," even those with valid health complaints, and treats them with indifference.

Emotional exhaustion, the most predominant dimension of burnout, refers to when a person feels wrung out or used up emotionally because of day-to-day role demands (Maslach and Jackson, 1981). Caregivers may face great pain and suffering for extended periods of time as they provide care for patients, especially those with serious conditions (Meltzer and Huckabay, 2004). For example, Sam, a pediatric nurse working at a children's hospital, may encounter great tragedies in the course of caring for sick children and their families. In addition, she finds herself constantly attending to the emotional needs of her subordinates and coworkers, comforting, encouraging, and nurturing them through difficult cases. This ongoing demand leaves Sam exhausted and unable to care for her own family's emotional needs. In order to protect her dwindling emotional resources, Sam feels she must either detach herself from work or leave her job for a less emotionally draining environment.

Box 4.2 Communication in Practice

Recognizing the Signs of Burnout
Professionals working in health organizations face a variety of stressors that, over time, can lead them to occupational burnout. Sometimes, it is difficult for people who are dedicated to caring for others to identify and/or admit burnout in themselves. Burnout may be recognized by a number of physical, behavioral/communicative, emotional, and work-related symptoms. The following signs, adapted from Figley (1999), provide a useful starting point:

Physical

- Problems sleeping
- Low energy and weariness
- Prone to illness

Behavioral/Communicative

- Dehumanization of patients
- Reduced communication with colleagues or patients
- Aggressive and/or defensive interactions with others
- Communication that shows callousness and/or cynicism

Emotional

- Depressed
- Apprehensive or worried

Work-Related

- Late for work
- Absenteeism
- Reduced or ineffective job performance
- Turnover

To summarize, burnout is a complex, multi-faceted phenomenon that poses significant threats to caregivers and negatively influences caregiver communication. The next section examines the powerful, harmful effects of burnout on health workers and health organizations.

Costs of Burnout

For individual health professionals, burnout has been linked to myriad physical and mental health problems that affect quality of life. Increased illness, reduced morale and self-esteem, and anxiety are just a few of many outcomes of burnout that personally affect those working in the health professions (Steiger, 2006). Burnout can also affect caregivers' communication, potentially making them less empathetic and responsive to the needs of others (e.g., patients and their families, other caregivers) (Halbesleben and Rathert, 2008: Jenkins and Elliott, 2004). Perhaps most disturbing is the link between burnout and depression, a condition that causes personal distress, work disability, substance abuse, and sometimes even suicide (Fahrenkopf et al., 2008; Park, Wilson, and Lee, 2004; Rada and Johnson-Leong, 2004).

These negative individual responses to burnout pose significant problems for health organizations, particularly in terms of caregiver turnover. Burned out employees tend to suffer from job dissatisfaction, reduced organizational commitment, and low organizational identification, factors that all contribute to turnover (Apker and Ray, 2003). The financial costs associated with turnover have been well documented in the research literature.

For instance, Hayhurst, Saylor, and Stuenkel (2005) conclude that the cost of replacing one nurse ranges from $25,000 to $65,000, while Atencio, Cohen, and Gorenberg (2003) estimate this cost to range from $90,000 to $135,000 per nurse. Workers who are burned out but remain in their jobs also pose problems for their institutional employers, with studies finding that burnout reduces organizational productivity and leads to negative job performance (Park, Wilson, and Lee, 2004).

Burnout has significant human costs for health organizations as well. A growing body of research indicates that burnout contributes to ineffective working conditions that reduce patient care quality (Taris, 2006). The link between burnout, turnover, and healthcare personnel shortage is the most deleterious. Turnover intent and burnout have been linked to quality of care, a factor correlated with patient mortality and failure to rescue (death following the occurrence of an adverse event during hospitalization) (Aiken et al., 2008). In 2007, the Agency for Healthcare Research and Quality (AHRQ), a leading U.S. government health institution, concluded that nurse turnover and absenteeism associated with burnout contributed to lower nurse staffing rates and higher incidents of adverse patient outcomes.

Other patient care problems exist in addition to those associated with turnover and staff shortage. For example, physician depersonalization results in lower patient satisfaction and longer post-discharge recovery time (Halbesleben and Rathert, 2008). Among social workers, burnout has been found to negatively affect the quality and consistency of client services (Kim and Lee, 2009). Self-perceived medical errors were associated with heightened burnout among medical residents (West et al., 2006). Burned-out nurses in a geriatric care facility reported inadequate preparation to meet the emotional needs of their clients (Kennedy, 2005).

Stress and burnout have far-reaching implications affecting health professionals and organizations. Communication scholars have increasingly turned to the study of social support in the search for solutions to these problems. Before exploring the specific types and sources of supportive communication, let's take a closer look at how to understand social support from a systems perspective.

A Systems Perspective on Social Support

In his influential article, "Caring for the Caregivers," Kahn (1993) uses a systems approach to explain how primary caregivers may be "filled with or emptied of the emotional resources necessary for their caregiving in interactions with other agency members" (p. 539). Arguing that organizations must provide a system of caregiving so workers can better manage or even avoid workplace stressors, Kahn calls attention to the importance of positive superior-subordinate relationships to such a system. He argues that managers and leaders must do more than provide resources (e.g., support groups, stress management workshops). They should also support subordinates and protect them from burnout. Key communication behaviors such as empathy, consideration, and validation create a caregiving system that replenishes caregivers' emotional resources.

training

Supportive communication consists of exchange and **feedback** processes that allow health professions to better handle work stressors and display behaviors that can prevent or deal with burnout. For example, Krishna is a new first-year medical resident who is overwhelmed by the intensity, complexity, and amount of his work at a busy urban hospital. Emily, a third-year resident who supervises Krishna, sees that he is "stressed out" and takes him aside one day to find out how she can help. The two exchange information—Krishna describes workplace stressors and Emily listens, empathizes with, and validates his experiences by recalling her own days as a struggling medical student. Further, Emily provides feedback on how Krishna can improve his time management skills and reduce workload stressors. She also encourages him to leave work on time in order to see friends and family. In these interactions, Emily has created a system that helps Krishna feel supported in ways that build his resilience to burnout.

Characteristics and Sources of Social Support

Albrecht and Adelman (1987) provide an enduring definition of **socially supportive communication,** conceptualizing it

Table 4.2   Forms of Social Support and Examples

Social Support Type	Description	Health Organization Example
Instrumental	The provision of tangible or visible assistance such as physical help, money, or restructuring of job tasks.	Nurse passes medications for a struggling peer. Supervisor gives an employee a paycheck in advance to cover debts. Nursing home executive pushes back a project deadline for stressed-out managers.
Informational	The provision of knowledge, data, advice to reduce and/or buffer a person's stress.	Physical therapist manager explains to subordinates how hospital restructuring will impact PT care, thereby reducing their uncertainty about change. Nursing aide gives a stressed-out peer ideas for relaxation techniques.
Emotional	The display of care and concern in the form of showing encouragement or empathy.	Occupational therapist praises team members for a job well done. A social worker shows compassion and concern for coworkers dealing with difficult caseloads.

as interaction that reduce perceptions of ambiguity and helps foster a sense of control over stressors. Albrecht and Adelman further argue that individuals who actively participate in seeking/ providing social support and stay well informed of organizational uncertainties and changes tend to cope best with workplace stress. While most considerations of social support acknowledge that individuals are not just passive recipients of supportive messages, there is growing recognition that it is more likely that social support helps people *manage* rather than *reduce* uncertainty (Babrow, 2001).

Social support takes several forms (Table 4.2). While this section addresses concepts of informational, emotional, and instrumental support separately, it's important to note that individuals tend to seek and receive multiple types of supportive communication simultaneously.

Two major types of relationships—supervisor-subordinate and peer—are most salient in health organization research.

Supervisor-subordinate relationships refer to formal reporting structures (e.g., nurse manager to staff nurse, attending physician to resident physician, dentist to dental hygienist). Since vertical hierarchies remain prevalent in health organizations (Lammers, Barbour, and Duggan, 2003), it is not all that surprising that supervisor-subordinate relationships have been identified as a popular source of supportive communication. Those in leadership positions often have knowledge that can help their subordinates cope with or manage stress. For example, Chan is vice president for patient care services at a large health network challenged by economic downturn, forcing consolidation of facilities, restructuring, and downsizing. From his participation in executive-level decisions, Chan can provide informational support in the form of sensemaking to mid-level managers who are anxious about job changes. He explains the systemic contingencies that created the organization's financial woes and resulting institutional changes. Chan's position of power also affords him the ability to provide instrumental support to his mid-managers to help them manage stress, such as adding temporary workers to severely understaffed facilities.

Supervisor support plays a key role in quality of work life and burnout in health organizations (Kim and Lee, 2009). Both Angermeier et al. (2009) and Aiken et al. (2008) argue that leaders who provide adequate information and share decision making with subordinates create working conditions conducive to reduced employee burnout. Apker's (2002) study of managed care stressors found that nurse managers perceived instrumental support from nurse executives that helped manage conflicting role expectations and work overload. Other studies of nurses found that supervisor social support influences staff nurse burnout and intent to leave (Apker, Ford, and Fox, 2003; Hayhurst, Saylor, and Stuenkel, 2005; Ray and Miller, 1994). Kim and Lee (2009) argue that supervisors who welcome and value subordinates' input reduce employee role stress and burnout.

Peer relationships refer to lateral or parallel relationships between employees that lack a formal reporting authority structure. Because peers work in a shared organizational setting (and may be doing the same type of job), the informational support they provide serves an important sensemaking function (Ellis and Miller, 1994). Peers are intimately familiar with an organization's unique stressors, making them more common sources of support than nonwork relationships. For example, Teri works as physician assistant (PA) in a mental health hospital where she has extremely stressful daily encounters with mentally and emotionally disturbed patients. Teri avoids retelling patient "horror stories" to her family because they lack experience in the organization and she doesn't want to scare them. Teri instead turns to other PAs employed at the hospital for support. They listen to each other's job frustrations and provide tips on how to cope with difficult patients, thereby helping Teri cope with her role stress.

Studies provide empirical support for the salience of peer-based social support in health organizations. Ellis and Miller (1994) argue that positive coworker communication creates supportive work environments that foster beneficial individual and organizational outcomes. They conclude that "social support from coworkers can be a potent antidote to the stress inherent in the nursing profession" (p. 91) and advocate that health organizations implement strategies to facilitate instrumental and informational support among direct caregivers. Miller, Joseph, and Apker (2000) conclude that peer support groups provided nurse care coordinators with an important outlet for understanding the meanings of new role identities. Shared discussion created joint interpretations among the coordinators which helped them cope with stressors that accompanied new, undefined roles. Among medical students, peer interactions provide affirmation and foster relational bonding that helps ease the intellectual, emotional, and physical rigors of medical training (Zorn and Gregory, 2005). The importance of peer support in reducing burnout also extends across specializations in the interactions between professional associates. For instance, positive nurse-physician relationships play a critical part in creating supportive work environments that retain nurses (Rosenstein and O'Daniel, 2005).

Box 4.3 Communication in Practice

Individual and Organizational Coping Strategies
Burnout affects more than the individual concerned—the condition influences their personal relationships, working conditions, and job outcomes. The Health Resources and Services Administration (HRSA, 2007) provides the following tips:
Individuals can:

1. **Take time out**: Make sure to step away from the stressors contributing to burnout. This may involve changing up work duties or taking time off from work.
2. **Connect**: Establish and maintain supportive relationships with others both in and outside of the workplace. Supportive communication in different forms is a powerful defense against occupational strain.
3. **Exercise**: Physical activity functions as a mood enhancer and immunity builder, among many other benefits.
4. **Vent**: Let emotions out when needed to give the body a release from pent-up stress and tension.
5. **Sleep**: Lack of sleep may reduce the ability to cope so recharge your batteries with adequate sleep on a daily basis.

Organizations can:

1. **Know the signs**: Leaders should become aware of and look for symptoms of burnout.
2. **Offer assistance and solutions**: Help workers with social support before burnout creates significant damage. Assist with problem-solving and/or providing access to resources (e.g., online training, support groups).

> 3. **Foster professional autonomy**: Provide employees with opportunities to assert control over their work and have more accountability. Doing so may yield a sense of purpose and independence helpful to reducing perceptions of work-related stress.
> 4. **Promote participation**: Give employees opportunities to participate in decision-making, especially in matters that affect their work.

Social Support Functions and Dysfunctions

Two sets of findings emerge from the research literature. First, social support functions to **buffer or shield** health workers from stress and burnout (Keeton et al., 2007; Miller et al., 1990; Apker and Ray, 2003). For example, in the historically high burnout and turnover social work profession, research by Kim and Lee (2009) shows that providing job-relevant data (informational support) to caregivers provides them with coping mechanisms to deal with role stress. Second, social support helps health professionals manage workplace stress, thereby minimizing burnout. For instance, studies in communication show that social support has a valuable sensemaking function, enabling health workers to understand organizational uncertainties such as role ambiguity, institutional restructuring, and unit policy changes (Apker, 2001; 2004). In other work, Ford and Ellis' (1998) study of novice nurses suggests that memorable supportive messages (i.e. specific pieces of discourse that have lasting effects on the recipient) help newcomers manage the stress encountered during the initial phase of organizational assimilation.

The research literature in health contexts shows mostly positive outcomes associated with supportive communication with a great deal of this work done in nursing. Ellis and Miller (1994) found that emotional support was positively associated with organizational commitment and intent to remain among hospital nurses. Apker, Ford, and Fox (2003) found that high levels of social support from managers improved staff nurses' identification with their hospital employer, an important predictor of turnover. A supportive work environment increases nurses' job satisfaction, promotes nurse retention, and reduces emotional exhaustion, a major predictor of burnout (Hayhurst, Saylor, and Stuenkel, 2005; Jenkins and Elliott, 2004). Outside of nursing, a study of hospital workers by Park, Wilson, and Lee (2004) found that regardless of position or specialization, social support is associated with greater job control and performance.

Supportive communication has numerous benefits for health organizations. However, social support has a "dark side" that can contribute to dysfunctional organizational dynamics. Ray's (1993) compelling critique of social support research questions commonly held assumptions that supportive communication yields positive relational links and outcomes. She argues that while "supportive communication can be the lifeline among organizational members, these same links may become chains" (p. 107).

Extending Ray's work in a study of memorable messages in nursing, Ford and Ellis (1998) label the dysfunctional communication identified above as nonsupport messages. They found that communicating dependency and reciprocation, especially when received from supervisors, were detrimental to the socialization experiences of nurses. In their study of health workers, Ray and Miller (1994) conclude that support may be stressful because it can create dysfunctions such as those identified earlier by Ray (1993) as well as foster a contagion effect in which the solicitation of support serves to heighten a person's emotional exhaustion.

Chapter Summary

Stress, burnout, and social support remain highly salient issues for health organizations, particularly those institutions and professions struggling with staff turnover and shortage. The range and complexity of role, emotional labor, and organizational stressors suggests that no single answer provides an adequate remedy. Rather, health organizations must approach stress and burnout from a variety of perspectives and with a repertoire of strategies. Social support offers a promising avenue of assistance that can complement other efforts (e.g., physical work environment improvements, financial compensation) to make working conditions better and, ultimately, enhance the quality of work life for health professionals.

5

Change and Leadership

You may be familiar with the phrase "the only constant in organizations is change" and this sentiment certainly sums up the current state of the U.S. health system. Advancements in medical technology, innovations in healthcare delivery, and reforms to healthcare services are just a few major shifts. As employees, patients, or health consumers, you have already encountered significant changes in the health system as health organizations continually adapt in order to survive and thrive. Health organizing has changed a great deal from what our grandparents (or parents) experienced and it appears likely that future generations will face a vastly different health landscape than what we have today. What you will learn in this chapter may help you anticipate and participate in the transformations occurring in health organizations.

Dramatic changes occurring in the health system create a need for people who can lead successfully during challenging times. Health leaders must "create direction, win commitment of followers and other key stakeholders, and influence others to do what needs to be done" (Manion, 2005, p. ix). Learning about leadership will add to your understanding of the complexities facing today's health leaders (and their followers) and provide you with insights into how to enhance your own leadership skills in health contexts.

The chapter begins by presenting change from a systems perspective, discussing general models of change and innovation, and identifying major categories of health organization change. Next, you will gain a greater understanding of change management. The chapter examines how people react to change and the communication processes that facilitate change implementation. The second half of the chapter addresses leadership. After considering leadership from a systems perspective, you will learn about the challenges facing health leaders and the foundational leadership theories that inform their behaviors. The chapter concludes by discussing key attributes of effective leader communication.

A Systems Perspective on Change

According to change scholar William Bridges (2003), **change** is situational and emphasizes the outcome produced by the change. It is accompanied by **transition**, a psychological process that people experience as they leave old situations and identities behind and come to terms with new circumstances and selves brought about by change. Bridges argues that changes, even ones that are welcome, involve a transition from old habits to new behaviors and this shift requires time and effort from all organizational members.

Contingencies such as those you learned about in Chapter 1 create external conditions that stimulate change in health organizations. For instance, managed care has altered care delivery by introducing third-party payers into care decisions, grouping patients into plan populations subject to insurance contract requirements, and prospectively setting reimbursement rates. Healthcare providers must adapt to these changes because managed care is the health system's predominant form of health organizing. Healthcare providers that avoid or refuse to participate in managed care risk obsolescence.

Most visibly, change creates a disruption to the balance of health organization systems. These disruptions can range from relatively minor policy modifications such as mandatory hand washing for clinicians before and after patient encounters to dramatic structure transformations such as cutting or combining units following an institutional merger. To succeed in the constantly shifting landscape of health delivery, health organizations must display an ability to maintain **dynamic homeostasis**—a steady state which simultaneously adapts to change. Achieving dynamic homeostasis requires **openness** between health organizations and the embedded environment allowing the institutions to anticipate and react to contingencies appropriately. Openness is also necessary within health organizations as information about change (e.g., change development and implementation) flows among components.

Understanding Organizational Change

Health organizations that desire long-term sustainability recognize the importance of anticipating and responding to varying environmental conditions. Models of organizational change lend insight into how organizations implement and experience change. Next, you will consider models of change and then explore the responses and communication processes associated with change.

Models of Organizational Change

Based on an interdisciplinary literature review, van de Ven and Poole (1995) present a typology of four theories to explain change

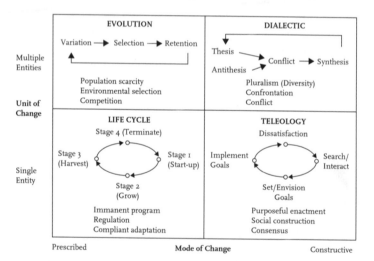

Figure 5.1   *Typology of Theories of Change and Innovation*
(Source: van de Ven, A. H., and Poole, M. S. Explaining development and change in organizations. *The Academy of Management Review*, 20, 1995, 510–40. Copyright 1995. Reproduced by permission of Academy of Management [NY].)

development in organizations (Figure 5.1). Each approach depicts change as driven by different event sequences or catalysts. In addition, the typology describes how change progresses and affects organizations.

The typology spans two dimensions: unit of change and mode of change. Unit of change refers to whether change develops in a single entity (e.g., organization, unit) or in the interactions between multiple entities. Mode of change refers to whether the sequence of events is established before the change process begins or if its progression emerges as the change process develops. While each theory offers conceptual and applied value, the life-cycle and teleological approaches are primary explanatory frameworks for organizational change (Poole and van de Ven, 2004). Table 5.1 summarizes each theory and provides examples.

Forms of Health Organization Change

Change takes a variety of forms and degrees of complexity in health organizations. **Structure change** involves arrangement of people and reporting structures within an organization as well as an institution's physical or material transformations. A visible example of structure change is an organization merger or acquisition. **Process change** involves adaptations of individual and group behaviors, beliefs, and attitudes, such as with shifts in organizational policies and in how work gets accomplished. **Culture change** entails adjustments in the assumptions and values of an organization as well as corresponding artifacts and/or behaviors. For instance, to improve patient safety culture, health organizations may reinforce the value of reporting mistakes and reward employee behaviors that prevent errors. While the forms of change are considered here separately, it is important to note that changes can and do occur simultaneously. Table 5.2 presents change categories and examples.

Managing Planned Change

Most organizational change is planned or intentional as leaders and followers implement innovations in anticipation of or in response

Table 5.1   Change Models in Health Organizations and Examples

Approach	Description	Health Organization Example
Life-Cycle	Change is imminent; it evolves from internal responses to external environmental events and processes. It is an organic process consisting of stages such as start-up, growth, maturity, and decline or death. Change is prescribed and regulated by institutional rules or programs.	A hospital changes its policies and procedures in order to meet federal standards for patient care, such as those mandated by the Joint Commission on Accreditation of Healthcare Organizations.
Teleological	Change is intentional, emerging from purposeful actions and communication of an envisioned end state. Change occurs as a cycle of goal formulation, implementation, evaluation, and modification of actions and goals.	A public health department implements service provision changes based on goals shared by employees, legislators, and community members. Changes are made, evaluated, and modified through ongoing dialogue between these stakeholders.
Dialectical	Conflicts among opposing entities collide to produce a synthesis, which over time becomes the foundation for the next cycle of dialectical progression. Change emerges through efforts to manage conflict, contradictions, and tensions.	Physicians in a large, multi-group practice experience tension between a need for professional identity based on medical specialization and a desire to be part of a collective. The ways in which physicians handle the conflict influences organizational change.
Evolutionary	Change is comprised of a repetitive sequence of variation, selection, and retention events among entities in a certain population. The evolutionary cycle is driven by competition for scarce environmental resources.	A cancer center responds to managed care changes by selecting and retaining practices that allow the organization to successfully compete for scarce financial resources.

(Adapted from Poole and van de Ven, 2004)

Table 5.2   Forms of Health Organization Change:
Categories and Examples

Structure Change	Process Change	Culture Change
• Organization consolidation and integration • Organization mergers and acquisitions • Reorganization from vertical to flat management • Redesign and/ or renovation of facility buildings, units, office space, patient rooms, etc. • Introduction of new equipment and technology	• Continuous quality improvement efforts to enhance patient care • Patient safety initiatives • Heightened participation in decision making and shared governance • Streamlining procedures to increase efficiencies in patient flow • Policies regarding patient-clinician communication, patient confidentiality, etc.	• Initiatives that espouse team collaboration rather than professional dominance • Efforts to reduce status hierarchy based on position and/or specialization • Instituting organizational ceremonies, rituals, rewards, etc. that support professional collaboration

to contingencies. **Planned organizational change** is defined as "change that is brought about through the purposeful efforts of organizational members as opposed to change that is due to environmental or uncontrollable forces" (Lewis, 1997, p. 456). Change research focuses on **change implementation**—the formal and informal activities designed and executed to bring about change. This literature explains that people function as **change implementers** who manage the change process whereas **change users** are people who have direct and indirect contact with a change through their organizational activities.

Managing planned change involves intensive and ongoing efforts from change implementers and users. Even then, successful adoption is not always guaranteed. Communication influences how organizational members understand change and plays a predictive role in change outcomes. Drawing on organizational communication concepts, let's consider potential responses to change in health organizations before discussing specific change communication processes.

Reactions to Change

Perceptions of change affect people in varied ways. These differences are perhaps most pronounced in the emotional and behavioral reactions of change users. Users understand change in unique ways due to individual qualities, distinct group characteristics, and organizational cultures. Further, they experience change in different stages of implementation and with varying implications for their identities, roles, and relationships (Lewis, 2006). However, several pervasive emotional and behavioral reactions can be identified, despite distinctions among and across users.

The most common reaction is **uncertainty** as change can be an unknown phenomenon that fosters ambiguity about the future. Uncertainty can bring about fear, sadness, depression, anxiety, and anger. Ambiguity and its resulting negative emotions can contribute to problematic outcomes such as heightened dissatisfaction, stress, and burnout among health professionals (Bazzoli et al., 2004; Rosen et al., 2006). Further, uncertainty can motivate members of health organizations to resist change. Consider the various ways in which managed care has affected physician uncertainty. To varying degrees, managed care limits clinician decisions, reduces payment of medical services, and sets defined patient population boundaries. To some, managed care erodes physicians' professional autonomy, decreases control over work, and lessens occupational status (Hafferty and Light, 1995). Due in part to these changes, there is an uncertainty among physicians about the future of the medical profession. Uncertainty helps stimulate physicians' resistance to managed care through behaviors such as refusing to participate in managed care changes, circumventing managed care rules and structures, and, in extreme cases, leaving their occupations for nonmedical careers (Mechanic, 2003). However, the effects of change-based uncertainty are not all bad for health organizations. Miller, Joseph, and Apker's (2000) study of nurse role ambiguity during organizational change suggests that, in times of uncertainty, change users may develop innovations which best meet individual and organizational goals.

Change may also bring out **conflict** because it affects how and with what resources people do their jobs, creating conditions which exacerbate professional differences (Bridges, 2003). Consider Leicht, Fennell, and Witkowski's (1995) study of how hospital mergers affect health personnel. The study findings demonstrated that hospital nurses must absorb the most deleterious effects of mergers (e.g., reduced staffing, heightened patient volume) and such workplace pressures make nurses resistant to mergers. Nurses' responses differ from those held by physicians, who are in positions largely protected from similar job stressors. Leicht et al. argue that such disparate reactions reveal professional conflicts influenced by traditional power imbalances and status differentials favoring physicians. Change may also expose opposition to institutional values and assumptions. Rosen et al.'s (2006) investigation of a nursing home's new treatment protocol discovered that even though staff feedback was publicly encouraged, the organization's culture reinforced upper-management decision-making. The researchers conclude that the change to a new protocol failed because leaders did not change the organization's cultural values to support employee participation.

The tension or conflict created by change can offer benefits to health organizations. Medved et al. (2001) identify the tensions present in community health change efforts that promote dialog between change implementers and users. They argue that such openness reduces resistance to change. Similar conclusions are drawn by Bess et al. (2009) in their study of collaboration between a non-profit public health organization and its community constituents. Here, constructive participant dialog about agency-community relations yielded community empowerment, participation, and commitment to prevention.

Finally, users may respond to change through **resistance** or lack of cooperation. Change users may resort to overt tactics such as directly challenging change implementers, working around the change, and/or refusing to participate. Hoff and McCaffrey (1996) found that self-employed physicians were more likely to resist economic control by managed care organizations than salaried physicians employed by HMOs. Other resistance reactions are less active, such as showing apathy, ignoring/avoiding innovations, ridiculing change, and displaying skepticism. For instance, in Barley's (1990) study of the introduction of a new medical technology, physicians resisted change by not consulting more knowledgeable, but lower-status, technical staff. Lacking the requisite knowledge allowed the physicians to avoid using the new technology. These forms of resistance, taken singularly or together, can contribute to change failure.

Change Communication Processes

How communication affects organizational innovations is critical to understanding and predicting the results of change. Four major processes emerge as most salient to change communication in health organizations: disseminating information about change, encouraging the participation of all organizational members, coping with change, and making sense of change. Let's explore these processes in greater detail.

Disseminating information refers to how implementers transmit information to persuade, explain, interpret, and evaluate change—usually in an effort to reduce uncertainty and anxiety. It has been found that any information communicated about change, even negative information, decreases ambiguity and contributes to more cooperative attitudes (Miller and Monge, 1985). Lewis (2006) identifies several key change communication behaviors:

- Creating and articulating vision
- Channeling data between implementers and users
- Providing social support
- Addressing and managing user resistance
- Assessing and promoting results

She argues that when change implementation lacks these qualities, apathy and resistance can arise among change users in ways that predict the failure of the change.

Box 5.1   Communication in Practice

Making Innovation an Organizational Reality
Health organizations must engage in continuous transformation in order to anticipate and respond to significant shifts in healthcare delivery and public health. According to healthcare change experts Jack Silversin and Mary Jane Kornacki (2003), change implementation requires overcoming resistance, such as the following barriers:

- **The vice-like grip of the status quo**: People get comfortable with current routines and business as usual. Even simple innovations may involve learning new responsibilities and skills, modifying roles, and altering relationships.
- **Lack of shared vision**: The picture of the future must be clear, desirable, and encompass the perspectives of multiple groups.
- **The corrosive effect of cynicism and pessimism**: A history of failed changes contributes to indifference and skepticism. People don't believe they can affect change.

Silversin and Kornacki argue that effective communication helps health organizations overcome barriers and implement innovations for continuous improvement and organizational longevity. Consider the following strategies:

- **Increase the sense of urgency**: Understand dissatisfaction with the status quo and perceptions about what can be done to resolve unhappiness.
- **Ensure visible sponsorship**: Identify innovation "champions" who have authority and will advocate for change.

> • **Use feedback to keep the change on track**: Reinforce new behaviors by providing feedback. Let people know they are making a difference.

The relevant research in health organizations primarily examines what change implementers can say or do to disseminate information successfully. Scholars generally agree that effective change comes from 1) developing and sharing a vision for change; 2) coordinating efforts within and across multiple areas of an organization to support change; and 3) aligning organizational goals, roles, resources, actions, and accountability systems. A study of a quality improvement program initiated in the U.S. Veterans' Administration Health System (VAHS), one of the nation's largest, most complex healthcare organizations, provides an illustrative example (Stetler et al., 2008). VAHS leaders successfully brought about change by continually communicating the program's vision and values and seeking buy-in from employees. Leaders also created communication tools which integrated innovations, matched program goals with existing staff, facilities, and funds, as well as fostered shared accountability.

Participation is particularly useful in the context of health organizing, where numerous and often disparate occupational groups must work together. Each profession may have its own unique perspective on change and desire to voice its opinion on proposed innovations. Managing successful change then, means considering the needs, opinions, and knowledge sets of different health personnel groups and including them in change decisions. Change implementers must show responsiveness to professional cultures and develop change initiatives that reflect shared values rather than divergent and potentially divisive occupation-based perspectives.

Participation should be provided throughout change management from development and planning to execution and monitoring. Input from change users should be solicited through multiple communication mediums. Timmerman (2003) advocates using several strategies simultaneously (e.g., discussion groups,

Table 5.3 Coping with Change: Sample Communicative Responses

Coping Tactics

- Talk with coworkers who are against and/or who are in favor of the change
- Speak with others about how the change will affect unit work activities
- Enlist cooperation from professional associates
- Point out negative/positive qualities of the change
- Teach others about how the change should work
- Refuse to participate in the change
- Work out change-related problems
- Go along with the rules of change
- Attempt to learn new work techniques in order to make the change work better
- Try to convince administration to stop the change

informational meetings, face-to-face interactions) for optimal results. Such outreach typically takes time and effort, but it is usually a wise investment. Outcomes include improved decision quality, increased commitment, reduced uncertainty and anxiety, and decreased resistance to change.

Coping refers to change users' responses to becoming involved in and understanding an innovation. Change users are not passive recipients of change; rather they are actively engaged in dealing with the process and its consequences. Table 5.3 presents a list of sample coping behaviors drawn from a larger set of responses developed by Lewis (1997). Notice how coping consists of multiple types of communication choices, such as information-seeking in various ways, resisting or accepting change through different kinds of behaviors, and educating and persuading interested parties in an effort to adopt or reject change.

Sensemaking refers to the ways in which change users talk with peers, leaders, and other professional associates in order to understand the development and consequences of change. For example, hospital nurses experiencing workplace transformations due to managed care used sensemaking to achieve role clarity in turbulent organizational conditions (Apker, 2004). By interacting with key role set members (physicians, other nurses, patients, etc.) nurses were able to confirm or modify role requirements to better respond to managed care change. Separate studies of hospital-based change, by Callister and Wall (2001) and Dutton et al. (2001), underscore the influence of boundary spanning in the sensemaking process. These studies' findings show that by making social connections between different groups of health professionals within the same organization, boundary spanners gain information from multiple change users, share different perspectives on change, and influence perceptions about adopting or resisting change.

While executing change requires time, effort, and commitment on the part of all organizational members, it depends most visibly on support and direction from leaders. In the constantly shifting health system, change management is one of the most critical communication responsibilities performed by health leaders. Next, you will take a closer look at health leadership and learn more about the specific challenges, theoretical approaches, and communication skills involved.

A Systems Perspective on Leadership

Leadership has been conceptualized in multiple ways as scholars and practitioners attempt to better understand how to lead groups and organizations. Several definitional properties appear as common themes across these interpretations of leadership: 1) it is a process—a dynamic phenomenon; 2) it involves influence—affecting the behaviors, attitudes, and beliefs of others; 3) it occurs in a group setting—involving multiple individuals; and 4) it concerns collective goal attainment—working together to achieve shared aims. Leadership is "a process whereby an individual influences a group of individuals to achieve a common goal" (Northouse, 2007, p. 3). Leadership connects with systems concepts of goals, subsystems, and order.

Leaders define **goals** for their organizations by creating a vision or desirable future reality that followers can believe in and share. Effective leaders do not determine goals in isolation; rather, they invite followers to provide input so that goals are shared throughout an organization. Collaboration with followers enables leaders to set specific objectives for individuals and groups that help the organization accomplish defined goals and achieve a shared vision.

Leadership occurs in a group context, drawing attention to the systems concept of **holism**. Both leaders and followers are necessary sets of components; leaders do not exist without followers and vice versa. Patterns and messages of influence found in leader-follower interactions contribute to the interrelationships which form a unified whole. The relationships between leaders and followers, constructed in communication, greatly determine the success of leaders' effectiveness and, ultimately, affect the success of the entire system.

Leadership creates **order** by introducing a structure to components and subsystems by which activities may be organized. Leadership may be assigned, such as in official reporting structures, or emergent, occurring over time through communication rather than from an assigned position. Both forms of leadership create order by identifying who is in charge and how specific components or units fit into the larger organization.

Next, you will learn about specific leadership challenges occurring in health organizations and the role of leadership theories as a lens through which to understand the qualities and behaviors of leaders. The chapter concludes by discussing the communication competencies necessary for effective leadership in health organizations.

Leadership Challenges and Theoretical Approaches

As you read this book, you are becoming more aware of the multi-faceted nature of the health system and its contingencies. Successful leaders are people who can bolster health organizations' resiliency and ability to thrive in times of significant change as well as during times of stability. A more complete understanding of leadership in health organizations begins by considering the challenges leaders encounter in their roles.

Leadership Challenges

Leaders of health organizations encounter immense challenges as they strive to lead their organizations effectively. **Contextual challenges** encompass financial, operational, and informational/technological factors. Rapidly escalating healthcare costs combined with problems in patient access and patient demand present significant financial pressures. Health organizations are institutions with complex operational structures. They typically consist of state-of-the-art equipment and facilities, multiple units organized bureaucratically, and employees who vary by occupation, training, and specialization. To remain competitive, health leaders must make changes to improve organization efficiency (e.g., mergers, downsizing personnel, program/unit elimination or consolidation). Finally, health organizations must keep up with advancements in information technology in order to attract and retain patients as well as qualified employees. It is up to leaders to manage innovation implementation while taking into consideration the effects of change on employees, organizational structures, and financial concerns (Porter-O'Grady, 2010).

Workforce challenges refer to issues such as personnel shortage, lack of diversity, and organizational culture management. As mentioned in Chapter 2, the shortage of health professionals presents health organizations with particular problems. Such shortage has major human and financial costs, affecting care quality and continuity. Leaders recruit and retain qualified personnel by creating and maintaining positive work environments. Currently, there is a lack of diversity in health leadership and staff positions. Greater diversity will help health organizations adapt to changing patient and consumer populations as well as better represent the communities they serve (Institute of Medicine, 2004a). Leaders must make diversity a priority and develop structures and processes that emphasize diversity. Leaders also face challenges in regards to managing organizational cultures so that their organizations embody desired shared values (DeLellis, 2006). It is up to health leaders to collaborate with followers to develop and maintain collective values (Chaudry et al., 2008).

Box 5.2   Communication in Practice

Leading through Cross-Cultural Respect
Developing an organizational culture of mutual respect is a critical responsibility for leaders of health organizations, argues Anthony DeLellis, an administrator and professor in the school of nursing at Virginia Commonwealth University. In a *Health Care Manager* article, DeLellis (2006) states that achieving respect depends on recognizing differences while simultaneously focusing on similarities shared by all cultural groups. He encourages health leaders to establish cross-cultural respect as a core organizational value in an effort to promote collaboration, coordination, and cooperation.

Health leaders need to first help organizational members develop structured understanding by raising their awareness of universal social institutions (e.g., religion, family). Leaders must also help others recognize that health organizations have unique subcultures—based on factors such as race, ethnicity, age, socioeconomic status—and bring those subcultures into the mainstream. Subcultures should not be eliminated. Rather, leaders should create environments where groups experience compatibility between their subculture's values and the mission of the larger organization. Open discussion and consensus among employees regarding respected professional behaviors is a positive first step toward a collective identification with cross-cultural respect.

DeLellis offers guidelines to help healthcare leaders build organizational cultures of respect and replace homogeneity with cultural synergy, including the following:

1. Recognize and respect cultural differences, but focus on similarities.

2. Know that every person has unique attributes that differentiate that person from others.
3. Strive for consensus on norms of respectful behavior that align and support the organizational mission.
4. Establish consensus on what constitutes respect-worthy behaviors.
5. Develop a system of rewards that reinforces respect.

Professional challenges consist of factors that affect leaders as they take on and advance in leadership roles. Two major professional challenges are dual-tracks of institutional leadership and lack of leadership training. Dual tracks refers to when organizations have health administrators responsible for finance, business operations, human resources, etc., as well as clinical leaders who hold positions of authority based on their clinical expertise (e.g., medical director, chief nursing officer). Both tracks of leadership are intimately intertwined, but may represent different, and opposing, views about health organizing. For example, clashes can exist between administrators and clinical leaders based on conflicts about market-driven values versus traditional caregiving perspectives. While clinical leaders have broad and deep clinical expertise, they may lack the management knowledge and experience necessary for their leadership roles (Rowitz, 2006). To overcome such problems, leaders from both sides are encouraged to be sensitive to professional differences and find areas of shared interest and mutual cooperation (Martin and Keogh, 2004). Institutional employers must also help clinical leaders by providing education curricula and employer-based training programs that emphasize the development of leadership skills.

Healthcare leadership researcher and consultant Jo Manion (2005) identifies seven major demands which characterize twenty-first-century health leadership (Table 5.4). These demands require two skill sets that depend upon effective leadership communication. First, leaders must demonstrate **systems**

Table 5.4   Demands on Health Organization Leaders

Contingency	Description and Leader Role
Rapidity of change	Leaders must prioritize the changes most likely to achieve organizational goals and forego unnecessary efforts that sap resources. Leaders need to know their organizations' resilience and make alterations accordingly.
Workforce shortages	Lack of qualified healthcare professionals in a wide range of professions continues to dominate the healthcare landscape. Leaders must recruit top candidates and retain them by creating desirable work environments.
Rise of free-agent mentality	Outsourcing, temporary staffing, part-time employment, and shortage contribute to reduced loyalty to institutional employers. Leaders must influence and gain commitment from workers who lack strong organizational ties.
Diversity in the workplace	A diverse health workforce brings together individuals of varying ages, ethnicities, and cultures. Leaders need to foster work environments of respect and appreciation for differences.
New organizational structures	Health organizations need to move away from bureaucratic, vertical structures and adopt models such as teams, networks, and/or flattened hierarchies. Leaders must guide these reorganizations and reinforce participation.
Turbulent business environments	The financial and economic climate of healthcare delivery can be volatile and unpredictable. Health organizations that succeed are those led by leaders who constantly read business conditions and make adjustments.
Leader's energy capacity	Managing challenges requires a high degree of vitality. Leaders who can effectively manage their personal energy will be best equipped to avoid burnout and energize their organizations.

(Adapted from Manion, 2005)

thinking which necessitates that they see the "big picture" or how their organizations are interdependent with the embedded environment as well as how organizational components are interconnected. Systems thinking emphasizes that leaders collaborate to develop a shared vision, use inclusive decision-making, and solve problems collectively with followers. Second, leaders must display **interpersonal skills** to build positive relationships with followers. The leader is a coach who guides others rather than an autocratic leader who controls and dominates them. Key coaching behaviors include providing useful feedback, creating consensus, delegating to empower others, and building successful teams.

Leadership Approaches

Organizations, individuals, and situations in the health system continue to evolve and require ongoing study of leadership. The theories/models you will learn about below are useful for understanding and explaining leader qualities and behaviors.

Trait leadership is epitomized by the phrase "natural born leader." Developed in the early part of the twentieth century, this approach argues that leaders possess innate or inborn characteristics necessary for successful leadership. Self-confidence, determination, integrity, intelligence, and sociability are considered major, advantageous personality traits that contribute to a person's ability to lead (Northouse, 2007). Effective leaders have these desirable traits while those who lack them are ill suited for leadership roles. Classic studies by Ralph Stogdill (1948; 1974) dispute this notion of universal traits. Stogdill argued that leadership was influenced by situational factors *in addition* to personal leader traits. The traits displayed by leaders may vary in effectiveness across settings and relationships. Further, having desirable leader personality traits does not necessarily guarantee successful leadership behaviors.

Leadership style considers how individuals translate leadership traits into actual behaviors. This approach focuses on what leaders say and do in various contexts and with different groups of subordinates (Blake and Mouton, 1985). Leaders exhibit different styles consisting of varying degrees of task and relationship behaviors. Task behaviors emphasize goal accomplishment and help others achieve objectives whereas relationship behaviors help individuals become more comfortable with themselves, others, and different situations. Style theorists generally advocate a balance between task and relational needs as the "ideal" manner of leadership. The style approach is evident in health organizations when leaders are described in terms such as "democratic," "autocratic," or "laissez-faire," or when achieving a balance of concern for people and concern for productivity (exemplified in collaboration and teamwork) are desired leader behaviors (Frankel, Leonard, and Denham, 2006).

Situational leadership centers on how leaders adjust their leadership style to the demands of different situations (Hersey and Blanchard, 1977). No one leadership approach works best. Rather, leadership effectiveness depends on the match made between a situation—conceptualized as the competence and commitment of followers—and the leader's style. This approach tells us that leadership is made up of supportive and directive dimensions. Supportive behavior includes activities such as listening, encouraging, and communicating trust and respect, whereas directive behavior consists of providing rules and instruction and monitoring others. In healthcare contexts, ideas from the situational approach are visible when leaders are encouraged to tailor their communication according to follower needs. Leaders develop leadership behaviors which meet the needs of diverse health professionals and teams as a way of reducing conflict, fostering teamwork, and developing positive workplace climates (Dreachslin, Weech-Maldonado, and Dansky, 2004).

In the search for ways to inspire and empower workers, health organization scholars and practitioners have increasingly turned to ideas of **transformational leadership**. This approach centers on a leader's ability to influence followers to go above and beyond role requirements in order to benefit their organizations. The following list presents the key concepts (Avolio and Bass, 2002):

Idealized influence: leaders are trusted role models with high standards for moral and ethical behaviors; leaders provide a persuasive vision and mission.

Inspirational motivation: leaders motivate followers through setting high expectations and encouraging commitment to a shared vision.

Intellectual stimulation: leaders stimulate followers intellectually and creatively and encourage followers to challenge organizational beliefs and assumptions.

Individualized consideration: leaders recognize individual differences and pay attention to each follower's needs by serving as a mentor and coach.

Communication behaviors associated with transformational leadership in health organizations include supporting and recognizing staff, building connections that foster motivation, sharing leadership with others, listening, and determining and espousing a vision (Aarons, 2006).

Transformational leadership has been linked to numerous positive outcomes for health organizations. Given the current and projected nursing shortage, nursing studies have emphasized how transformational leader behaviors build positive leader-follower relationships and develop workplace environments conducive to nurse retention and commitment. These findings are consistent across levels of leadership. For instance, Leach (2005) found that transformational nurse executives positively influence staff nurses' commitment to their teams and organizational employers. Separate studies of nurse managers indicate that a transformational approach has a positive effect on staff nurse retention, morale, job satisfaction, and organizational identification (Raup, 2008; Robbins and Davidhizar, 2007).

Similar trends have been found in other health professions. In medicine, transformational leadership is positively associated with staff physician extra-role behavior and job satisfaction (Xirasager, Samuels, and Stoskopf, 2005). Menaker and Bahn's (2008) survey of physicians working at the Mayo Clinic found that transformational leadership qualities correlate highly with physician

Box 5.3   Ripped from the Headlines

Leading the Global Movement to End Breast Cancer
Calling her passion and determination a "blessing to all those whose lives have been touched by breast cancer," President Obama awarded Nancy G. Brinker, founder and chief executive officer of Susan G. Komen for the Cure, with the Presidential Medal of Freedom, the United States' highest civilian honor (Sanchez and Malveaux, 2009, para. 197). Brinker received the award for her leadership in transforming the nation's approach to breast cancer and guiding a global movement to end the disease.

Beginning with $200 grocery money and a list of friends, Brinker set out to fulfill a promise to her sister, Susan G. Komen, to prevent other families from suffering from breast cancer the way that her family had. Komen died of breast cancer in 1980 at the age of 37. Brinker now leads more than 120 affiliate organizations and supervises an institution that has spent more than $1.3 billion in research and outreach (Susan G. Komen for the Cure, 2009). Komen's success is a joint effort—shared by advocates, volunteers, employees, sponsors, and others—but it is largely due to Brinker's leadership, which is best captured in the transformational approach.

Consider her speech to the 2008 Susan G. Komen for the Cure Affiliate Leadership Conference (Susan G. Komen for the Cure, 2008). Here, Brinker demonstrates *idealized influence* when she talks persuasively of the organization's vision to "end this ugly disease forever" and discusses how, "After years of aspiring to be a global leader, we have become that leader." She is a vivid role model of passion and determination as she speaks of starting Komen with only a "handful of volunteers."

She displays *inspirational motivation* when she talks about her promise to "a woman named Susan" that is now a promise shared by all members of the organization as they work to help those suffering from breast cancer. Brinker sets high standards to fulfill that promise. She emphasizes that Komen must be "one organization, telling one story, in one voice. Without it, we risk becoming another nameless, faceless breast cancer group."

Brinker's *intellectual stimulation* is evident when she explains the need for organizational improvement through constant innovation. "We have to evolve or perish," Brinker explains as she challenges advocates to change Komen through new models, collaborations, communities, and donors.

Brinker's desire to "break the mold, throw out all the old playbooks" is articulated in her *individual consideration* of her followers. She encourages advocates to replace themselves in order to make way for the next generation of organization leaders. She urges them to give up familiar roles and to try new experiences. "It's hard to let go of something you're doing that you love . . . but if it's not showing results or increased results it's time to try something new," she states.

Discussion Questions
1. Given what you know about health organizations, what are the characteristics necessary for effective health leadership?
2. What major challenges will health leaders experience? What suggestions could you give health leaders to anticipate and/or adapt to such challenges?
3. What do you think of Brinker's leadership approach? Would her style work in a different health organization or in a different industry? Explain your response.

satisfaction, a key factor in intent to stay. Findings also show that the transformational attributes most valued by staff physicians—idealized influence and individual consideration—were the least often displayed by physician leaders. The authors conclude that physician leaders must develop these qualities to create workplaces conducive to physician recruitment and retention.

The theories and models considered here provide different perspectives in which to understand leader behaviors and skills. Across these varied conceptualizations, leadership communication is a central theme.

Leaders' Communication Competencies

Health leaders must display a wide variety of communication competencies. Four major competencies particularly relevant to leadership in health organizations are empowerment, conflict management, collaboration, and influence.

Empowerment refers to leader communication that encourages participation, involvement and autonomy in ways that develop competence, ability, and personal authority among followers (Chiles and Zorn, 1995). Health leaders demonstrate empowerment when they create opportunities for participation in decision-making and actually use follower feedback in decisions of mutual interest. Further, leaders empower others when they provide messages of support and encouragement, build feelings of self-efficacy among followers, and create positive networks that give subordinates access to power (Laschinger and Finegan, 2005).

Empowerment is of critical importance in health organizations due in part to the myriad challenges facing health leaders. No one leader can effectively meet all organizational demands alone. Empowering communication encourages leadership skills among all members of an organization and develops leaders throughout an institution, regardless of formal position. Thus, health leaders who empower subordinates are making their organizations better equipped to address contextual, workforce, and professional challenges.

For instance, in a study of Latina nurses working in U.S. and Mexico, Baker et al., (2007) found that empowerment instills a sense of ownership of decisions and accountability among employees. Kahaleh and Gaither's (2007) study of pharmacists found correlations between empowerment and outcomes such as loyalty, identification, commitment, and turnover. In a study of a non-profit community health agency, Wolff et al. (2004) found that leaders who create empowering workplaces enable followers to feel confident to act on their own decisions, thereby furthering the goals of the organization. Manojlovich (2007) concludes that empowered nurses experience better health, more job satisfaction, less job strain, and reduced burnout.

Conflict management refers to interpersonal communication that negotiates the interactions of individuals who are interdependent yet have incompatible goals (Putnam and Poole, 1987). Leaders are often third-party conflict managers because they supervise some or all of the individuals who are in disagreement. Conflict is a natural part of life in health organizations, as individuals with different backgrounds, cultures, qualifications, etc., attempt to work together to achieve organizational and individual goals. Major factors that contribute to conflict include varying specializations and diverse cultures among health professionals, the complex and demanding nature of caregiving work, and the predominance of team-based care which requires individuals to work closely together. Given these organizational conditions, it is not all that surprising that effective conflict resolution is a desirable competency for health leaders.

Managing conflict successfully in health organizations depends on multiple communication qualities. First, health leaders must establish trust so followers feel comfortable sharing information and opinions without fear of negative repercussions (Wolff et al., 2004). Trust is reinforced when leaders deal with conflict directly and respectfully, rather than avoiding disagreements or handling them with hostility. Second, leaders must keep the lines of communication open between themselves and subordinates and be willing to listen and to mediate conflict. Openness is particularly critical in healthcare teams where team members must defuse dysfunctional conflict and work together for the good of the patient (Chaudry et al., 2008). Openness requires willingness to discuss

conflict and refraining from giving negative feedback and discon-
firming responses. Third, conflict resolution requires diplomacy
and negotiation so that followers feel their perspectives are recognized and attempts are made to meet their needs appropriately
(Duncan, et al., 2007). Conflict management takes time and effort
but the outcomes can benefit health organizations by improving
clinical staff retention, team morale, and work culture.

Collaboration entails working together, typically in a shared
intellectual effort. Unlike division of labor where individuals divvy
up tasks and work independently, collaboration requires people
to work interdependently on responsibilities of mutual interest.
Leaders and followers collaborate when their interactions enable
their knowledge and skills to synergistically influence decisions
and/or work. Teamwork allows leaders and followers to generate more and better quality solutions than would be produced by
working alone.

Collaborative leadership is well suited to the health professions because it draws upon the expertise, energy, and efforts of
multiple constituencies (e.g., health professionals from various
occupations and specializations) who are working on accomplish-
ing the same or similar goals (e.g., ensuring quality patient care).
Communication takes center stage as leaders and followers share
information, solve problems, provide feedback, coordinate activities, etc., to accomplish shared objectives. Frankel, Leonard, and
Denhamet's (2006) case study of WalkRounds, a twice-daily,
multidisciplinary rounding at Brigham and Women's Hospital in
New York City, provides a useful example of effective collaborative
leadership in action. Clinicians from multiple professions and specializations visit patients together and have an opportunity to hear
about the care being provided. WalkRounds provides opportunities
for all caregivers—nurses, residents, and senior medical staff—to
have an input and speak their minds without fear of negative
repercussions.

Factors and outcomes of collaboration are similar to those
pertaining to empowerment and conflict resolution. That is,
collaboration is best achieved in leader-follower relationships
characterized by trust, openness, respect, and participation.

Collaboration has been associated with increased clinical staff retention and autonomy, more functional healthcare teams, and greater organizational commitment.

Influence is the essence of leadership as leaders continually shape the attitudes and behaviors of others to achieve goals (Northouse, 2007). Establishing and maintaining healthy relationships through positive communication behaviors—such as those found in empowerment, conflict resolution, and collaboration—are the first steps in developing the ability to influence. Leaders are better able to persuade and gain compliance when they have a strong, mutually beneficial relational foundation with followers.

While influencing others enables leaders to get things done, it is perhaps most critical to achieving a vision or sense of direction and purpose for an organization. Having a clear vision is especially important in the continuously shifting healthcare environment, where leaders must constantly anticipate and respond to new contingencies as well as guide followers through organizational adaptations. A leader's vision also drives health organization culture and plays a crucial part in the quality of work-life conditions which factor in employee retention, morale, job satisfaction and job involvement (West et al., 2003).

Chapter Summary

Health organizations are constantly changing in order to meet the needs of multiple constituencies and contingencies. Managing planned change successfully can be a difficult, long-term endeavor that involves multiple communication strategies and responses. Working together, leaders and followers can more effectively navigate the change process and bolster their organizations' resilience to environmental turbulence. Leadership takes on heightened importance in the current health system as leaders face complex demands that require a wide repertoire of communication behaviors. Positive, relationally centered leader-member communication is a cornerstone for the effective leadership of today's health organizations.

6

Health Teams

Health organizations provide countless settings in which to observe teams and teamwork in action. One of the most visible and dramatic contexts in which to observe teams in action is an operating room. Here, teams consist of multiple health professions—surgeons, nurses, anesthesiologists, and others—who work together to perform surgical interventions. In some instances, the clinicians have had little or no prior experience working together but their tasks demand precise and interconnected team activities. The success of the operation and the health of the patient depend on collaboration.

According to Dr. Atul Gawande (2009), a Harvard Medical School professor who is also a cancer surgeon and best-selling author, surgical teams could often use a little help in getting teamwork—and team communication—right. He proposes that teams use a checklist which provides protocol guidelines to run through prior to surgery. A key benefit of the checklist is that it requires team members to interact. The simple act of team member introductions can improve team communication during an operation. Gawande says knowing names produces an activation phenomenon that encourages team members to speak up if they notice a problem. He argues that speaking up reduces surgical complications which can contribute to patient deaths.

Gawande's findings call attention to the vital role that teams perform in health organizations. Teamwork done right can save lives. Poor or ineffective teamwork can have negative and possibly deadly repercussions. Achieving optimal teamwork can be challenging given complexities such as increased patient volume and diversity, heightened pressures to speed up work, and rising patient health disparities. Health teams must find better ways to work together to overcome such barriers and facilitate collaboration.

Today's health teams are increasingly diverse, consisting of team members representing various professions, specializations, demographic characteristics (e.g., age, ethnicity/race, gender) and other cultural variables. This diversity has implications for team communication as the influence of culture plays out in team dynamics. Participating in health teams requires knowledge about cultural influences, sensitivity to cultural differences, and communication skills to work with others from varied cultural backgrounds.

This chapter begins by considering health teams from a systems perspective and exploring defining qualities of healthcare teams. Next, you will learn about how communication contributes to effective teamwork or synergy and the discursive processes that lead to team conflict. The second half of the chapter takes a closer look at cultural diversity by examining major cultural variables that affect health teams. The chapter addresses culturally competent communication before exploring the unique role of medical interpreters, a position designed to improve team cultural communication competence.

A Systems Perspective on Health Teams

Team refers to a small number of people with complementary skills who are dedicated to common objectives and performance goals for which they are mutually accountable (Katzenbach and Smith, 1993). Even though the term "team(s)" is used pervasively, groups that actually embody the above-mentioned qualities are not all that common in health organizations. It is perhaps more accurate to say that health teams are collectives that both exemplify "teamness" as well as those which *intend* to achieve team ideals but may not actually do so (Poole and Real, 2003). **Teamwork** refers to the ways people work together cooperatively and effectively, primarily through collaboration (Manion, Lorimer, and Leander, 1996).

Interdependence refers to the reliance that team members have on one another, creating relationships necessary for survival. Team members rely on each other to varying degrees—sharing occupational expertise, experience, and skills—to reach individual and group goals. Interdependencies are developed as health professionals interact to coordinate work efforts, make decisions, and build relationships.

Feedback refers to interactions that regulate team behaviors, relationships, and outcomes. Timely, clear, and useful feedback provides team members with information critical to the ongoing success of the team. Two forms of feedback are important to teams. First, positive feedback encourages team growth and development so that the team can better meet system changes. Second, corrective feedback regulates individual and collective efforts to align with team norms and expectations, thereby maintaining system functioning.

Next, you will explore the unique qualities of health teams and investigate different types of teams. You will also consider health team communication and effectiveness.

Health Teams Overview

Health teams are characterized by several distinct qualities and specific configurations that vary within and across health organizations. The unique features of health teams and the multiple types of team structures play a role in team communication.

Types of Health Teams and Qualities of Clinical Teams

In their review of the research literature, Poole and Real (2003) distinguish six generic types of groups or teams (Table 6.1). The most visible kind of team in health organizations is **multidisciplinary**— consisting of health professionals who come together, report/share information on specific patients, and work side-by-side on individual tasks (Pecukonis, Doyle, and Bliss, 2008). Such teams may be so large and complex that embedded teams naturally develop (Ellingson, 2003). **Embedded teams** consist of dyads or triads of health professionals who communicate in constant but fleeting interactions. For instance, a long-term-care staff nurse may form

Table 6.1   Types of Groups and Teams in Health
Organizations and Examples

Group/Team	Description	Health Organization Example
Ad hoc group	Created for restricted time period to address a problem and disband upon resolution and/or goal achievement.	A fertility clinic forms a team consisting of clinician, support, and administrative staff to develop plans for redesigning and expanding existing facilities.
Nominal care group	Patient care is provided through the autonomous consultation of health professionals directed by a primary care physician.	A patient suffering from chronic back pain receives treatment from a massage therapist and a physical therapist under the direction of the patient's internal medicine physician.
Uni-disciplinary group	Organized around a single profession with relatively permanent and formal boundaries; these groups may have support personnel who play a subordinate role.	Physicians known as pediatric hospitalists provide care for children who are inpatients. They are a distinct professional group within a hospital setting.
Multi-disciplinary team	Made up of health professionals from multiple occupations and/or specializations that work together but function independently – often work sequentially rather than simultaneously.	A state health department provides immunizations to low-income children. Health educators meet with parents to explain the program and answer questions. Public health nurses perform the vaccinations at a separate time and location.
Inter-disciplinary team	Consist of multiple practitioners who work interdependently in the same settings. Members agree upon performance goals, show mutual accountability, and share a common approach to work.	A regional public health program consists of physical therapists, occupational therapists, audiologists, and speech pathologists. They work together to help at-risk children meet developmental milestones.

Table 6.1   (continued)

Group/Team	Description	Health Organization Example
Trans-disciplinary team	Interdisciplinary teams where members are sufficiently cross-trained to develop knowledge and skills to provide care across traditional professional domains.	Social workers and chaplains provide end-of-life counseling, spiritual support, and coordinate community resources with faith-based organizations for hospice patients.

(Adapted from Poole and Real, 2003)

an embedded team with a nursing assistant because they care for the same patients and routinely talk throughout the course of their shifts together. The nurse and nurse assistant develop close task and relational bonds while still communicating with other team members (e.g., physical and occupational therapists, dieticians, social workers, and physicians) albeit on a less frequent basis.

Clinical health represents the majority of team-based organizing in the health system and, as such, much of the research has specifically examined teams in clinical settings. Such groups are characterized by several unique qualities, which are summarized in Table 6.2 along with illustrative examples. While non-clinical teams may share these identified features in some ways (e.g., dispersed geographic locations, multiple domains of professional expertise), it is the existence of all or most of these qualities that make clinical teams distinct from other forms of team structures in health organizations (e.g., administrative teams, leadership teams).

The unique qualities of clinical teams have profound implications for team communication. For instance, team duration is patient-centered. Team members may flow in and out of the team as well as work together for limited time periods. Communication may be fragmented, inconsistent, and lacking in relational qualities (e.g., trust, support) which can ultimately negatively affect team cohesion and decision-making

Table 6.2   Unique Qualities of Clinical Teams and Examples

Quality	Description	Health Organization Example
Team assignment	Assignment to team primarily based on patient care needs and outcomes. The focus is on the patient, not the team.	A primary care physician may work with oncology physicians and nurses to provide specialized treatment and monitor care for cancer patients.
Team membership	Multiple experts from different professions and specializations; consists of varying levels of education, training, and experience.	A hospice team relies on the shared contributions of physicians, nurses, chaplains, and social workers. Team members jointly make decisions and solve problems about end-of-life care.
Team tasks	Consist of repetitive, relatively stable behaviors done multiple times with the same or varying patients. Work is altered based on the patient's condition.	Pharmacists and pharmacist technicians fill medication orders, interact with patients, and advise clinicians.
Team leadership	Not always defined by hierarchy, may emerge as team members take the lead on tasks pertaining to professional affiliation. Therefore, the individual who actually performs the task may not be the one ultimately responsible.	Surgical attending physician delegates trauma resuscitation to a surgical resident. The resident actually runs the resuscitation and leads the team but the attending is legally responsible for the procedure and outcome.
Team roles	Defined in relation to professional affiliation and/or expertise although roles may blur as tasks overlap between professions.	Social workers and nurses may perform discharge planning tasks which coordinate outpatient care.

(Adapted from the following sources: Porter-O'Grady and Wilson, 1998; Manion, Lorimer and Leander, 1996; Parker, 2002; Yun et al., 2003)

(Parker-Oliver, Bronstein, and Kurzejeski, 2005). Further, the co-existence of multiple professions influences team interactions. Cross-disciplinary communication has been found to improve team decision-making, enhance problem-solving, and build team cohesion; however, it may also promote team conflict. You will learn more about these communication dynamics later in the chapter.

Teamwork and Health Team Effectiveness

Teams generally maximize the contributions of multiple professionals in ways that improve health institutions' abilities to address problems. A great deal of the research literature has focused on links between team communication and team effectiveness. Scholars have primarily explored how teamwork—open, respectful, cooperative, and collaborative communication—enhances individual and organizational outcomes. Table 6.3 presents sample findings from this literature, spanning medicine, nursing, health communication, dentistry, and allied health research.

Building teams that yield such outcomes is not an easy or straightforward task. Successful teamwork requires time, energy, and a commitment to constructive communication processes. Next, you will learn about the communication processes that contribute to achieving and maintaining teamwork in health organizations.

Team Communication Processes

If teams form the foundation of health organizations, then "communication is the cement which holds teams together" (Poole and Real, 2003, p. 396). While effective health team communication can take many forms, depending on the nature, function, and context of the group, two processes are consistently recognized as being essential to optimal teamwork. Below, you will explore aspects of team synergy before learning about team conflict resolution.

Table 6.3   Research Summary of Teamwork and Health
                 Team Effectiveness Indicators

Indicators	Sample Findings	Authors
Patient care	Lower patient mortality and reduced patient length of stay. Heightened care quality and clinical team decision-making. Enhanced care continuity Patient referrals from team correlated with higher quality. Greater understanding of the "big picture" regarding patient condition.	Fewster-Theuente and Velsor-Friedrich (2008) Haeuser and Preston (2006) Parker (2002) Parker-Oliver, Bronstein, and Kurzejeski (2005) Yun et al. (2003)
Quality of work life	Higher satisfaction and lower burnout among nurses. More team cohesion Novice clinicians experienced reduced uncertainty, greater satisfaction, and more team appreciation. Improved nurse retention. Reduced work stress.	Fewster-Theuente and Velsor-Friedrich (2008) Grumbach and Bodenheimer (2004) McGrail et al. (2008) Rosenstein (2002) Propp et al. (2010)
Health organization functioning	Improved innovation, information flow, and decision-making. Greater ease of medical technology adoption. Increased dental team productivity and member empowerment. Heightened flexibility to adapt to change.	Colón-Emeric et al. (2006) Edmondson (2003) Chilcutt (2009) Ellingson (2003)

Synergistic Communication

Building and maintaining an effective health team requires **synergy**, an idea that draws upon the systems concept of interdependence. Synergy calls attention to the fact that teams are more than just structures which combine the skills, knowledge, and abilities of individuals (Porter-O'Grady and Wilson, 1998). Rather, synergy occurs when each team member plays a part in the overall effort of the team and each team member's quality of contribution is improved as a result of others' ideas and efforts. Promoting team synergy inherently involves communication as team members with different backgrounds, education, and roles must interact to form a coherent whole for the good of the patient.

Consider the experience of Jenna, a patient who is expecting her first baby and desires a natural childbirth setting within a hospital environment. During delivery, Jenna works with a nurse midwife who is trained in natural birthing philosophy and procedures. Because Jenna is giving birth at a community hospital she also receives consultations from a labor and delivery nurse and an obstetrician-gynecologist (OBGYN), with the nurse midwife serving as her primary caregiver. When Jenna experiences complications, her requirements shift from a natural delivery to a surgical intervention. Consequently, the labor and delivery nurse and OBGYN physician must step in to assume treatment responsibilities. They collaborate with the nurse midwife who continues to care for Jenna's emotional and spiritual needs. Together, the team contributes information, skills, and knowledge that achieve a successful birth. The sum of their collaborative actions is greater than the combined force of their separate efforts.

Wright, Sparks, and O'Hair (2009) have presented a model of synergistic healthcare teams that illustrates the centrality of communication to team development (Figure 6.1). Building effective teams requires inculcating a sense of personal accountability to the overall goals of the team and patient care (e.g., instilling a sense of ownership), setting and maintaining performance standards (e.g., becoming performance based), and contributing to the sum of the team's efforts (e.g., developing team synergy). Wright et al. argue that these three essential characteristics offer the "greatest potential for improving outcomes and elevating organizational and system effectiveness" (p. 267).

Health professionals must display a repertoire of discursive skills to accomplish and maintain team synergy. For instance, McGrail et al. (2008) found that synergy requires physicians

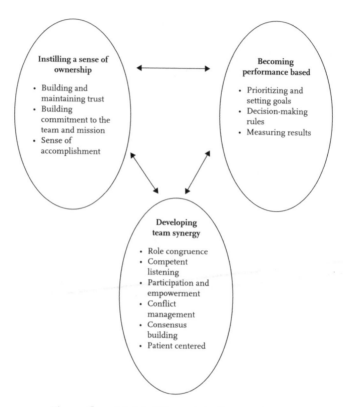

Figure 6.1   *Model of Synergistic Communication*
(Source: Wright, K. B., Sparks, L., and O'Hair, H. D. *Health communication in the 21st century*. Malden, MA: Blackwell Publishing, 2008.)

and nurses to communicate technical expertise as well as show interpersonal competence in their interactions. A series of studies by Apker and colleagues regarding nurse-team communication highlights multiple communication behaviors that contribute to optimal team synergy (Apker, Propp, and Ford, 2005; Apker et al., 2006; Propp et al., 2010). Table 6.4 describes nine synergistic communication behaviors from this research.

Effective **participation in decision-making** is a hallmark of team synergy. Recall from Chapter 5 that participation is a key factor in leader-member communication; it also figures prominently in

Table 6.4   Promoting Team Synergy

Communication Behavior	Description
Coordinating the patient-care team	Assigning team member responsibilities and managing team members' information needs to enhance task accomplishment.
Mentoring team members	Teaching, guiding and supporting team members, particularly novices, in work tasks and communication with others.
Empowering lower-level team members	Encouraging team members to speak up and share ideas as well as valuing their contributions to the overall efforts of the team.
Advocating on behalf of others	Giving voice to the needs of team members of lower status and standing up for them in light of power differences due to medical hierarchy.
Managing conflict constructively	Dealing with conflict in a direct, professional manner, listening to others' perspectives with courtesy, and remaining objective, rational, and calm.
Listening actively to team members	Displaying openness to other team members' ideas and questions and addressing team concerns in a nonjudgmental manner.
Fostering a positive climate	Modeling optimism through friendly, warm, cheerful, and humorous interactions with other team members.
Managing workplace stress	Providing team members with calming and comforting talk during times of stress, thereby bringing order to chaotic conditions.
Pinch hitting for team members	Helping team members with tasks when they are overwhelmed by the demands of the care environment.

team communication. In teams, participation in decision-making involves practices such as team members providing solutions to problems (e.g., brainstorming), giving feedback when implementing proposed ideas, and evaluating performance of change. Berteotti and Seibold's (1994) study of hospice team communication identifies three central team decision-making qualities: 1) share the decision-making process; 2) listen to the opinions of

Box 6.1   Communication in Practice

Consensus Decision-Making in Health Teams
Decision-making by consensus is one way in which team members can contribute their ideas, opinions, feelings, and interpretations for the good of the team. Health management researchers and consultants Tim Porter-O'Grady and Cathleen Krueger Wilson (1998) explain that consensus is not agreement or voting in support of one way of doing things. Rather, consensus consists of give-and-take as teams recognize, deliberate, and solve problems. The goal is to maximize team member contributions through ground rules such as:

1. Share all relevant information: Facts and emotions are important. Convey information to enhance others' understanding of your views.

2. Be specific; use examples: Verbally portray the observable actions and/or results that will be achieved if the team adopts your position.

3. Explain the reasons behind statements, questions, and behavior: State your rationale to ensure that others interpret your behavior correctly.

4. Disagree openly with team members: Constructively challenge other team members' assumptions and inferences (e.g., play devil's advocate).

5. Test disagreements: Compare disagreements objectively. Where is the common ground?

others; and 3) openly discuss feelings. Frequently, these critical communication processes occur in the "clinical backstage" away from patients and members of the public. Research suggests that backstage communication bolsters participation by providing team members with discursive spaces where they can freely share information and informal impressions, build relationships, and adjust to changing clinical demands (Ellingson 2003; 2007;). Box 6.1

identifies specific communication practices that bolster team decision-making through consensus building.

Conflict Communication

Drawing upon Putnam and Poole's (1987) classic definition of organizational conflict, **team conflict** is defined as the interaction of interdependent team members who perceive an opposition concerning goals, objectives, and values, and who see the other team members as possibly interfering with the attainment of these goals. Conflict is a natural part of team life in health organizations, particularly when team members work in multi-disciplinary or interdisciplinary teams which represent varying specializations, education and training, roles, and communication styles. Such team member differences may contribute to underlying conflict conditions and influence how team members communicate during disputes.

The first characteristic that can promote team conflict is **profession-centrism**—a preferred, narrow worldview held by a particular professional group which is created and reinforced through training (Pecukonis, Doyle, and Bliss, 2008). This worldview affects a profession's communication preferences and styles. For instance, in Chapter 2 you learned that the culture of medicine values autonomy and authority and those values are reinforced in medical education (e.g., teaching students about who gets to talk and when, not to question senior physicians). Over time, physicians may come to believe that their cultural values are superior to others, such as professional collaboration, and these perceptions influence how they communicate in a team. Consider Lindsey, a physician who becomes defensive when lower-status team members share their professional opinion, because she perceives their attempts at collaboration as encroaching on her medical autonomy. Her hostility shuts down future team member participation in decision-making, which may ultimately reduce the quality of care.

The second characteristic is **role overlap** or the blurring that occurs when multiple health professionals engage in the same or similar work activities in ways that threaten disciplinary territoriality (Reese and Sontag, 2001). Role overlap can be a source of conflict as team members' role expectations and responsibilities clash with actual behaviors. For instance, the liaison and counselor role of social workers may also be performed by nurses, thereby creating conflict due to role confusion, duplication of effort, and competition for resources (Kennedy and Lyndon, 2008). Social workers and nurses may voice conflict over when tasks should be done and by whom, which can negatively affect the team.

Third, **role and organizational stressors** can predispose health professionals to engage in conflict more readily (Chapter 4). Heightened time and financial constraints, the severity of a patient's illness, higher workload, and rising emotional labor are just a few of the pressures that contribute to latent conditions that may lead to team conflict. For example, faced with more work to do with less time and staffing, team members may be more apt to communicate in destructive ways (e.g., blaming, ignoring, yelling) in order to achieve their goals. Such behaviors reduce team trust and respect, undermining the positive relationships necessary for team synergy (Davidhizar and Dowd, 2001).

Conflict management acknowledges that the characteristics and accompanying communication such as the ones identified above are an inherent part of team dynamics. It is generally advised that health teams should handle conflict openly and directly and avoid behaviors that ignore, discount, or indirectly deal with conflict (Freire et al., 2008). Appropriate conflict management not only identifies problems that impede teamwork, it provides health teams with strategies to handle conflict effectively and to improve team dynamics. Runde and Flanagan (2008) argue that teams must display **conflict competence**, a concept that involves:

- **Perspective taking**: listening to and taking on board another person's point of view about conflict; displaying empathy for others.
- **Expressing emotions**: respectfully and candidly discussing feelings in ways that do not blame and/or criticize others.
- **Reflective thinking and delaying response**: cooling down feelings and slowing down conflict in order to create emotional distance and promote objective decision-making.

Conflict competence enables teams to engage, speak, listen, hear, interpret, and respond constructively so members are able to "leverage conflict rather than be leveled by it" (Runde and Flanagan, 2008, p. 116).

To provide health teams with practical strategies to manage conflict successfully, researchers have explored how to create safe team climates founded on positive communication principles. Kupperschmidt (2006) explains that health professionals must care enough about themselves and their team members to "carefront" with respect rather than show hostility. Through behaviors such as making eye contact, using courtesies, and paying attention, carefronting conveys a respect for self and other that promotes positive team relationships. Haeuser and Preston (2006) argue that communicating common ground, listening, empathy, and providing consistent, constructive, and honest feedback are central to building trust in health teams. These techniques must be reinforced by institutional policies. Together, team and institutional efforts may go a long way in helping team members handle conflict more effectively.

To summarize, teams are central to how health organizations function with team synergy figuring prominently in creating effective team environments. Conflict is an inherent part of team life and stems from multiple sources. Even though conflict can have deleterious effects on teamwork, constructive conflict management strategies can enhance team performance. The remaining sections of this chapter focus on cultural diversity, with a continued emphasis on teams. You will first learn about major cultural variables present in health teams before exploring the topic of culturally competent communication. The chapter concludes by considering the unique role played by linguistic interpreters in team-based care.

Cultural Diversity in Health Teams

United States health organizations are diverse institutions, consisting of teams with wide-ranging memberships that serve an increasingly diverse patient population (Chapter 1). Health teams consist of many cultures and are common sites for cross-cultural encounters. **Culture** refers to members of a social group who have commonly held beliefs, values, and attitudes that shape and direct their behaviors (Kreps and Kunimoto, 1994). **Multiculturalism** is the representation—typically in a collective such as an organization or a team—of people with different group affiliations of cultural importance (Cox, 1994).

In health teams, members from various cultural groups may have distinct—and at times divergent—understandings of health and illness and perceptions of health encounters. Their unique perspectives play out in team communication behaviors and can eventually affect patient care and quality of work life. Below, you will learn more about the effects of profession/specialization as a cultural variable.

Profession/Specialization

Regarding **profession/specialization**, recall that health teams, especially clinical teams, consist of a range of health workers who come together to achieve collective goals. Team members bring different orientations to care and team life based on their respective professional cultures. These differing and potentially conflicting perspectives are likely to have their roots in variations of education and training (Kreps and Kunimoto, 1994). For instance, research into physician-nurse interactions shows that the two occupations have different approaches to care (Baggs et al., 1999). Nurses tend to take a holistic approach, caring for the physical dimensions of disease as well as the social/emotional aspects of illness; physicians tend to center on the physical manifestations of disease. A nurse may advocate taking time with cancer patients to address feelings of uncertainty before conveying the technical aspects of the disease, whereas a physician may be more interested in diagnostic efficiency and immediate discussion of treatment steps. These cultural influences play out in nurse-physician interactions with potential outcomes such as disagreements or, more positively, in the form of professional collaboration.

Cultural influences may also vary among caregivers within the same profession who are on the same team. For instance, two different specializations within the medical profession—a surgeon and a family practice physician—may come into conflict over the removal of a patient's gall bladder. The surgeon may immediately advocate surgical procedures as a first line of treatment to relieve the patient's extreme and long-term discomfort and digestive trouble (among other symptoms) whereas the family physician may advocate a wait-and-see approach involving non-surgical treatments such as prescription medications, lifestyle changes, etc. Their perspectives are consistent with their respective professional cultures and the two clinicians may be unwilling to negotiate because their worldviews have solidified through years of education and training. The cultural clash can lead to team conflict as well as patient confusion about next steps in care. Box 6.2 identifies strategies that may help improve communication among health professionals in team settings.

Gender and Race/Ethnicity

The second major cultural variable is **gender and race/ethnicity**, and the following statistics from the three largest health professions—medicine, nursing, and pharmacy—illustrate recent growth trends. In regards to gender, increasing numbers of women comprise the once male-dominated professions of medicine and pharmacy. Nearly one in four physicians and approximately half of pharmacists are female (Health Resources and Services Administration [HRSA], 2008a; 2008b). While still underrepresented in nursing (approximately 6% of the total nursing population), the number of male nurses rose 14.5% from 2000 to 2004 (HRSA, 2006a).

While there is still a long way to go to achieve racial and ethnic representation on a par with the greater U.S. population, more racial and ethnic minorities have joined health professions. Consider these statistics:

- The number of Black and Hispanic physicians was 9% in 2008, up from 8.5% in 2000 (HRSA, 2008a).

Box 6.2   Communication in Practice

How to Get Along in Diverse Health Teams
Health teams consist of many different cultural variables such as profession/specialization, race/ethnicity, age, and gender. Each team member comes to the team with unique backgrounds and different cultural perspectives. This diversity may contribute to cultural misunderstandings and/or conflict that are further heightened by negative team communication behaviors. The strategies listed below, selected from Davidhizer and Dowd (2001), provide suggestions on ways health professionals can promote positive interpersonal relationships in diverse teams:

1. Know the person/professional you are dealing with: Take time to know team members on a personal and professional basis; show interest in people.

2. Utilize techniques that promote cooperation: Show receptivity to others by open posture, consistent eye contact, and friendly facial expressions.

3. Time communications strategically: Consider when and where to best approach team members; it is better to converse privately during "down time" about a controversy rather than talk publicly in a hectic environment.

4. Avoid reacting with anger: Anger alienates people and escalates conflict; avoid these obstacles through wait time and communicating in a calm, objective manner.

- In 2007, 25% of pharmacists indicated they are in a racial minority group, an increase of 7% from 2000 (HRSA, 2008b).
- In 2008, 16.8% of nurses were from non-White groups (Asian, Black/African-American, Native American/Alaska Native, and/or Hispanic); a 12.2% increase from 2004 (HRSA, 2010).

The most significant growth has occurred in the number of international medical graduates (IMGs) who work as practicing physicians in the U.S. Currently, IMGs comprise 25% of the physician population, the majority of whom are racial or ethnic minorities coming from India, Pakistan, Mexico, and the Philippines (American Medical Association, 2010).

Teams with racial and ethnic minority members are often able to yield better quality and quantity of patient information, therefore enhancing the quality of care they provide. Taylor and Lurie (2004) argue that because racial and ethnic minority patients feel more welcome and comfortable with clinicians of similar backgrounds, there is greater openness, information sharing, and joint decision-making in health encounters. Ultimately, these positive communication behaviors can lead to greater patient satisfaction with care, heightened adherence to treatment, and improved patient outcomes (Smedley, Stith, and Nelson, 2003). Team members who share racial/ethnic cultures with patients may be better able to understand and adapt to cultural norms that facilitate patient-team communication.

Racially and ethnically diverse health teams may also promote greater sensitivity to racial/ethnic cultural differences in ways that reduce uncertainty among team members and improve team effectiveness. Ulrey and Amason (2001) explain that many individuals enter healthcare professions wanting to help people, but for a variety of reasons (lack of exposure to cultural diversity in education and life experiences, etc.) they may not be well equipped to deal with intercultural differences once they are in their jobs. Communication with racially/ethnically diverse peers and professional associates in a team can provide health professionals with a context in which they can learn about culture differences and gain experience interacting with individuals from different cultural backgrounds. For these reasons, Smedley, Stith, and Nelson (2003) argue that greater team diversity may reduce stereotyping, biased, or discriminatory treatment of patients based on race, culture, and language proficiency.

Educational and training opportunities offer promise in fostering greater understanding of gender and racial/ethnic

diversity issues. Increasing numbers of health education institutions offer formal curricula in cultural diversity (e.g., patient
simulations, discussion groups, development of language skills)
which is reinforced in on-the-job training (Rosenberg et al.,
2006). Some schools require students to earn credit hours
through service to racially/ethnically diverse communities.
Students provide care to racial/ethnic minority patients and
gain work experience in diverse teams, thereby increasing
multiculturalism.

Today's health teams are complex structures consisting of multiple and diverse cultures. The team-based health
environment demands communication knowledge and skills
from health professionals. Cultural competence has emerged
as a topic which can foster beneficial cross-cultural relationships within health teams and between team members and
others. Next, you will explore cultural competence and team
communication.

Culturally Competent Communication in Health Teams

Cultural competence implies having the capacity to function
effectively as an individual, team, and organization within the
context of multicultural beliefs and behaviors (Cross et al., 1989).
Although the term "competence" may imply goal mastery, cultural competence is best understood as the ongoing development
of cultural attitudes, knowledge, and skills performed by health
professionals. Recognized first as a tool to enhance physician interactions and relationships with patients from different cultures,
cultural competence is a key concept in building and maintaining
positive dynamics throughout multicultural health organizations.
Culturally competent communication consists of the ability to
influence and customize communication in order to reduce ambiguity among the various components of the health system (Moore
and Thurston, 2007).

Attributes of Cultural Competence and Benefits to Health Teams

Most considerations of culturally competent communication rely on the individual health professional to develop cultural awareness and flexibility when interacting with a multicultural patient population (Pecukonis et al., 2008). The benefits of culturally competent communication are well documented, with findings reporting associations between good patient-health professional communication and heightened patient satisfaction, increased adherence to treatment recommendations, and improved patient health outcomes (Office of Minority Health, 2005). This research suggests that culturally competent messages in health promotion and delivery contribute to reducing ethnic and racial health disparities (see Smedley, Stith, and Nelson, 2003).

There is increased understanding, however, that competence is not just an attribute of health professional-patient encounters; it also involves groups and organizations. Health professionals communicate in culturally diverse teams as well as interact with people of different cultures across the units of an institution (Perloff et al., 2006). Consider a public health department's mobile medical unit that provides information and treatment to HIV/AIDs patients and those at high risk of getting the disease. The unit team consists of multiple health professionals—physicians, nurses, medical interpreters, and community health workers—as well as different ethnic and racial cultures. Team effectiveness depends on demonstrating principles of cultural communication competence in team interactions as well as when talking with a diverse patient population. Further, team members must display cultural competence when they communicate with the public health department's diverse employees in order to coordinate and implement the activities of the mobile medical unit.

At the **individual level**, culturally competent communication depends on the health professional's educational background, the quality of his/her messages, cultural understanding, and self-awareness of bias (Niemeier, Burnett, and Whitaker, 2003). Through behaviors such as displaying empathy, accepting differences, and conveying messages of trust and respect, health professionals can improve their relationships with patients and professional associates of different cultures. Competence at the **team level** is dependent on team members who show knowledge of different cultures and languages, display positive affective and behavioral skills, and manage cultural uncertainty and ambiguity (Matveev and Nelson, 2004). It is the discourse that incorporates personal diversity experience, awareness, and sensitivity into everyday team practice behaviors. To be most effective, teams' cultural communication competence requires support at the **organizational level** (Brach and Fraser, 2000). Examples of institutional initiatives instrumental to creating team environments of cultural competence include caregiver education and training, use of medical interpreters and community health workers, and policies that reflect communication patterns related to cultural differences. Table 6.5 provides sample lists of culturally competent communication characteristics for individuals, teams, and organizations.

Medical Interpreter-Team Communication

The heightened role of medical interpreters represents one visible organizational response designed to improve health team cultural communication competence. **Medical interpreters** are bilingual individuals whose clinical role is to facilitate communication between patients and health professionals (Dysart-Gale, 2005; 2007). This emerging occupation bridges cross-cultural gaps between patients and team members that are due to differences in language, worldviews about health and illness, etc.

In the context of health teams, the research literature has mainly explored the role of professional interpreters (in contrast to informal or untrained interpreters, such as relatives and friends) as they manage information exchange and relationship development between health professionals and patients. Patient-health professional encounters mediated by interpreters represent the intersection of different domains of expertise. Health professionals bring the clinical expertise while medical interpreters (who may be

Table 6.5   Sample Cultural Competence Characteristics by
Health Organization Levels

Individual	Team	Institution
• Recognizing potential differences between own culture's and other cultures' healthcare values, beliefs, and behaviors • Being aware of feelings of difference • Accepting that differences may exist between cultures' understandings of time and urgency • Valuing the salience of culture as a causal factor in health; the existence of varying perspectives about health/illness	• Acknowledging variety in the communication styles of team members from different cultures • Adapting communication behavior to resolve conflict • Feeling comfortable when interacting with others from different cultures • Understanding and clearly articulating team objectives, roles, and norms in a multicultural team • Showing patience and empathy in intercultural situations	• Creating environments of openness and esteem for diverse personnel and patients • Providing staff with access to a range of professional interpreters • Employing culturally diverse workers that ideally mirror its patient population • Supplying cultural competence education for all staff members • Offering services that meet the needs of diverse patient populations

*(Adapted from University of Michigan Health System Program for Multicultural
Health, n.d.; Matveev and Nelson, 2004; Management Sciences for Health, n.d.)*

novices in medical knowledge) provide the linguistic and cultural
proficiency necessary for quality healthcare encounters.

Conceptualizations of medical interpreter-health team communication have emphasized two very different perspectives (Hsieh,
2006a; 2006b). The traditional approach views interpreters as
conduits of information, neutral participants in the transmis-
sion of information between patients and health professionals.
Interpreters strive to achieve message reliability and accuracy

from a position subordinate to the health professional leading the clinical encounter. More recent understandings have recognized that interpreters actively influence patient-provider interactions to achieve particular goals (e.g., a greater understanding of the patient's culture) (Schapira et al., 2008). The interpreter is the most influential person in a bilingual clinical encounter because he/she is the only person who understands the two languages, filters information based on relevancy, and has the right to interrupt others.

The work of communication scholar Elaine Hsieh (2007; 2010) has been particularly influential to current understandings of the active role interpreters play in managing encounters between patients and members of the health team. This research emphasizes the complex repertoire of communication skills interpreters display as they attempt simultaneously to meet the relational needs of patients and health professionals within the clinical encounter. Hsieh argues that interpreters may function as co-diagnosticians with other team members, a role that attempts to balance the clinician's goal of diagnostic efficiency with the cultural needs of the patient. Table 6.6 identifies five co-diagnostic communication practices and example:

Interpreters are also important providers of emotional support to patients, a role that is especially critical in light of clinician time constraints and lack of cultural sensitivity. By spending time with patients and showing compassion and concern for their health, interpreters can develop positive relationships that lead to greater patient disclosure and a more complete picture of the patient's physical and emotional distress.

While interpreters and health team members work interdependently for the good of the patient, this collaboration is not without its tensions. Hsieh (2010) found that clinicians and interpreters have differing expectations regarding the role and authority of interpreters in clinician-patient interactions. For example, physicians who are used to controlling conversation may become defensive when interrupted by the interpreter or when their medical language is manipulated for cultural purposes (e.g., revising a sensitive topic so it is culturally appropriate). While some clinicians may view

Table 6.6 Medical Interpreters' Co-Diagnostic Behaviors

Communication Behavior	Description	Example
Assuming the provider's communicative goals	The interpreter autonomously determines whether information is complete and the health professional's objectives have been met.	Upon hearing incomplete information about diet from the patient, an interpreter asks follow-up questions without consulting the nutritionist.
Editorializing information for medical emphasis	The interpreter evaluates and prioritizes the speaker's message for medical relevancy.	After listening to a patient's concerns, the interpreter downplays personal information that he/she believes has little medical value to a nurse practitioner.
Initiating information-seeking behaviors	Unsolicited by the clinician, the interpreter directly seeks information from the patient in the presence of the clinician.	The interpreter questions a mother about her baby's sleeping habits in the presence of a lactation consultant who is coaching the mother about nursing.
Participating in diagnostic tasks	The interpreter contributes to the diagnosis by investigating information, examining the patient, and identifying illnesses.	Collaborating with a physician by researching a patient's medical history and providing this data for use in diagnosing the patient.
Volunteering medical information to the patients	In effort to conserve clinician time, the interpreter may give patients information independently of what they receive from clinicians.	Following a brief encounter with a social worker, the interpreter spends time with an elderly patient to describe options for nursing home care.

(Adapted from Hsieh, 2007)

Box 6.3   Ripped from the Headlines

Connecting Public Health Teams with Communities
Similar to the professional medical interpreters you read about in this chapter, community health workers (CHWs) bridge the cultural gaps between patients and health teams, most notably the teams working in public health. CHWs differ from the majority of health professionals in that they are typically volunteers who are indigenous residents of the populations they serve. Trusted and respected community members, CHWs communicate the needs of their communities to health teams as well as provide health promotion and disease prevention information to members of their communities. They are considered a positive force in reducing health disparities in medically underserved populations.

A *Milwaukee Journal Sentinel* story about Latina *promotoras*—community outreach workers—in West Allis, WI, depicts the important role CHWs play in spanning boundaries between public health teams and at-risk communities (Montaño, 2009). Like many other U.S. cities, West Allis has experienced a dramatic growth in its Latino population, many of whom are immigrants. Local and state public health departments had limited success serving immigrant families due to parents' limited English speaking skills, lack of insurance, and little, if any, familiarity with the healthcare system. Members of public health teams received cultural competence training and the health departments also provided interpretation services and document translation. Although these efforts helped, public health officials were concerned that immigrant families were still not accessing services or getting the care they needed.

Success depended on greater involvement from the Latino community. City health administrators approached

several Latina mothers to get involved in a health pro-
moter training program. The women went through an
intensive course covering health issues and the services
available to the Latino community. As promotoras, the
women partnered with public health teams to inform
community members of services, promote illness prevention, and discuss sensitive topics in comfortable, familiar
community group environments.

The promotoras' efforts have been instrumental in connecting members of the Latino community with public
health professionals and Spanish-speaking caregivers
as well as educating community members about how
the U.S. health system works. Furthermore, promotoras convey community member needs to public health
workers that might not be accessible through other channels (e.g., face-to-face visits between Latino patients and
public health team members). According to public health
officials, promotoras are "[a] bridge between the community and service providers. They are able to represent
the community's needs and communicate them to us"
(Montaño, 2009, para. 19).

interpreters as equal partners in care provision, difficulties emerge
when clinicians believe interpreters are overstepping their role
boundaries and/or violating norms of medical hierarchy (Hsieh,
2006b; 2010). Despite these challenges, it is apparent that medical
interpreters are of rising significance to teams as health organizations strive to meet the needs of increasingly diverse patient
populations.

Chapter Summary

This chapter began by considering the defining qualities of
teams and the importance of effectiveness in health organizations. Conflict and teamwork are opposing team communication

processes inherent in health teams that influence team dynamics and ultimately patient care. As health teams become increasingly diverse and serve greater numbers of patients from various cultural backgrounds, team members must demonstrate greater understanding of key cultural variables such as profession/specialization, gender, and race/ethnicity, as well as the influence of each on team dynamics. Developing team environments that display cultural communication competence and the successful integration of medical interpreters in teams are major steps toward meeting the diverse needs of health organizations and of populations they serve.

7

Health Organization Quality

The Institute of Medicine (IOM) issued two landmark reports, *To Err is Human: Building a Safer Health System* (2000) and *Crossing the Quality Chasm: A New Health System for the 21st Century* (2001), addressing quality-related issues in health organizations. The IOM (2001) concluded: "Quality problems are everywhere, affecting many patients. Between the health we have and the care we could have lies not just a gap, but a chasm" (p. 1). This body of documentation regarding unacceptably high and pervasive medical errors spurred health professionals, regulators, and payers into action. Since the IOM reports were published, significant improvements have been made in an attempt to achieve higher quality care in our nation's health system, yet achieving consistently good patient care system-wide remains a monumental challenge.

The IOM's findings also drew national attention to a growing body of research showing that the current state of organized health delivery poses risks with regard to the treatment of patients. This literature demonstrates several types of quality problems: 1) regional and organizational variation in health services; 2) fragmented, inconsistent care within and between institutions; 3) the failure of current practice to keep pace with advancements in scientific knowledge and technological innovation; 4) underuse of services by millions of Americans who need healthcare but cannot afford it; 5) overuse of services by millions of Americans who receive unnecessary care, increasing overall system costs and potentially endangering their health; and 6) lack of capacity to meet the needs of patients with chronic conditions (IOM, 2001; Agency for Healthcare Research and Quality [AHRQ], 2002).

Enhancing care quality begins by recognizing the current health-care system flaws and taking steps to redesign ineffective work practices and structures within and across health institutions. It is increasingly recognized that a key component of quality improvement lies in changing outdated and ineffectual communication processes at varying levels of health organization interactions (e.g., dyads, groups/teams) (IOM, 2003b). This chapter explores care quality in health organizations and the role of communication in quality improvement efforts. You will begin by learning about health organization quality from a systems perspective. Then, you'll review considerations of quality from the research literature by first understanding quality culture. The chapter concludes by exploring safety and patient-centeredness, two key areas in which communication figures prominently in quality scholarship.

A Systems Perspective on Quality

Quality in health organizations is often understood from the standpoint of the receiver or the user of a particular health product or service. Patients, health professionals, consumers, and others represent major groups who are concerned with health organization quality. Quality has mainly been defined as it pertains to **patient care**, referring to the degree to which health services increase the likelihood of positive health outcomes and are consistent with current professional knowledge (Lohr, 1990). It is care delivered over a lifetime that helps people stay healthy, recover from illness, live with chronic disease or disability, and cope with death and dying (AHRQ, 2008). Table 7.1 identifies features of quality patient care which commonly appear in the research literature.

Quality has also been considered from the vantage point of **quality of work life** by those employed by health organizations. Here, employees' overall satisfaction with their work experiences are explored by studying issues such as communication processes, working conditions, and organizational structures (e.g., reporting relationships, policies). This line of research concludes that improving quality of work life will ultimately enhance the overall

Table 7.1   Quality of Care Characteristics

Characteristic	Description
Safe	Avoiding errors and injuries to patients arising from the care intended to help them.
Effective	Delivering services based on scientific knowledge that prevents underuse and refrains from overuse.
Timely	Reducing wait times and sometimes harmful delays for receivers and providers of care.
Patient-centered	Delivering care in a respectful, responsive manner that takes into consideration patients' preferences, needs, and values; making sure patient values guide clinical decision-making.
Efficient	Avoiding waste (of, e.g., equipment, supplies, ideas, and effort).
Equitable	Providing care consistently, regardless of differences such as gender, ethnicity, geographic locations, and socioeconomic status.

(Adapted from IOM, 2001)

quality of care (Gershon et al., 2004). Work by Linda Aiken and colleagues exemplifies this line of research by investigating the effects of nurse quality of work life (e.g., staffing levels, patient acuity, salary, interactions with physicians and other health professionals) on patient care outcomes (see Aiken, et al., 2008; Rogers et al., 2004. Table 7.2 presents major communication themes that contribute to improved quality of work life.

Quality is a central goal of today's health system; to achieve quality requires successful interrelationships between system components (typically people). Systems concepts of goals and subsystems are particularly relevant in examining health organization quality. Quality is the fundamental **goal** of the health system. Goals typically involve **structural quality**—a health organization's capacity to provide quality care; **process quality**—the interactions between patients and health professionals as well as between health professionals in the delivery of health services; and **outcomes quality**—evidence about changes in patients' health status related to the provision of health services (IOM, 2001).

Quality depends on how well the **subsystems** work as distinct

Table 7.2   Quality of Work Life Communication Themes

Characteristic	Description
Participation in decision-making	Communication that invites and values input from others; opinions and ideas are used in decision-making.
Supportiveness	Discourse that reduces perceptions of uncertainty, that helps foster a sense of control over stressors, and that creates a climate of encouragement.
Empowerment	Interactions that encourage involvement and independence in ways that develop competence, ability, and personal authority.
Trust	Dialog that conveys a belief in the integrity, ability, or character of others.
Teamwork	Communication that solicits and maintains collaboration; team members cooperate to synchronize team activities and achieve team goals.
Respect	Talk that demonstrates an esteem for others' viewpoints and feelings and a willingness to understand and appreciate differences.

entities as well as how they function interdependently. For example, most patients receive care from health professionals working in small groups or units (e.g., an outpatient surgery center, a clinician's office, a radiology clinic). The quality of that care depends on the effectiveness with which each group of health professionals work together, over time, to do what's needed for the good of patient. Large, complex health organizations such as hospitals are made up of multiple interrelated subsystems that serve a shared population of patients/consumers. Quality will also be largely determined by how well the larger organization coordinates activities across subsystems to achieve desired outcomes.

Quality is a vital issue that affects how health organizations manage and deliver health services to patients and consumers as well as how they develop positive work environments for employees. As a research topic it has held the attention of health scholars and practitioners for decades, with health organization culture figuring prominently as a key contributor to quality. Next, you will explore this combined approach to quality and health organization culture.

Quality and Health Organization Culture

Studying quality and health organization culture gained popularity in the 1980s as researchers and health institution leaders searched for ways to improve quality of care for patients and consumers as well as enhance the quality of work life for health professionals. The publication of the IOM reports (2000; 2001) mentioned at the beginning of this chapter contributed to a renewed interest in quality culture, and particularly the communicative aspects of the organizational environment pertaining to patient safety. The quality culture literature in health contexts draws heavily on notions of organizational culture, which has a long history in organizational studies. To begin, let's briefly review some major organizational culture concepts before considering their application to health organization quality.

Organizational Culture Levels

Scholars tend to rely on traditional understandings of organizational culture as a starting point for studying quality culture in health organizations. A representative view is articulated by Helmreich and Merritt (2001), who define **organizational culture** as "the values, beliefs, assumptions, rituals, symbols, and behaviors that define a group, especially in relation to other groups or organizations" (p. 109). Organizational culture is shared across an organization and plays a central role in guiding the behaviors, sensemaking, and identity development of organizational members. People learn culture by observing others, participating in organizational life, and experiencing formal and informal socialization.

Organizational culture consists of three distinct, yet interrelated levels (Figure 7.1), an understanding largely influenced by the work of management scholar Edgar Schein (2004). He argues that an organization's underlying assumptions are embodied by its values, which, in turn, are reflected by its visible artifacts. Let's take a closer look at how the three levels interrelate to form organizational culture.

Artifacts—the visible and tangible representations of cultural

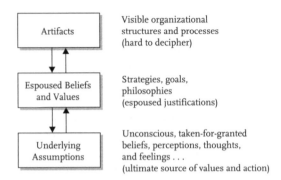

Figure 7.1   *Schein's Levels of Organizational Culture*
(Source: Schein, E. H. *Organizational culture and leadership*, 3rd ed. San Francisco: Jossey-Bass, 2004.)

values—form the outermost layer. Artifacts are the things people see, hear, and feel during their organizational experiences and what newcomers first notice. For instance, it is commonplace to see physicians wearing "whites" as they work in health organizations. Wearing white attire began because it symbolized values of quality, specifically cleanliness and sterility. While this symbolism is less relevant today, the tradition of wearing "whites" continues in medicine and it is now difficult to conceptualize the physician profession without thinking of white coats.

Values refer to the policies, goals, principles, and/or characteristics that are considered ideal, worthwhile, or desirable. While not explicitly stated or highly visible, values are often displayed in people's behaviors and influence their communication. To understand values, let's consider the organizational culture at a pain clinic that places a high value on collaboration among employees as well as between employees, patients, and their families. To achieve this, clinic leaders routinely solicit formal and informal feedback from employees on how to improve quality of care and quality of work life. Patients and their families are considered central figures in the healthcare team and they are actively involved in decisions about treatment. Patients also have a great deal of access to clinicians (e.g., face-to-face visits, email communication, telephone follow-up) which encourages patient input.

Assumptions form the core of culture, which in turn affects the values and artifacts of an organization. Assumptions are the taken for granted, deeply held ways in which people understand themselves, their relationships with others, and work. They provide a logic which guides organizational members' values, beliefs, and behaviors. For example, in a study of communication at a dialysis clinic, Ellingson (2003) observed that physicians were rarely challenged or questioned by lower-level employees, especially in front of patients. Physicians also were afforded more work space and access to technology than other clinicians despite a crowded clinic environment. Such behaviors reinforce values of status hierarchy which are based in part on long-held assumptions of medical expertise, professional power, and role authority.

Organizational Culture Contributions to Quality Performance

Organizational culture is a contributor to quality in terms of both quality of work life and quality of care (Gershon, et al., 2004). Two organizational culture approaches are present in the literature regarding health quality. The **prescriptive approach** reflects the business and management literatures, viewing quality culture as an attribute, something that an organization has along with other attributes such as structure, size, strategy, personnel, etc. This viewpoint considers how culture can be manipulated to satisfy organizational goals (usually those espoused by leaders). Culture change is seen as a having commercial or other technical ends that can involve altering values and artifacts. The **descriptive approach** has its roots in anthropology, understanding quality culture as something that an organization is. In this perspective, cultural values and assumptions are reproduced through the social interaction of members. Culture is unique and complex; not easily manipulated or changed nor transferred to other organizations (Scott-Findlay and Estabrooks, 2006).

The majority of quality culture studies in health organizations borrow ideas from both approaches rather than adhering to one set of theoretical principles. That is, researchers describe and assess quality culture by considering organizational artifacts, behaviors, and/or values as a means to identify their contributions to quality performance. Performance outcomes span a range of quality of care and quality of work life indicators (e.g., patient satisfaction, clinical results, employee retention and commitment). This line of scholarship emphasizes that managing culture is an essential lever or tool for health system quality improvement that begins with a thorough understanding of culture as a socially constructed phenomenon (Scott et al., 2003). Thus, measures taken to enhance quality culture often start with studying interactions occurring in health teams, between patients and health professionals, and among different organization units.

Communication norms, patterns, and processes are commonly examined as artifacts that represent deeply held values and assumptions that ultimately affect quality performance. In regards to quality of work life for members of health organizations, positive communication environments improve employee well-being, satisfaction, and morale and reduce burnout and turnover (Safran, Miller, and Beckman, 2006). The converse of this relationship appears to also be true. Separate culture studies conducted in physician group practices, nursing homes, and hospitals point to the negative effects of highly centralized, bureaucratic communication on teamwork, care coordination, and employee involvement (Scott-Cawiezell et al., 2005; Vina et al., 2009).

There is also increasing evidence that communicative aspects of organizational culture are related to quality of care issues. For example, clinical settings with a stronger group culture orientation—characterized by high collegiality, information sharing, cohesiveness, and trust—are generally associated with enhanced patient care outcomes and clinical decision-making (Meterko, Mohr, and Young, 2004). In contrast, dysfunctional hierarchical cultures—characterized by rigid leadership, top-down communication, and dominance by those in authority positions—contribute to poor quality care (Helmreich and Merritt, 2001).

To summarize, organizational culture has contributed a great deal to understanding and managing quality in health organizations. Health organization research tends to bridge prescriptive

Box 7.1   Communication in Practice

Developing Culture to Optimize Quality
Recent interest in the culture of healthcare organizations has started to address the importance of culture in quality improvement efforts. Researchers argue that culture drives both the quality of work life and the quality of care in health organizations. By describing, evaluating, and managing cultural elements, health organizations can enhance quality performance.

A study conducted by Scott-Cawiezell et al. (2005) of 32 nursing homes explores organizational values that optimize quality performance. These authors assess nursing staff and leaders on the following value categories:

- **Group**: dominance in this area shows shared values and goals, cohesion, participation, and inclusive identity. Teamwork and employee development guide patient care.
- **Developmental**: organizations that rate highly in this value are flexible; able to adapt quickly to change.
- **Hierarchy**: working conditions reflect a high priority on formalization and structure. Activities driven by rules, defined roles, and centralized decisions.
- **Market**: A results-focused environment in which profitability, competitiveness, and productivity supersede the needs and preferences of employees and patients.

Group culture was the most frequently reported cultural value (84% of the nursing homes studied), a result that indicates the presence of an optimal context for working conditions supporting quality improvement. Nursing homes in which hierarchy was a frequently reported value were found to have problems with staff morale, teamwork, and quality improvement implementation. Developmental organizations were identified as settings in which quality improvement thrives.

The authors encourage health organizations to promote group and developmental cultures through the following communication strategies:

To Promote Group Culture:
1. Increase involvement by seeking input of staff when making clinical changes.
2. Send messages of inclusion to all levels of staff; let employees know their feedback is welcome and valued.
3. Encourage problem-solving at the local level (e.g., health teams) rather than centralized decision-making by institutional managers.

To Promote Developmental Culture:
1. Create work environments that celebrate risk-taking to solve problems.
2. Promote and reward creative problem-solving.
3. Stress flexibility and the ability to change.
4. Support new ideas through implementation and encourage staff to go beyond crisis management mode to executing changes to achieve an organization vision.

and descriptive approaches to culture by describing and evaluating key communication processes, patterns, and behaviors in order to bring about and manage quality improvement. It can be concluded from this literature that improving communication is an important factor in enhancing quality in health organizations. In the next section, you will take a closer look at the relationship between communication and two key areas of quality.

Communication and Quality

Quality in health organizations largely depends on what happens to patients as they experience various health delivery subsystems (family practitioner, emergency department, intensive care unit, home-based care, etc.) that comprise their care over time. Communication constitutes these experiences, consisting of patient-health professional interactions as well as interactions occurring between the members of health institutions who are involved in many aspects related to care provision. A rich body of research has specifically explored two major health organization quality indicators—safety and patient-centeredness—from a communication perspective. This literature shows that achieving quality in safety and patient-centered care requires continuous efforts to improve health organizations' communication.

Safety

Safety refers to freedom from accidental injury; establishing an operational system of processes that minimize the likelihood of error and maximize the likelihood of intercepting errors when they occur (IOM, 2000). Despite the best efforts of health professionals and their institutional employers, healthcare delivery poses significant patient safety risks, ranging from medication errors to surgical mistakes and from missed diagnoses to treatment delays. Communication is at the heart of the problem. According to the Joint Commission on Accreditation of Healthcare Organizations (2005), poor communication is the root cause of most sentinel events, medical mistakes, and "near misses" (unplanned events that did not result in injury or illness but had the potential to do so). It is not all that surprising, then, that improving communication is an often-reported strategy to improve patient safety in health organizations.

Healthcare professionals spend their days in settings where they must respond to constantly changing conditions, time pressures, and uncertainties. While they strive to avoid errors and achieve desirable patient outcomes, numerous sets of communication obstacles exist in health organizations (Table 7.3). **Clinical environment obstacles** refer to aspects of the physical environment that can impede communication in ways that exacerbate patient safety risks. **Professional obstacles** consist of relational barriers between health professionals, due to factors such as specialization, status hierarchy, and power differences that contribute to dysfunctional communication patterns and behaviors. **Information obstacles** are barriers in poor communication content and delivery typically as displayed in interpersonal interactions among health professionals.

Hospital emergency departments (EDs) provide a visible example of how such communication challenges can contribute to patient safety threats. According to Eisenberg et al. (2005), emergency medicine is "largely a communicative activity and medical mishaps that occur in this context are too often the result of vulnerable communication processes" (p. 390). Over-crowded conditions contribute to work overload, time pressures to speeding up work activities, and subsequent clinical multi-tasking. The shift-based nature of the work means that care is handed off between multiple clinicians during a patient's length of stay. Such an environment is conducive to disruptions, hurried and/or fragmented conversations, and multiple opportunities for information to get dropped along the chain of communication. Information barriers further create problems for ED communication and resulting patient safety. Apker, Mallak, and Gibson (2007) found that information exchange in the ED often consists of incomplete, omitted, and delayed data. Clinicians must work with a high level of ambiguity, lacking background information about patients (patients present with little or no medical history, test results may not arrive in time for medical decisions, etc.), while caring for multiple patients simultaneously. Time pressures may encourage clinicians to rely on one-way information dissemination rather than dialog with peers that could clarify areas of uncertainty.

Professional communication barriers can compound environmental and information problems. ED settings bring multiple professions and specializations together as the variety of patients' care needs requires external consultations (e.g., surgeons,

Table 7.3 Communication Obstacles Contributing to Patient Safety Risks

Clinical Environment	Professional	Information
• Constant interruptions disrupt flow of communication; heightens dropped communication exchanges. • Time pressures and work overload foster multi-tasking; creating distractions that can impede communication. • Ambiguity about patient condition (e.g., patient presents with little or no medical history on record; patient health status changes abruptly; uncertain diagnoses). • Shift-based nature of caregiving requires multiple handoffs among health professionals; increases potential for data to "fall through the cracks."	• Conflicting information expectations due in part to contrasting professional approaches to care orientation/ specialization. • Power and status differences may prevent those in subordinate roles from asking questions and/ or challenging faulty assumptions. • Desire to show professional competence and gain approval of others may pressure clinicians into displaying certainty and confidence even when they are unsure of decisions. • Dysfunctional bureaucracies characterized by isolated silos of professional specialization; authority by position rather than expertise; fixed rules and decision-making designed to preserve the status quo.	• Insufficient, incomplete, and/or omitted information. • Poor communication flow among clinicians; delayed information, mistimed data exchange. • Inaccuracies and information overload. • Failure to allocate sufficient time to communicate data. • Clinicians rely on "one-way" communication in which information-giving dominates in order to expedite interactions; reduces give-and-take that can clarify areas of uncertainty.

(Adapted from Morath and Turnbull, 2005; Agency for Healthcare Research and Quality, 2008)

cardiologists) and may involve long-term hospital stays involving inpatient physicians and nurses. Expectations for the content and delivery of communication vary across professions and specializations and, when expectations are not met, conflict can result that ultimately impacts on care quality (Eisenberg et al., 2005). EDs also exemplify a traditional medical hierarchy in which those in positions of authority typically have the most power. Status differences may prevent people in subordinate roles from asking questions and challenging faulty decisions. Further, concerns about positive face—the desire to be publicly approved of others—may pressure those in low-status positions from sharing their uncertainty about decisions and/or admitting mistakes. Such a professional atmosphere exacerbates conditions that place patients at risk of medical errors (Murphy et al., 2008).

Creating safe health institutions involves developing discursive processes and tools which reduce faulty and inadequate communication and corresponding safety threats. Research findings suggest that qualities of trust, openness, respect, and appreciation foster teamwork that facilitates patient safety. For instance, Safran, Miller, and Beckman (2006) found that heightened collaboration is associated with reduced hospital patient mortality, shorter length of stay in inpatient care settings, and lower wait times in the emergency department. In the United States Veterans Administration Hospital System, an organization recognized for innovations in safety research, Hartmann et al. (2009) found that certain organizational attributes promote patient safety more than others. For example, they found that social support, innovation, and adaptability are significantly and positively associated with safety climate. Similarly, Odwazny et al. (2005) argue that health organizations which promote continuous learning, mistake-prevention efforts, and teamwork provide safer and higher quality patient care. Box 7.2 provides an illustrative example of such communication characteristics in action.

Growing numbers of scholars and practitioners have called for changes in health organization culture, advocating that institutions develop "blame-free" or "blameless" cultures. Such environments encourage health professionals to report errors and near misses

Box 7.2   Ripped from the Headlines

Enhancing Patient Safety Through Teamwork
More than a decade ago, the Institute of Medicine reported that as many as 98,000 deaths occur in United States each year due to medical errors (IOM, 2000). Many errors are linked to communication failures and most are shown to be preventable (Joint Commission, 2005; Eisenberg et al., 2005). While significant measures have been taken nationwide to improve patient safety, miscommunication continues to result in medical tragedies such as the following:

- A 17-year-old girl died at Duke University Medical Center after receiving donated organs of a wrong blood type. Follow-up investigations revealed that a lack of verification by surgeon, hospital, and the organ donor system regarding donor-matching criteria was a major factor in her death (Comarow, 2003).
- Rhode Island Hospital surgeons operated on the wrong side or place of patients' heads on three separate occasions in less than a year. Hospital precautions were thwarted by "ego and overconfidence on the part of surgeons, and timidity on the part of nurses too afraid to speak up when they see something about to go wrong" (Smith, 2007, p. A4).
- At Johns Hopkins Children's Center, a young toddler suffering from extreme dehydration died after receiving an injection of a narcotic, despite orders that she receive no further medication (Rein, 2009).

In the search for ways to improve communication and patient safety, scholars and practitioners are recognizing the importance of organizational culture. According to the Joint Commission, a leading U.S. government health agency, health organizations must develop a culture of safety consisting of teamwork, communication, and collaboration.

In a 2008 article, "Behaviors that Undermine a Culture of Safety," the Joint Commission argues that intimidating and disruptive behaviors displayed by health professionals, regardless of gender and/or specialization, impair team functioning in ways that create patient safety risks. Such behaviors include:

- Overt actions such as verbal outbursts and physical threats, condescending language or voice intonation; and impatience with questions.
- Passive activities such as refusing to perform assigned tasks or quietly exhibiting uncooperative attitudes during routine activities; reluctance or refusal to answer questions, return phone calls or pages.

The Joint Commission further argues that cultural factors such as authority, autonomy, empowerment, and the roles or values of professionals on the healthcare team contribute to unprofessional behaviors. Raising awareness and educating team members about such communication problems, reinforced by organization interventions, zero-tolerance policies and disciplinary actions, can go a long way toward reducing practices of intimidation and disruption and creating workplaces favorable to patient safety. Furthermore, health organizations must foster cultures that value team trust and respect.

Discussion Questions

1. Think about your own organizational experiences where you have observed disruptive and/or intimidating behaviors. What did the person(s) say and/ or do? How did those behaviors affect others? Think about outcomes such as effects on performance, quality, etc.

2. How did the culture of the organization contribute to the intimidation/disruption you witnessed? What was the role of artifacts, values, and assumptions?

3. What do you think of the Joint Commission's general suggestions to reduce unprofessional behavior? What other strategies could team members and health organizations use to combat the problem of disruption and intimidation?

rather than "blame, shame, and punish" those at fault (Morath and Turnbull, 2005, p. 84). The following qualities are associated with blame-free culture (Roberts and Perryman, 2007):

- **Mindful interactions**: talk that encourages alertness and vigilance; people notice and if necessary stop unexpected events from occurring.
- **Collaborative sensemaking**: communicating about circumstances and one's own perceptions with others as a way to make sense of events and the environment; considering alternatives and weighing the pros/cons of different courses of action.
- **Cultivating communication values**: appreciating and displaying behaviors such as information sharing, joint decision-making, responsiveness, respect, and listening.

What communication mediums best convey the messages of a blame-free culture? The research in this area recommends using a variety of channels and employing techniques accepted in local contexts. For example, a study by Parker et al. (2009) of frontline caregivers found that staff desired face-to-face, group discussions with supervisors and patient safety experts. These meetings are most effective when they are held frequently and followed up by group interactions with peers. Communication technology also supports patient safety initiatives. Using email alerts and electronic health records has been found to promote information sharing and care coordination as well as to encourage the dissemination of patient safety guidelines organization-wide (Odwazny et al., 2005).

Patient-Centered Care

Patient-centered care evolved from the biopsychosocial approach (Chapter 1), due in part to growing recognition that improvements in quality will flow from organizing health delivery around patients rather than medical institutions (IOM, 2001). According to the Agency for Healthcare Research and Quality (AHRQ 2008), patient-centered care is "health care that establishes a partnership among practitioners, patients, and their families (when appropriate) to ensure that decisions respect patients' wants, needs, and preferences and that patients have the education and support they need to make decisions and participate in their own care" (p. 127).

Six core communication functions form the foundation of patient-centered care (Table 7.4). These overlapping functions have implications for patient quality of care and health professional quality of work life (Epstein and Street, 2007). Advocates argue that health organizations using a patient-centered approach are more likely to achieve improved care outcomes and patient adherence to treatment (IOM, 2001). Patient-centeredness also enhances working conditions to bolster employee satisfaction, retention, and performance, factors that contribute to quality care (Aita et al., 2005).

It is increasingly understood that successful patient-centered care extends beyond medical encounters between physicians and patients to involve the greater organizational context of healthcare

Table 7.4 Communication Functions of Patient-Centered Care

Function	Description	Sample Behaviors
Fostering healing relationships	Communicating to convey trust, respect, and mutual understanding about roles and responsibilities. Interactions reflect clinician self-awareness and well-being.	• Share agenda-setting • Active listening • Convey empathy and warmth
Exchanging information	Discovering the patient's information needs; understanding what the patient knows; sharing clinical evidence and interpretations so patients can make sense of their health status.	• Use everyday language • Allow adequate time for discussion • Ask patients to paraphrase information to ensure understanding
Responding to emotions	Recognizing and reacting to the emotions (e.g., fear, anger, sadness) displayed by patients and their families; addressing emotional distress with compassion.	• Legitimize feelings as natural • Validate emotions as justifiable responses • Show empathy by voicing emotions
Managing uncertainty	Dealing with the complex, inconsistent, and unpredictable aspects of illness; acknowledging ambiguity.	• Engage patients in vigilant self-monitoring • Allow space for hope • Help patients manage uncertainty (e.g., patient education)
Making decisions	Articulating and taking into account the patient's needs, values, and preferences; involving the patient in decision-making as they desire.	• Check understanding • Offer involvement opportunities • Support patient participation
Enabling patient self-management	Helping patients solve health-related problems and improve their health; removing barriers so patients can care for themselves.	• Advocate for patients • Help patients navigate the healthcare system (e.g., referrals)

(Adapted from Epstein and Street, 2007)

delivery. Patient-centered care encompasses the multiple interactions patients have with members of health organizations (e.g., direct caregivers, administrative personnel, support staff) as well as the communication occurring across a broad spectrum of health worker interactions. Thus, the health organization itself is responsible for carrying out patient-centered communication, and health professionals working individually and in teams contribute to an institution's patient-centeredness.

Coordination (also known as clinical integration) is a hallmark of the patient-centered health organization. Coordination refers to "the extent to which patient care services are coordinated across people, functions, activities, and sites over time so as to maximize the value of services delivered to patients" (Shortell et al., 2000, p. 129). Rather than approaching care as a series of separate events occurring over disparate locations and clinical environments, coordination emphasizes combining individual health service components and wrapping care around patients to form seamless care provision. Coordination enables continuous healing relationships between patients and caregivers and promotes care designed around patients' needs and preferences. It has been found to increase clinical efficiency and optimize patient outcomes as well as facilitate positive work environments for health professionals (Epstein and Street, 2007; McCauley and Irwin, 2006).

Let's consider the example of Emily, an oncology nurse navigator, to illustrate care coordination in action. Due in large part to medical advancements in treatment and knowledge, cancer no longer is an immediate terminal illness. Rather, cancer is a chronic illness which patients can live with for years or even decades and often involves myriad health professionals. The employment of oncology nurse navigators such as Emily became popular following the recognition that cancer patients needed assistance finding their way through the healthcare system as they experienced initial diagnosis, treatment, and survivorship. Emily's role is multifaceted; she provides not only clinical expertise (answering patients' questions, helping them prepare for chemotherapy) but also relational support (showing compassion and nurturing during the highs and lows of the disease). Further, Emily functions as the hub of the patient care team, linking clinicians together so they are constantly informed and updated on a patient's health status and treatment. Emily's job doesn't end with the conclusion of treatment. She follows patients into survivorship, supporting their efforts to self-manage their care and providing a consistent point of contact between survivors and clinicians.

Communication is at the heart of coordination. Health professionals must know how and when to communicate with each other and with their patients to deliver quality patient care. This characteristic is perhaps most apparent when examining the role of care coordinators such as Emily. In their case study of quality improvements in the U.S. Veteran's Administration Health System, Harris, Dresser, and Kreps (2004) identify feedback as central to coordinated care. They list three defining communication activities of care coordination:

1. **Assessment**: care coordinator and patient discuss the patient's clinical needs, functional status, and the social and environmental context in which care occurs.
2. **Matching**: the care coordinator communicates with various clinicians involved in a patient's care, matching health services to the needs of the patient.
3. **Monitoring**: an ongoing feedback loop, such as in-home monitoring equipment, assesses a patient's health status, quality of life, satisfaction, and needs. Working with other clinical team members, the care coordinator may deploy various information and communication technologies, depending upon the patient's needs and preferences.

Coordination fits well with the team-based structures present in modern health organizations. Recall the importance of synergistic team communication to successful healthcare delivery (Chapter 6). Team synergy depends on coordinated activities in which the team's collective effort is greater than the sum of team members' individual activities. Patients depend on the members of the healthcare team to coordinate services—tests, consultations, or procedures—to make sure that information is communicated accurately, appropriately, and in a timely manner. Further, effective coordination often requires smooth interorganizational transitions as patients move along the care continuum to receive care at different locations, institutions, and caregivers (McCauley and Irwin, 2006). Positive interpersonal skills, as detailed in previous chapters (e.g. active listening, empathy, respect), and collaboration are vital to the success of a team's coordination efforts.

Patient-centered team coordination highlights the importance of including patients and their families as key members of the healthcare team (Epstein and Street, 2007). The patient-centered approach recognizes that patients bring a certain expertise derived from their own health and illness experiences and, along with their families, have important knowledge that no one else on the team has (e.g., how a person reacts to medications, the severity of symptoms). Team coordination, then, involves looking for opportunities to involve patients and their families in decision-making by offering choices where all parties can find common ground (Michie, Miles, and Wienman, 2003). Since patients are often the main link in their care continuum, team coordination also means keeping patients and their families updated on health status, treatment, etc., and ensuring that this information is understood so it can be communicated appropriately in patient encounters with different caregivers (IOM, 2001).

McCauley and Irwin (2006) argue that the degree to which a health organization is patient-centered influences the success of team coordination. Their study of an intensive care unit shows the importance of institutional and unit communication to promoting patient-centered team coordination between health professionals, patients, and their families. Table 7.5 lists these discursive work environment qualities.

Communicating in ways that improve health literacy is increasingly recognized as a key component of patient-centeredness and quality in health organizations. **Health literacy** refers to the degree to which individuals have the capacity to obtain, process, and understand basic health information and the services needed to make appropriate health decisions (Parker, Ratzan, and Lurie, 2003). Health literacy includes but is not limited to reading ability

Table 7.5   Work Environment Qualities that Promote
Patient-Centered Team Coordination

Institutional Qualities	Unit Qualities
• Multi-disciplinary patient care rounds are accepted practice and decisions are made with each profession making a contribution. • Patients and their families, when able, are included in decision-making; patient desires and values figure prominently in planning processes. • Team members are encouraged and supported in challenging care practices perceived to be inconsistent and/or inaccurate with patient-centered care. • Team members seek out educational opportunities to improve their teamwork communication skills; professional associates role model positive team behaviors and hold each other accountable when poor communication occurs. • Problems in team collaboration are dealt with directly and respectfully; teams provide support to members who need to improve their teamwork skills.	• Create task forces consisting of health professionals from multiple disciplines to develop processes and guidelines for collaborative multi-disciplinary patient-care rounds. • Implement education programs at the unit level in which representatives from different health professions teach others about new and interesting patient-centered care strategies. Participants in such programs should involve all professions with patient contact, not just physicians and nurses. • Invite team members from all health professions to attend and contribute to unit social events. Establishing rapport promotes getting input from all levels of unit staff and sets a positive tone for collaboration. • Develop a unit orientation program for all new caregivers so they can learn how to contribute to patient-centered care within health care teams.

(Adapted from McCauley and Irwin, 2006)

and comprehension, oral communication, word recognition, and numeracy (e.g., interpreting graphs and tables, understanding risk) (Schapira et al., 2008). Regarding communication, consider the following skills needed for health literacy (IOM, 2004b):

- Asking questions and requesting clarification
- Participating in encounters with caregivers about treatment
- Discussing medical decisions based on information received
- Advocating for safety, patient rights, and/or needed care and services

Health literacy affects patient outcomes, health costs, and working conditions. For example, patients with low literacy have less knowledge about their health and treatment and decreased ability to participate in medical decision-making (IOM, 2003b). Consequently, they may be less involved in self-management of their own health and illness, increasing their reliance on the health system and heightening healthcare costs. When low literacy patients seek out health services they are less likely to adhere to treatment recommendations. Health worker safety is also affected by health literacy; workers who cannot understand safeguards (e.g., processing hazardous materials, following procedures for safely dealing with patients) may be at risk for job-related injuries and accidents. In addition, they may not be able to understand and/or fully engage in safety education.

Health organizations contribute to health literacy by functioning as major sources of health information. Due in part to advancements in health communication technologies and changing expectations about self-management, people are taking more active roles in their health and illness. They tend to seek information from health organizations, particularly when interacting with individual caregivers, regarding their current health status, prognosis (what will happen in the future), and treatment plan. However, problems may arise when patients cannot adequately participate in those interactions because low health literacy prevents them from understanding the nature of their illness, the risks and benefits of treatment, and the implications of health behaviors (Parker and Gazmararian, 2003). Further, health institutions frequently provide patients and consumers with written materials, yet those efforts may fail if messages do not take into consideration users' literacy abilities. Even skilled individuals may encounter confusion and frustration due in part to the growing complexity of modern healthcare delivery and financing and they turn to health organizations for help.

Health organizations also play a role in health literacy because they are the primary contexts in which patients and consumers communicate about health and illness; yet multiple literacy barriers exist (Mayer and Villaire, 2007). Signage is difficult to understand and consists of jargon unfamiliar to those who lack formal health training or experience. Finding one's way around can be a challenge when an organization doesn't provide adequate directions and relies on medical terms (rather than plain language, universal symbols, or caregiver names) to identify clinical units and offices. Office staff, the first line of contact with patients and consumers, may fail to recognize or ignore low health literacy and not offer assistance in reading or filling out printed materials. Caregivers rely on medical jargon, don't adapt instructions and explanations to facilitate understanding, and can shut down opportunities for patient participation.

What can health workers and their organizational employers do to combat the problem of low health literacy? The research literature identifies many promising responses that can make health settings more favorable to patients and consumers (Rudd, Comings, and Hyde, 2003; Rudd et al., 2004). Literacy efforts begin by recognizing that all members of health organizations— from bedside caregivers to people working behind the scenes in technical roles and administrative positions—are responsible for making health environments user friendly. Those with direct patient contact can participate in training to detect the signs of low health literacy and hold discussions about what is essential information to communicate to patients and their families so medical encounters avoid information overload. Forms, instructions, and other written materials can be revised to meet low rates of reading ability and comprehension. These forms of print communication can be further enhanced by audiovisual aids, cartoons, and pictures. Verbal communication must use plain language, allow opportunities for give-and-take, and include efforts to confirm patient understanding (Mayer and Villaire, 2007). Such initiatives enable health organizations to make a positive difference in improving health literacy among patients and consumers.

Box 7.3   Communication in Practice

Speaking in Plain Language
Low health literacy is a significant problem that has far-reaching effects. Approximately 90 million adults may lack the necessary literacy skills to successfully use the U.S. health system (IOM, 2004b) and nearly 9 out of 10 adults lack the proficiencies needed to manage their health and disease (Office of Disease Prevention and Promotion, n.d.). Low health literacy has been linked to poor health outcomes and rising health costs and it tends to affect those already most at risk of health disparities (e.g., the poor, the elderly, racial/ethnic groups, individuals with limited English proficiency).

Solving the health literacy problem requires improvements in how health messages are communicated to patients and consumers so that health information and services are used and understood by all. Communicating in plain language plays a prominent role in reaching and involving adults with limited literacy skills in their personal well-being. Rudd et al. (2004) offer these suggestions:

- Replace multi-syllabic terms and jargon with commonly used words
- Revise complex sentences and, if needed, restate using two or three sentences to convey the same idea
- Use "we" and "our" to convey collaboration and personal rapport
- Make complex charts, tables, and graphs simpler (e.g., separate ideas into different visuals, use color coding; provide users with a glossary of terms)

Chapter Summary

Chapter 7 examined the importance of quality in health organizations. Quality is a complex, multifaceted issue that has been commonly associated with health organization culture in the research literature. Scholars and practitioners describe and assess indicators of institutional culture as a means to improve organizational performance in patient care quality and quality of work life for employees. Communication is a process central to quality improvement, figuring prominently in patient safety and patient-centered care. While discursive obstacles present significant safety threats, communication plays a key role in facilitating safety efforts throughout health organizations. Patient-centered care depends on coordinated communication as patients experience multiple caregivers, locations, and organizations in their care continuum. Patient-centered organizations promote health literacy by using a repertoire of communication techniques to educate and involve patients and consumers in their personal well-being.

8

Health Communication Technologies

What kinds of technologies do you use to access health information and communicate with others about your health? If you are like growing numbers of patients and health consumers, you probably turn to health technologies. For example, you may go to internet websites to gather facts about particular health conditions, access expert medical opinions, and develop relationships with others who share similar health interests and/or concerns. Further, you may use email to communicate with your physician or access your health insurance online to check coverage, deductibles, and copayments. You may have also observed health professionals access and add to your personal health records via a laptop computer.

If you work in a health organization, health communication technologies (HCTs) are a pervasive part of your organizational life, allowing you to access health information quickly and conveniently to inform your interactions with patients, consumers, and professional associates. You probably use databases such as Medline for research and you may communicate via wireless communication devices to consult with peers, talk to team members, and improve your work efficiency and effectiveness. Perhaps you participate in online forums or discussion groups to discuss health issues of interest. You may have even used telemedicine technologies that allow clinicians and other health professionals to bridge time and geographic location constraints to exchange patient information and provide health services to underserved patients.

HCTs function prominently in the lives of users—patients, consumers, healthcare professionals, and others—to provide them with continuous, interconnected, and convergent communication (Rice, 2001). HCTs offer users **continuous access** to and availability of health information. Users can retrieve timely information when and where they need it, as well as input, convert, and store information to share. HCTs provide nearly **limitless interconnectivity** within health organizations and between health institutions and other entities (e.g., individual patients/consumers, other organizations). Such connections link fragmented components of the health system and offer the potential for seamless information integration. Finally, HCTs provide spaces for **convergence**. Individuals, groups, and organizations can turn to a single repository on a single storage media to gain data from text, images, audio, and video sources.

This chapter explores the significant, encompassing, and ever changing role that HCTs play in health organizations. You will begin by understanding HCTs from a systems perspective before learning more about e-health, a broad spectrum of digital database-based HCTs that has transformed communication processes in health organizations. The influence of HCT applications extends worldwide, contributing to new ways of communicating about health on a global scale. Thus, the chapter concludes by investigating how HCTs intersect with health globalization.

A Systems Perspective on Health Communication Technologies

Health communication technologies refer to tools and processes that store, influence, and communicate health information both at the local organization level and at a distance (Pluyter-Wenting, 2002). HCTs represent a range of complexity, ranging from simple telephone and email exchanges between patients and clinicians to sophisticated electronic health records that integrate comprehensive clinical data throughout a patient's lifespan (Wechsler, 2008). Openness and input-throughput-output concepts usefully apply to HCTs in health organizations.

Openness describes system permeability that allows messages and other sources of information to flow within organizations and between organizations in the greater, embedded environment. For example, HCTs have dramatically improved access to health data once reserved primarily for certain health professionals such as physicians. Patients and consumers easily and conveniently search online for information about health conditions, treatments, and prevention efforts which promotes open dialogue and more detailed conversations during patient-caregiver interactions. Members of health teams separated by time and space are better able to collaborate because computerized information systems provide access to integrated patient data which can be shared internally and externally such as in consultations with other clinical experts.

The openness created by HCTs has also heightened transparency and accountability in health organizations (Landry, Mahesh, and Hartman, 2004). Consider electronic health records (EHRs) which display clinical actions and interpretations. The presentation of this information shows lines of clinical responsibility through which health team members are clearly accountable for patient care decisions. Further, the visible presentation of this data may encourage questions and other forms of information-seeking less likely to occur with the use of paper files.

Input-throughput-output is a process by which messages and other data come into the system from the embedded environment, are altered by components for system use, and leave the system as an end product. HCTs increase the ability of health organizations to put information and communication in the hands of employees, patients, and others whenever and wherever needed (input). Technologies help individuals and groups within and across organizational units to understand and take action on data received (throughput). In addition, HCTs provide a mechanism to facilitate organizational outcomes (outputs) such as decisions, policies, and improved health services and products. In short, health technologies provide the connectivity that allows input-throughput-output to occur between often-fragmented health system links.

A telemedicine videoconference provides an illustrative example of the input-throughput-output capabilities of HCTs. Hector is a 35-year-old father of three children who suffers from chronic back pain that severely limits his quality of life. He lives in a rural area that lacks many medical specialties, such as the neurological services necessary to treat his herniated disk problem. Hector's primary caregiver, a nurse practitioner (NP), sets up videoconference consultation with a neurologist who works in a major university hospital 200 miles away. The NP faxes Hector's medical records for the specialist to examine in advance of the meeting. During the videoconference, the neurologist examines Hector's back in real time with the help of the NP. The medical records and real-time examination function as inputs. The neurologist uses her university's medical databases and decision-making support tools to form an opinion about treatment options. She calls the NP to discuss Hector's case. The independent research and peer conversation represent throughput. The two clinicians form a consensus that Hector needs physical therapy rather than a surgical intervention (output).

Communication technologies heighten openness and input-throughput-output processes in ways that improve health system integration, data convergence, and information access. Never before have there been so many ways in which health professionals, patients, consumers, and health organizations can communicate. Next, you will learn about e-health, the HCT that has perhaps most profoundly transformed communication in health organizations.

E-health Communication

E-health refers to "the use of emerging information and communication technology, especially the Internet, to improve or enable health and healthcare" (Eng, 2001, p. 1). This term encompasses a range of related disciplines that pertain to the application of information and communication technology such as health communication, telemedicine, and health informatics. It also spans a broad spectrum of health communication strategies and applications which are in a constant state of evolution. Table 8.1 presents a list of sample e-health technologies. While this list is categorized by patient-centeredness and health professional-centeredness to facilitate ease of understanding, overlaps exist in terms of who uses particular e-health technologies. For example, a health organization may make electronic health records (EHRs), which are primarily used by its workers, available to patients for review and commentary. Or a public health outreach worker may research websites

Table 8.1   List of E-health Technologies

Patient/Consumer Centered	Health Professional Centered

• Health-related websites
  o Managed care websites
  o For-profit organization websites devoted to health products and/or services
  o Non-profit websites addressing specific diseases
  o Blogs
• Online support groups/ forums
• Web-based call centers
• Social networking groups
• Distribution lists and email
• Computer tailoring
	• Continuing health education
	• Web databases/portals
	• Electronic health records
	• Online collaborative communities
	• Telemedicine
	  o Teleradiology/telecounseling
	  o Video conferencing
	  o Store-and-forward technology (e.g., still images/video clips of patient visit)
	• Satellite technology
	• Web clearinghouses
	• Email

(Adapted from the following sources: Neuhauser and Kreps, 2003; Wright, Sparks, and O'Hair, 2008; Maheu, Whitten, and Allen, 2001; Rice, 2001)

mainly designed for patients/consumers to learn more about public needs, expectations, and perceptions about a health issue or disease.

E-health provides healthcare professionals, patients, and consumers with almost limitless opportunities to collect, manage, and share health information. Below, you will consider major forms of e-health technologies that have figured prominently in the research literature and learn about the benefits and drawbacks of each for communication in health organizations.

Telemedicine

Telemedicine is "the provision of healthcare services, clinical information, and education over a distance using telecommunication technology" (Maheu, Whitten, and Allen, 2001, p. 2). Health organizations have used telemedicine for decades (see Turner, 2003, for a review) most visibly since the 1990s when advancements in telemedicine technology and rising interests in health cost containment drove its use among health providers. Popular technologies include the following:

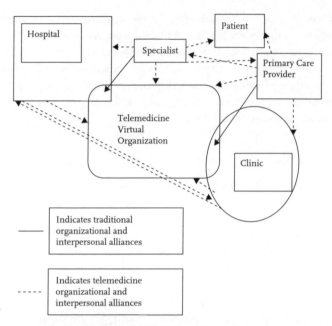

Figure 8.1   *Model of Telemedicine Relationships*
(Source: Turner, J. W. Telemedicine: Expanding health care into virtual
environments. In T. L. Thompson, A. Dorsey, K. I. Miller, and R. Parrott
(eds), *Handbook of health communication*. Mahwah, NJ: Lawrence Erlbaum
Associates, pp. 515–36, 2003.)

- **Teleradiology and telepathology**: the electronic transfer of
  diagnostic and other clinical data from an area of low specialization to a center with clinical specialists.
- **Telecounseling**: the use of conferencing equipment such
  as videoconferencing enable real-time interactions among
  clinicians and between clinicians and patients.

For communication scholars, telemedicine is not simply about
technological applications such as those identified above, but
rather how discourse using these technologies makes up health
organizations. Turner (2003) argues that telemedicine creates a
virtual organization where health relationships change as interactions move from traditional face-to-face encounters to mediated

spaces (Figure 8.1). In their study of telemedicine communication between a university and a rural health facility, Whitten, Sypher, and Patterson (2000) found that participants perceived telemedicine as a dynamic form of organizing—providing patient access to healthcare, giving clinicians educational opportunities, offering opportunities for economic outcomes—rather than as just technological equipment and software.

Electronic Health Records

Electronic health records (EHRs) are computerized patient files that include a patient's vital health information generated by multiple health professionals working in different health institutions. EHRs provide clinicians at the point of service with data such as a patient's medical history, drug allergies, and existing conditions. Rather than relying on paperwork distributed among numerous caregivers and organizations, EHRs give immediate, up-to-date, and convergent information which can improve care continuity, safety, and efficiency (Brenner, 2006). Health organizations develop EHRs based on institutional needs and requirements. Minimum features typically include entry of clinical notes, prescriptions, test orders, and access to lab and imaging results.

Here's an example of how an EHR might be used in a medical encounter. Jordan, a 18-year-old student athlete, needs an annual physical exam in order to participate in high school sports and his physician's office uses an EHR system. Jordan's medical records are already entered into a computer when he arrives for his appointment. In the exam room, a physician assistant (PA) brings in a laptop and adds data that Jordan provides about changes in health status, medications, etc. The computer prompts the PA to ask Jordan questions to solicit more details about current conditions, medical history, and lifestyle issues which are also added to the record. The PA brings up X-rays and medical tests that Jordan received when he experienced a knee injury last year playing football. The two talk about his difficult recovery and the PA examines Jordan's knee again. The PA advises a renewed course of physical therapy from a clinician who works in the same health organization

Box 8.1   Ripped from the Headlines

Going Paperless at Kaiser Permanente
Electronic health records (EHRs) show great promise in contributing to more efficient, safer, and better quality healthcare. While many hospitals and other health organizations struggle to implement EHRs because of high start-up and maintenance costs, industry giants such as Kaiser Permanente (KP) are leading the way in adopting EHRs in medical offices and hospitals. As of 2010, each medical facility within the KP system was equipped with EHRs (Kaiser Permanente, 2010).

A *BusinessWeek* article (King, 2009) profiles the company's intensive efforts—involving billions of dollars and decades of work—to go paperless. The centerpiece of the program is Kasier Permanente HealthConnect, an EHR system that gives clinicians access to patient information and services needed for care delivery. HealthConnect has been credited with increasing communication and data sharing among care teams in ways that ultimately lead to better patient care. System features include bedside documentation, clinical decision support, and bar-coding for medication administration. Such EHR attributes reduce waste (e.g., reducing duplicate office visits and tests) and help clinicians make better treatment decisions.

Significant amounts of time, effort, and money have gone into achieving 100% adoption. KP owning all of its medical facilities and employing all physicians on salary are two favorable conditions that have helped the organization achieve this success. Thus, KP paid for all EHR costs and had the power to require physicians use it. The road to adoption has not been easy. Getting clinicians up to speed on the technology typically takes several weeks and facility installation needs about three months. Once the EHR system is in place, however, clinicians don't want to return to a paper-based approach.

The improvements extend beyond care teams and medical facilities to help KP members. In an online video accompanying the *BusinessWeek* story, KP chief information officer Phil Fasano explains that the member-accessible component of the EHR system directly connects members to their own health and well-being. Members log on to My Health Manager to perform activities such as scheduling appointments, emailing clinicians, viewing test results, and requesting prescription refills. Fasano argues that My Health Manager empowers patients to self-manage their health and also benefits clinician-patient communication.

KP's success provides compelling evidence for other health organizations to adopt EHRs. It is hoped that in the coming decades, EHRs will be a standard tool in the broad spectrum of e-health technologies used in health organizations.

Discussion Questions
1. What are your reactions to the KP story? Is their success possible at other health organizations? Explain your response.
2. How could EHRs improve the quality of work life for members of health organizations? How can this technology benefit patients?
3. What concerns might you have about the use of EHRs?

as the PA and who, as a result, has access to Jordan's EHR. This communication continuity allows the physical therapist to better understand and develop a therapy plan tailored to Jordan's needs.

EHRs can benefit health organizations in myriad ways, by improving communication continuity and efficiency in ways that ultimately increase care quality, producing $142 to $371 billion in efficiency and safety savings (Hillestad et al., 2005). However,

EHRs are not without problems, most notably lack of widespread adoption by health organizations and incompatibilities of EHR systems across institutions.

Email and Health Organization Websites

Email correspondence extends individual interactions to a mediated forum, transcending time and space to facilitate patient-patient, professional-professional, and patient-professional interactions. The store-and-forward capabilities of email allow users to retain sent messages for future use, save unfinished messages for further composition, and transmit information to others who may need data access and confirmation (e.g., setting up a telemedicine consultation between multiple clinicians and forwarding the message to the patient). Email's asynchronous quality enables communication without requiring that individuals be simultaneously present in the interaction, thus heightening communication and care continuity (Wright, Sparks, and O'Hair, 2008).

The usefulness of email depends on the degree to which it is adopted. Despite growing interest in alternatives to face-to-face clinical encounters, email contact between patients and health professionals remains limited, particularly with physicians (Houston et al., 2003). Professional-professional email is more prevalent in health organizations as individuals use the technology to communicate cheaply, quickly, and conveniently with peers. A study by Aspden, Katz, and Bemis (2001) demonstrates that increasing numbers of clinicians view email positively and value its contributions to their work.

Eighty percent of American internet users go online for health information and health organization websites rank among their top sources for information-seeking (Madden, 2006). The virtual presence of health organizations has profoundly influenced the ways in which people understand health and illness as well as engage in the health system. Rather than being passive recipients of health information and services, patients and consumers can use websites interactively in ways such as the following (Fox and Fallows, 2003):

- Research a diagnosis, treatment, or prescription
- Get advice from other health professionals and/or patients
- Give and receive social support
- Keep family and friends updated on a loved one's condition

Increasingly, managed care organizations are using their websites to provide patients and consumers with information not only about illness prevention but also education about their health plans and costs of healthcare. For instance, patients can go online to take health assessments and receive advice about lifestyle changes based on their assessment results, track benefit usage, and find answers to frequently asked questions about health insurance coverage.

Health professionals join patients and consumers in turning to health organization websites for their health information needs (Aspden, Katz, and Bemis, 2001). For instance, clinicians may use websites sponsored by medical research institutions and government agencies to keep up with current information about health conditions. Websites sponsored by large medical centers and teaching institutions can provide caregivers located in remote locations with access to consulting specialists as well as clinical data useful for diagnosis and treatment. In addition, health workers can search their employers' websites and/or intranets to learn more about benefits and services, network with professional associates, and participate in online education.

The e-health technologies described above provide patients, consumers, and health professionals with unprecedented access to health information in ways that have fundamentally transformed health organizations. Each form of technology has numerous communication advantages and disadvantages (Table 8.2). E-health attributes, both pro and con, influence health organizations' communication contexts, relationships, and processes.

E-health: Transforming Health Organizations

E-health has dramatically influenced and will continue to affect communication in health organizations. At an overarching, macro-level, e-health technologies change the organizational environment

Table 8.2   E-health Advantages and Disadvantages

Technology	Advantages	Disadvantages
Telemedicine	• Provides care to secluded and restricted patients and educates clinicians in remote areas. • Does not require real-time interactions; decreases scheduling problems. • Provides immediate and personal communication. • Multi-clinician contact bolsters professional collaboration.	• Inconsistent and/ or no interstate licensing, unclear legal liabilities, and variance in institutional credentialing of physicians. • Lack of reimbursement. • Multiple health professionals increase exposure of confidential patient records. • Limited knowledge and expertise among health professionals.
Email	• Asynchronous communication allows for give-and-take. • Connects people who might otherwise interact less often and/or less effectively. • Self-documenting communication.	• Concerns about excessive time and workload demands by clinicians, particularly physicians. • Lack of reimbursement for email consultations. • Concerns about patient privacy and confidentiality.
Health organization websites	• Unlimited access to health information at little or no cost to users. • Site interactivity facilitates user participation in health issues (e.g., assessments, decision-making). • Often chosen first for health information-seeking; adjunct to face-to-face conversations.	• Data overload for users leading to confusion and/or frustration. • Problems with sites' source credibility and data quality. • Lack of user knowledge about assessing quality of information (e.g., checking sources, timeliness of data).

Table 8.2 (continued)

Electronic health records	• Patient documentation is easier to access, manage, and transmit. • Information available at point of care. • Patient information maintained over time and across multiple organizations and caregivers.	• Lack of widespread adoption by health organizations. • Lack of support resources and technical training for users. • Concerns about patient record confidentiality and privacy due to security breaches.

(Adapted from the following sources: Fox, 2006; Hillestad et al., 2005; Houston et al., 2003; Matusitz and Breen, 2007, Maheu, Whitten, and Allen, 2001; Mechanic 2008; Weiner and Biondich, 2006)

in which health communication occurs. At the micro-level approach of individual and group interactions, technology alters the communication processes and relationships by which people develop and manage their interactions in health settings.

Changes in Communication Contexts

With the help of computers or wireless communication devices and web browsers, people can instantly use the internet to acquire an endless supply of data. This ready **access** has implications for communication in health organizations. First, navigating this ocean of information can be a daunting task, creating contexts in which patients, consumers, and even health professionals find it difficult to locate credible, accurate, and useful data (Fox and Fallows, 2003). Reputable health organization websites as well as members of trusted health organizations become important filters through which to help individuals better gather and interpret health information. For example, patients may bring internet printouts to medical visits and expect physicians to guide them through the information maze, and consumers return to familiar and credible websites that have been recommended by trusted clinicians.

Second, technological access heightens the demand for communication in health organizations to be timely, transparent, and accountable (Weiner and Biondich, 2006). Studies of telemedicine communication reveal that technology reduces wait time between clinician-clinician interactions as well as decreases the time it takes for patients to receive care by removing time and space constraints (see Turner, 2003). Electronic health records allow workers to access patient records and share the information with patients at point of service. Both EHRs and telemedicine allow users to view previously entered health information, thereby creating documentation that increases communication transparency (Mechanic, 2008). Alerts, reminders, and professional contacts listings build in redundancies that bolster accountability (Brenner, 2006).

The **interactive** nature of e-health has also altered the communication contexts of health organizations. Neuhauser and Kreps (2003) argue that health technologies extend people's ability to develop and manage their heath communication in structured ways, unrestricted by time and space. For instance, email allows members of health organizations to engage in dialogue with one another online, using a mediated forum to share information, make decisions, and collaborate. Clinicians increasingly use email to interact with patients and this communication has been found to save time during medical encounters, offer opportunities for patient education between visits, and increase patient satisfaction (Houston et al., 2003). Baur (2000) argues that health websites with interactive features (e.g., sites which host Q and A sessions between patients/consumers and clinicians) and email are important mediums for customized interpersonal communication. She encourages physicians and other healthcare professionals to use these technologies to develop positive relationships with professional associates and patients.

E-health interactivity is perhaps best exemplified by tailoring technology. Using mediums such as health websites, researchers and practitioners create and deliver messages to meet the specific needs of individual patients and consumers (Suggs, 2006). According to developers of the Michigan Tailoring System, one of the leaders in this technology, tailoring gathers information from participants related to particular health issues and creates messages designed to meet participant characteristics (University

Box 8.2   Communication in Practice

Using Email in Patient-Physician Interactions
Email is pervasive in health organizations, allowing users to transcend time and space constraints to access and share health information. Despite growing patient interest in email contact, the majority of physicians remain reluctant to interact with patients through this communication medium (Chang, 2008). Many reasons exist for their hesitance, including concerns about work overload, lack of reimbursement, and patient privacy. In addition, physicians may have little, if any, training about handling email communication with patients.

In *"Guidelines for the Clinical Use of Electronic Email with Patients,"* Kane and Sands (1998) provide advice on how physicians and other clinicians can use email to extend and enhance their communication with patients. These guidelines may also apply to clinician-clinician email, particularly in regards to patient care matters. Consider the following recommendations:

- Determine response time for messages and avoid email for urgent matters.
- Tell patients about privacy issues.
- Establish types of messages and sensitivity of content acceptable for email communication.
- Use the autoreply function to confirm receipt of messages and instruct patients to do the same. Send patients a new email to confirm completion of request.
- Use appropriate rules of professional etiquette. Avoid anger, sarcasm, etc.

of Michigan Center for Health Communications Research, 2008–2009). Based on participant responses, tailoring technology selects, tests, and delivers relevant messages in order to achieve an intended effect (e.g., adherence to treatment, cancer prevention behaviors). For example, members of a health insurance plan complete a health assessment on the plan's website. Their responses are filtered into a tailoring program's results and recommendations section to give specific feedback about their personal health. This specificity had been found to be more effective in achieving intended health outcomes than generic, one-size-fits-all messages, such as offering general guidelines on prominent health issues (Kreuter et al., 2000).

Changes in Communication Processes

E-health enhances **coordination** by making it easier and less time consuming for health professionals and patients to synchronize their communication as well as by improving reporting within and across institutions. EHRs and telemedicine are often-cited technologies that contribute to coordinated communication between health professionals (Pluyter-Wenting, 2002). EHRs link healthcare team members who may lack face-to-face contact because they work at different times and locations within the same institution. In addition, EHRs can improve coordination between health organizations because the technology allows medical information to accompany patients as they move from one place to another depending on their care needs. In a study of hospital patient handoffs and rounding, Van Eaton et al. (2005) found that EHRs enable physicians to coordinate their care activities in ways that ultimately heightened care continuity. Study participants reported quicker, more reliable transfer of information across shifts as well as more streamlined patient rounds because patient information was available in one centralized location.

Telemedicine communication creates virtual health organizations that consist of interorganizational and intraorganizational coordination. Technology has the potential to break down professional silos between health workers and facilitate interactions. For example, Bucher, Delledonne, and Kaczmarczyk (2009) found that use of home care telemonitoring—devices that connect the patient's vital signs to a central monitoring station—synchronized communication between nurses and physicians. Nurses were more likely to seek additional assessment and treatment recommendations when telemonitoring was used in patients' home care. In other studies, nurses reported that telemedicine and other e-health technologies enable them to coordinate care across the health continuum (Cashen et al., 2006; Wilkstrom, Cederborg, and Johanson, 2007).

E-health increases **participation** between health professionals, patients, and consumers (Harris, Dresser, and Kreps, 2004). E-health technologies enable patients and consumers to become more involved in their healthcare and personal well-being. Eysenbach (2008) argues that in the age of Medicine 2.0—an online phenomenon of health-related Wikis, personal health records, social networking platforms, blogs, and other participative internet applications—health professionals and their organizational employers will experience unprecedented levels of patient/consumer engagement and empowerment. These more recent e-health technologies, combined with established tools such as email and interactive health websites, provide patients and consumers with information and decision aids that can help them weigh the benefits and risks of alternative treatment options (Ball and Lillis, 2001). Further, participating in online communities such as support groups gives patients and consumers forums in which to develop supportive relationships that can ease the difficulties of illness and disease.

Participation mainly pertains to consumers and patients but also applies to collaborative communication between health professionals. It is generally agreed that e-health technologies promote professional collaboration by facilitating shared decision-making and keeping health workers informed and integrated. For example, Houston et al. (2003) found that physicians perceive email as an efficient tool for communicating with professional associates about matters such as laboratory results, questions about medical information, and advice on chronic medical problems. EHRs combine the collective efforts of multiple team members into one centralized location and provide structured feedback loops (e.g., guidelines, prompts, reminders, and cautions) that encourage professional give-and-take (Harris, Dresser, and Kreps, 2004). Such collaborative effects of e-health technology have been shown to improve patient care.

E-health also promotes collaboration between health professionals across institutions. Mechanic (2008) identifies health websites such as the Cochrane Collaboration "which allows thousands of physicians to collaborate in reviews that bring together and assess controlled clinical trials and other studies from around the world" (p. 339). Medical databases such as Medline and PubMed allow researchers and clinicians to explore health issues and identify research connections with others.

Changes in Communication Relationships

The final set of changes you will consider pertains to how e-health technologies contribute to transformations in communication relationships. Here, empowerment and control figure prominently in the research literature, especially in regard to physician communication.

Easy access and availability of health information through the internet **empowers** patients/consumers to take more active roles in their health and well-being (Roter and Hall, 2006). Rather than relying on health professionals for information about diagnosis, prognosis, treatment, and prevention, patients and consumers go online to become more fully informed and to share decision-making. Further, using knowledge from the internet (e.g., health websites, online communities, research databases), patients/consumers feel empowered to demand choices in treatment options, health facilities, and caregivers. Bylund et al. (2007) found that patients who bring internet information to medical encounters are less likely to depend on health professionals to make their care decisions and are more likely to be satisfied when clinicians seriously consider and validate their internet research. Patients who email with their clinicians and have the ability to access and directly input data into their EHRs are more apt to initiate health-related discussions and participate in decision-making during medical encounters (Weiner and Biondich, 2006).

The trend toward heightened empowerment extends beyond the patient-health professional relationship to relationships between professional associates. It is argued that e-health technologies bolster the roles of nurses and social workers, professionals who have historically lacked physicians' power and authority in health organizations. For instance, telemedicine enables home care nurses to span boundaries between physicians and patients and play a central role in relaying physician feedback in follow-up care (Mun and Turner, 1999). Separate studies in nursing also point to the importance of online education, social networking, online communities, and wireless devices as tools for promoting professionalism in ways that ultimately increase nurse empowerment in their interactions with physicians and others (Brooks and Scott, 2006; Thompson, 2005). Parrott and Madoc-Jones (2008) argue that e-health technologies empower social workers by giving them the ability to transcend time and space constraints to collect information directly from patients and make decisions from that data.

Control within health organization relationships has shifted due in part to the readily available and rapidly increasing amount of health information that patients, consumers, and health professionals can access. Patients are taking control of their health, or at least are playing a major role in it, and accessing, managing, and disseminating health information is no longer solely the domain of health professionals (Lowery and Anderson, 2006). Now more than ever, the public desires health partnerships—or at least less paternalistic relationships—with clinicians. Particularly for physicians, the clinical role is changing from one of authoritative disseminator of health information to the position of an expert who helps informed patients make sense of data and reach decisions. For example, a survey conducted by Lee (2008) indicates that people's use of the internet increases the frequency of their contact with health professionals and, once in the context of the clinical encounter, patients seek help in understanding and using their internet research. In the absence of physicians, e-health technology such as telemedicine alters the traditional medical hierarchy in ways that may heighten non-physician caregivers' control in treating and communicating with patients (Turner, 2003; Whitten, Sypher, and Patterson, 2000).

Table 8.3   E-health Transformations in Health
Organizations

Changes	Description
Communication context Openness	Technology increases users' ability to seek and access health information from a broad spectrum of health-related sources.
Interactivity	Technology extends people's ability to develop and manage their health communication, unrestricted by time and space.
Communication processes Coordination	Technology makes it easier and less time consuming for health professionals and patients to synchronize their communication; improves reporting within and across institutions.
Participation	Technology enables patients and consumers to become more involved in their health care and personal well-being; promotes collaboration between health professionals.
Communication relationships; Empowerment	Technology encourages patients/ consumers to take more active roles in their health and well-being; bolsters health professionals who have historically lacked power and authority.
Control	Technology helps patient/consumers take greater control; accessing, managing, and disseminating health information no longer exclusive to health professionals.

To summarize, e-health has introduced a new era of communication, contributing to changes in organizational contexts, processes, and relationships (Table 8.3). The communication demands are high as health professionals, patients, and consumers constantly obtain, analyze, and share complex information in an environment of technological transformation.

Technological transformations extend to the global arena as HCTs enable health organizations to span boundaries to reach patients, consumers, and health workers on an international scale. Information about new therapies, treatments, and knowledge sets conveyed by HCTs has the potential to change global health in numerous ways.

Health Communication Technologies and the Globalization of Public Health

Globalization is a multidimensional process encompassing economic, social, cultural, political, and technological components that figure in the cross-border flow of goods, services, capital, people, information, and ideas (Murphy, 2008). It defines much of the environment in which health is determined and experienced, affecting a range of regulatory, market, cultural, environmental, and communication factors. Table 8.4 identifies the major globalization elements and provides examples of their influence on global health.

Technology facilitates access to and dissemination of health information and services across economic, geographic, political, and cultural borders. Technological applications offer new opportunities for enhanced participation in health issues and health organizations. In turn, globalization has resulted in the heightened speed with which information about new treatments, innovations and strategies is diffused from health organizations to reach health professionals, patients, and consumers worldwide (Edejer, 2000). Below, you will explore global public health organizing as an exemplar of how the combined forces of globalization and HCTs are reshaping health communication internationally.

Global HCT Improvements

HCTs improve the ways in which global public health services can contribute to meeting the needs of those living in medically

Table 8.4   Globalization Elements and Effects on the
Global Health Environment

Elements	Description	Example
New global governance structures	Globalization affects mutual dependence among nations as well as nation-state control, leading to (a need for) novel governance structures.	Global regulations that determine whether a country has the right to ban imported products for health reasons.
Global markets	Globalization consists of international changes in economic infrastructures and the creation of global markets and trading systems.	Heightened use of outsourcing and offshore health services (e.g., tele-radiology, medical transcription).
Global communication and diffusion of information	Globalization facilitates the sharing of information and experiences about common problems.	Increasing demand for and use of online health information to train and educate clinicians and other health professionals.
Global mobility	Global mobility is characterized by a rise in the frequency, intensity, amount, and variety of movement between nations.	The migration of health workers across borders such as the growth in international medical graduates who work as physicians in the U.S.
Cross-cultural interaction	Globalization influences the flow of interactions between global and local cultural elements.	International partnerships among researchers working to solve shared public health problems (e.g., HIV/ AIDs).
Global environmental changes	Global environment factors threaten world ecosystems such as global climate change and global decline in natural resources.	Growing recognition that ecosystem functions are central to sustaining physical health and basic human needs (e.g., clean air, water, and soils).

(Adapted from Huynen, Martens, and Hilderink, 2005)

underserved and/or hard to reach areas. Technology has opened new mediums of communication that facilitate openness between isolated areas where health needs are considerable and health organizations, typically located in urban centers, where experts have the requisite knowledge (Cartwright, 2000). For healthcare delivery and illness prevention, HCTs enable patients, consumers, and others to share health information, gain advice, or advocate for improved treatment. For health activism and crisis communication, use of traditional mass media has been replaced, or at least significantly reduced, by technologies such as mobile phones, email, and the internet as key tools to communicate health messages.

The research literature reveals that HCTs benefit public health organizations' care delivery efforts by providing communication networks that connect various stakeholders who share common interests and needs. Cellular technology, particularly the use of short message system (SMS) text, is an effective healthcare intervention in developing countries as it is more cost effective than other communication technologies such as the internet (Lucas, 2008). Further, mobile phones have high social value among users (in resource-poor areas, many people share phones to have access) and health messages can be rolled out fairly quickly. Thus, public health organizations increasingly use text reminders and alerts to individual patients (e.g., follow-up care, prevention messages) as well as send tailored messages to people living in communities with specific health needs/risks. Abbott and Coenen (2008) describe how nurses and other health professionals working for Phones for Health, a public health program located in Sub-Saharan Africa, use mobile phones to relay health information from localities to a centralized database for use by authorities to track public health data. These authors also explain that in Asia and Africa, nurses located in rural areas use personal data assistants (PDAs) and mobile phones to receive continuing education and network informally with peers worldwide.

The access and connectivity provided by HCTs has promoted global health activism and improved public health organizations' crisis communication efforts. Dutta (2008) argues that the internet has created a discursive space for activist groups to communicate with one another and to mobilize themselves internationally (e.g., signing petitions, participating in rallies and protest demonstrations). Health activist organizations also use the online platform to organize across publics separated by geographic location and to voice criticism of health policies without depending on traditional media gatekeepers. Consider separate studies (Pillsbury and Mayer, 2005; DeSousza and Dutta, 2008) that profile the efforts of grassroots non-governmental organizations (NGOs) to use HCTs to assist people in Africa and India, respectively, to better communicate about health issues such as HIV/AIDs. Research findings showed that internet applications such as e-forums, internet cafes, and electronic news-letters enabled members of separate NGOs to develop solidarity around shared issues of concern while simultaneously retaining their unique organizational identities. Further, NGO members' online communication conveys news, provides social support, and encourages future political activism. These results suggest that HCTs help make it possible for nontraditional organizations to become part of worldwide health activism.

Finally, HCTs offer great promise to improve public health service response to global health crises. The role of technology in the 2003 severe acute respiratory syndrome (SARS) crisis is a good example. During the first cases of SARS in China in 2003, the World Health Organization (WHO) initiated a digital virtual environment consisting of 11 laboratories in 9 countries (Abbott and Coenen, 2008). Using email and a secure website, researchers shared outcomes of their analyses in real-time to collaboratively identify and intervene in a severe public health risk. Global communication, including the creation of several websites to dis-seminate SARS-related information widely and quickly, is credited with helping many public health institutions effectively coordinate response efforts during a rapidly changing health crisis. Due in part to efforts to better communicate across health organizations and with the public, SARS did not lead to the worldwide devasta-tion that had been feared during the initial stages of the outbreak (Smith, 2006).

Box 8.3   Communication in Practice

Putting Information in the Hands of Healers
Public health organizations are turning to health communication technologies (HCTs) in their efforts to reduce global health problems. Satellife, an international not-for-profit organization, is generally recognized as a pioneer in effectively using HCTs for transnational distance care (Cartwright, 2000; Lucas, 2008). Satellife focuses on linking healthcare workers in developing countries to medical literature, databases, consultants, and colleagues in Europe and America.

Using technologies such as personal data assistants (PDAs) and mobile phones, Satellife disseminates health information to and collects data from health personnel working in areas where electricity, telephone lines, books, and the internet are not readily available (Satellife, n.d.). Major initiatives include establishing a network of PDAs, using cellular technology and wireless access points for health management information systems in Uganda and Mozambique. The systems electronically capture data and deliver health content to workers in remote locales as well as provide email so that health workers can access recent information about relevant topics (e.g., HIV/AIDs, malaria). In addition, remote health facilities can use HCTs to collect, analyze, and use data to aid medical decision-making and resource allocation.

Satellife also reaches out to health workers who lack access to reliable and updated health information available through free services on their website. Here, health workers can read e-newsletters featuring data from scholarly journals, participate in global dialog with colleagues who share mutual health interests, and link to several hundred health/medical websites that provide content specific to issues facing low income and developing countries.

> Achieving improved global health remains a complex, ongoing challenge involving a host of social, cultural, economic, and political factors. While HCTs alone will not solve global health problems, these communication technologies offer public health organizations a range of proven means to distribute health information, coordinate health services, and mobilize people to participate in their health and healthcare (Edejer, 2000). Organizations such as Satellife are leading the way in bridging borders and making a positive difference in developing countries.

Global HCT Implementation Issues

Public health organizations face considerable challenges when using HCTs to improve global health, especially in developing countries that have enormous public health demands yet lack the resources necessary for technology implementation. According to the World Health Organization, a broad spectrum of issues contributes to poor levels of HCT adoption. These factors include but are not limited to cost, misalignment of incentives, community resistance, an unskilled public health workforce, concerns about impact on productivity, and lack of standards and interoperability (WHO, 2006).

The communication aspects of the digital divide—economic, political, social, and cultural disparities that have resulted in large segments of low income and/or medically underserved populations being excluded from health communication technologies—figures prominently in the research literature (Lucas, 2008). To be successful, remote and/or disadvantaged communities must not only have access to health technology, they must receive ongoing support in how to understand and use the information. Edejer (2000) notes that people in developing countries need health information specific to their needs and cultural context. Public health organizations, then, should recognize local communities' attitudes, beliefs, and rituals about health and healthcare and develop messages which reflect those perspectives. She further argues that information ought to be communicated in the languages of users and at appropriate levels of literacy. Kaplan's (2006) content analysis of research regarding mobile phone adoption in developing countries shows that messages of technological integration must be adapted to the needs of individual users as well as be culturally and socially appropriate within their wider communities.

Dzenowagis, Pleasant, and Kuruvilla's (2004) case study of the Health InterNetwork India project, a public health initiative led by the WHO, offers the following strategies to help public health organizations bridge the digital divide:

- **Enhance connectivity**: facilitate information access and use through HCTs by meeting the needs of the physical infrastructure and cultural context.
- **Improve content**: provide timely, relevant, and high-quality information to motivate patients, consumers, and public health workers to use the technologies.
- **Build capacity**: help public health staff members develop skills in HCT management and use through formal computer/internet literacy efforts and supporting informal networks.
- **Change policy**: identify areas for improvement and realign resources (e.g., provide training of health personnel rather than purchasing additional computer hardware).

To summarize, HCTs are rapidly becoming a reality in the everyday lives of patients, consumers, and health workers, in both developed and developing countries. HCTs and globalization go hand in hand, providing opportunities for greater distribution of health information, services, and products in an increasingly interconnected world. While HCTs are not a panacea for solving the complexities of global public health, these technologies offer promising avenues in which to better deliver curative and preventative medicine, promote health activism, and respond to health crises on an international scale.

Chapter Summary

This chapter explored the range of health communication technologies (HCTs) present in health organizations and how they have changed organizational communication. The rise of e-health and other HCTs alters interactions within and across health institutions, playing an important role in shaping the communication contexts, processes, and relationships that constitute health and healthcare delivery. The transformative effects of HCT extend to the global public health arena, increasing the speed with which information about new treatments, technologies, and strategies for health promotion can be disseminated. Further, use of technology provides public health organizations with new opportunities to promote participation and inclusion in health issues within remote locales and/or medically underserved populations. These technological applications represent important advancements in understanding and addressing the multifaceted problem of worldwide health.

References

Aarons, G. A. (2006). Transformational and transactional leadership: Association with attitudes towards evidence-based practice. *Psychiatric Services*, 57, 1162–9.

Abbott, P. A., and Coenen, A. (2008). Globalization and advances in information communication technologies: The impact on nursing and health. *Nursing Outlook*, 56, 238–46.

Abramson, J. (1993). Orienting social work employees in interdisciplinary settings: Shaping professional and organizational perspectives. *Social Work*, 38, 152–8.

Accreditation Council on Graduate Medical Education (ACGME) (2006). Introduction to competency-based residency education. Retrieved from http:www.acgme.org/outcome/e-learn powerpoint.asp

Agency for Healthcare Research and Quality (AHRQ) (2002). Fact sheet: Improving healthcare quality. Retrieved from http://www.ahrq.gov/news/qualfact.htm

Agency for Healthcare Research and Quality (AHRQ) (2007). Questions and answers about health insurance. Retrieved from http://www.ahrq.gov/consumer/insuranceqa

Agency for Healthcare Research and Quality (AHRQ) (2008). National healthcare quality report. Retrieved from http://www.ahrq.gov/qual/nhqr09/key.htm

Aiken, L. H., Clarke, S. P., Sloane, D. M., Lake, E. T., and Cheney, T. (2008). Effects of hospital care environment on patient mortality and nurse outcomes. *Journal of Nursing Administration*, 38, 223–9.

Aita, V., McIlvain, H., Backer, E., McVea, K., and Crabtree, B. (2005). Patient-centered care and communication in primary care practice: What is involved? *Patient Education and Counseling*, 58, 296–304.

Albrecht, T. L., and Adelman, M. B. (1987). Communicating social support: A theoretical perspective. In T. L. Albrecht and M. B. Adelman (eds), *Communicating social support*. Newbury Park, CA: Sage, pp. 18–39.

American Association of Colleges of Nursing (2008). *The essentials of baccalaureate education for professional nursing practice.* Washington DC: AACN.

American Association of Public Health (n.d.). What is public health? Retrieved from http://www.apha.org/NR/rdonlyres/80C2EDFC-15E5-4D63-A424-C7462F20F7D0/0/whatisPH.pdf

American Hospital Association (2009, April 13). Fast facts on US hospitals. Retrieved from http://www.aha.org

American Medical Association (2009). *Health care careers directory 2009–2010* (37th ed.). Chicago: American Medical Association.

American Medical Association–International Medical Graduate Section Governing Council (2010). International medical graduates in American medicine: Contemporary challenges and opportunities. Retrieved from http://www.ama-assn.org/ama1/pub/upload/mm/18/img-workforce-paper.pdf

Angermeier, I., Dunford, B. B., Boss, A. D., Boss, R. W., and Miller, J. A., Jr. (2009). The impact of participative management perceptions on customer service, medical errors, burnout and turnover intention. *Journal of Healthcare Management, 54,* 127–42.

Apker, J. (2001). Role development in the managed care era: A case of hospital-based nursing. *Journal of Applied Communication Research, 29,* 117–36.

Apker, J. (2002). Front-line nurse manager roles, job stressors, and coping strategies in a managed care hospital. *Qualitative Research Reports in Communication, 3,* 75–81.

Apker, J. (2004). Sensemaking of change in the managed care era: A case of hospital-based nurses. *Journal of Organizational Change Management, 17,* 211–27.

Apker, J., and Eggly, S. (2004). Communicating professional identity in medical socialization: Considering the ideological discourse of morning report. *Qualitative Health Research, 14,* 411–29.

Apker, J., Ford, W. S. Z., and Fox, D. H. (2003). Predicting nurses' organizational and professional identification: The effect of nursing roles, professional autonomy, and supportive communication. *Nursing Economics, 21,* 226–32.

Apker, J., and Fox, D. H. (2002). Communication: Improving RNs' organizational and professional identification in managed care hospitals. *Journal of Nursing Administration, 32,* 106–14.

Apker, J., Mallak, L. A., and Gibson, S. C. (2007). Communicating in the "gray zone:" Perceptions of emergency physician-hospitalist handoff communication and patient safety. *Academic Emergency Medicine*, 14, 884–994.

Apker, J., Propp, K. M., and Ford, W. S. Z. (2005). Negotiating status and identity tensions in healthcare team interactions: An exploration of nurse role dialectics. *Journal of Applied Communication Research*, 33, 93–115.

Apker, J., Propp, K. M., and Ford, W. S. Z. (2009). Investigating the effect of nurse-team communication on nurse turnover: Relationships among communication processes, identification, and intent to leave. *Health Communication*, 24, 106–14.

Apker, J., Propp, K. M., Wendy, S. Z. F., and Hofmeister, N. (2006). Collaboration, credibility, compassion, and coordination: Professional nurse communication skill sets in health care team interactions. *Journal of Professional Nursing*, 22, 180–9.

Apker, J., and Ray, E. B. (2003). Stress and social support in health care organizations. In T. L. Thompson, A. Dorsey, K. I. Miller and R. Parrott (eds), *Handbook of health communication*. Mahwah, NJ: Lawrence Erlbaum Associates, pp. 347–68.

Ashforth, B. E., Harrison, S. H., and Corley, K. G. (2008). Identification in organizations: An examination of four fundamental questions. *Journal of Management*, 34, 325–74.

Ashforth, B. E., and Tomiuk, M. A. (2000). Emotional labour and authenticity: Views from service agents. In S. Fineman (ed.), *Emotion in organizations* (2nd ed.). London: Sage, pp. 184–200.

Aspden, P., Katz, J. E., and Bemis, A. E. (2001). Use of the internet for professional purposes: A survey of New Jersey physicians. In J. E. Katz and R. E. Rice (eds), *The internet and health communication: Experiences and expectations*. Jossey-Bass: San Francisco, pp. 107–20.

Association of Schools of Public Health (2010). Frequently asked questions. Retrieved from http://www.asph.org/document.cfm?page=727

Atencio, B. L., Cohen, J., and Gorenberg, B. (2003). Nurse retention: Is it worth it? *Nursing Economics*, 21, 262–8.

Avolio, B. J., and Bass, B. M. (2002). *Developing potential across a full range of leadership*. Mahwah, NJ: Lawrence Erlbaum Associates.

Babrow, A. S. (2001). Uncertainty, value, communication, and problematic integration. *Journal of Communication*, 51, 553–73.

Baggs, J. G., Schmitt, M., Mushlin, A., Mitchell, P. H., Eldredge, D. H., Oaks, D., et al. (1999). Association between nurse-physician collaboration and patient outcomes in three intensive care units. *Critical Care Medicine*, 27, 1991–8.

Baker, C. M., McDaniel, A. M., Fredrickson, K. C., and Gallegos, E. C.

(2007). Empowerment among Latina nurses in Mexico, New York and Indiana. *International Nursing Review*, 54, 124–9.

Ball, M. J., and Lillis, J. (2001). E-health: Transforming the physician/patient relationship. *International Journal of Medical Informatics*, 61, 1–10.

Barbour, J. B., and Lammers, J. C. (2007). Health care institutions, medical organizing, and physicians: A multilevel analysis. *Management Communication Quarterly*, 21, 201–31.

Barley, S. R. (1990). The alignment of technology and structure through roles and networks *Administrative Science Quarterly*, 35, 61–103.

Baur, C. (2000). Limiting factors on the transformative powers of e-mail in patient-physician relationships: A critical analysis. *Health Communication*, 12, 239–59.

Baxter, L. A., and Montgomery, B. M. (1996). *Relating: Dialogues and dialectics*. New York: Guilford.

Baxter, L. A., and Montgomery, B. M. (1998). A guide to dialectical approaches to studying personal relationships. In B. M. Montgomery and L. A. Baxter (eds), *Dialectical approaches to studying personal relationships*. Mahwah, NJ: Erlbaum, pp. 1–16.

Bazzoli, G. J., Dynan, L., Burns, L. R., and Yap, C. (2004). Two decades of organizational change in health care: What have we learned? *Medical Care Research and Review*, 61, 247–331.

Becker, H. S., Greer, B., Strauss, A. L., and Hughes, E. C. (1961). *Boys in white: Student culture in medical school*. Chicago: University of Chicago Press.

Beitman, C. L., Johnson, J. L., Clark, A. L., Highsmith, S. R., Burgess, A. L., Minor, M. C., et al. (2004). Caregiver role strain of older workers. *Work*, 22, 99–106.

Berry, E. (2008, Feb. 25). Charting your patients' insurance: It's all in a simple grid. *American Medical News*. Retrieved from amanews.com

Berteotti, C., and Seibold, D. R. (1994). Coordination and role-definition problems in health-care teams: A hospice case study. In L. Frey (ed.), *Group communication in context: Studies of natural groups*. Hillsdale, NJ: Lawrence Erlbaum Associates, pp. 107–31.

Bess, K. D., Prilleltensky, I., Perkins, D. D., and Collins, L. V. (2009). Participatory organizational change in community-based health and human services: From tokenism to political engagement. *American Journal of Community Psychology*, 43, 134–48.

Blake, R., and Mouton, J. (1985). *The managerial grid III: The key to leadership excellence*. Houston, TX: Gulf.

Bonsteel, A. (1997). Behind the white coat. *The Humanist*, 57, 15–18.

Boswell, S., Lowry, L. W., and Wilhiot, K. (2004). New nurses' perceptions of nursing practice and quality patient care. *Journal of Nursing Care Quality*, 19, 76–81.

Bowles, C., and Candela, L. (2005). First job experiences of recent RN graduates. *Journal of Nursing Administration*, 35, 130–7.

Brach, C., and Fraser, I. (2000). Can cultural competency reduce racial and ethnic health disparities? A review and conceptual model. *Medical Care Research and Review*, 57, 181–217.

Brenner, R. J. (2006). To err is human, to correct divine: The emergence of technology-based communication systems. *Journal of the American College of Radiology*, 3, 340–5.

Bridges, W. (2003). *Managing transitions: Making the most of change* (2nd ed.). Cambridge, MA: Da Capo.

Brooks, F., and Scott, P. (2006). Exploring knowledge work and leadership in online midwifery communication. *Journal of Advanced Nursing*, 55, 510–20.

Brown, M. A., and Olshansky, E. (1998). Becoming a primary care nurse practitioner: Challenges of the initial year of practice. *The Nurse Practitioner*, 23, 46–66.

Brown, T. (2009, April 1). Good Grief, Nurse Brown. Retrieved from http://well.blogs.nytimes.com/2009/04/01/helping-nurses-cope-with-grief

Bucher, G. M., Delledonne, T. M., and Kaczmarczyk, L. (2009). Technology improves team communication and coordination of care in home health. *DNA Reporter*, 34, 6–7.

Bureau of Labor Statistics (2008). Occupational Outlook Handbook 2008–2009 Edition. Retrieved from http://www.bls.gov/oco/oco1006.htm#support

Bylund, C. L., Gueguen, J. A., Sabee, C. M., Imes, R. S., Li, Y., and Sandford, A. A. (2007). Provider-patient dialogue about internet health information: An exploration of strategies to improve the provider-patient relationship. *Patient Education and Counseling*, 66, 346–52.

Callan, V. J., Gallois, C., Mayhew, M. G., Grice, T. A., Tluchowska, M., and Boyce, R. (2007). Restructuring the multi-professional organization: Professional identity and adjustment to change in a public hospital. *Journal of Health and Human Services Administration*, 29, 448–77.

Callister, R. R., and Wall, J. A., Jr. (2001). Conflict across organizational boundaries: Managed care organizations versus health care providers. *Journal of Applied Psychology*, 86, 754–63.

Cartwright, L. (2000). Reach out and heal someone: Telemedicine and the globalization of health care. *Health*, 4, 347–77.

Casey, K., Fink, R., Krugman, M., and Propst, J. (2004). The graduate nurse experience. *Journal of Nursing Administration*, 34, 303–11.

Cashen, M. S., Bradley, V., Farrell, A., Murphy, J., Schleyer, R., Sensmeier, J., et al. (2006). Exploring the impact of health information technology on communication and collaboration in acute care nursing. *Studies in Health Technology*, 122, 575–9.

Cegala, D. J., and Broz, S. L. (2003). Provider and patient communication skills training. In T. L. Thompson, A. Dorsey, K. I. Miller and R. Parrott (eds), *Handbook of health communication*. Mahwah, NJ: Lawrence Erlbaum Associates, pp. 95–120.

Centers for Medicare and Medicaid Services (2008). National Health Expenditure Data. Retrieved from http://www.cms.hhs.gov/ NationalHealthExpendData/downloads/proj2008.pdf

Chang, A. (2008, April 22). It's LOL: Few US doctors answer e-mails from patients. *AP News*. Retrieved from http://www.thefreelibrary. com/_/print/PrintArticle.aspx?id=1611497507

Chaudry, J., Jain, A., McKenzie, S., and Schwartz, R. W. (2008). Physician leadership: The competencies of change. *Journal of Surgical Education*, 65, 213–20.

Cheney, G. (1983). On the various and changing meanings of organizational membership: A field study of organizational identification. *Communication Monographs*, 50, 342–62.

Cheney, G., and Christensen, L. T. (2001). Organizational identity: Linkages between internal and external communication. In F. M. Jablin and L. L. Putnam (eds), *The new handbook of organizational communication: Advances in theory, research and methods*. Thousand Oaks, CA: Sage, pp. 231–69.

Cheney, G., and Tompkins, P. K. (1987). Coming to terms with organizational identification and commitment. *Central States Journal*, 38, 1–15.

Chilcutt, A. S. (2009). Exploring leadership and team communication within the organizational environment of a dental practice. *Journal of the American Dental Association*, 140, 1252–8.

Chiles, A. M., and Zorn, T. E. (1995). Empowerment in organizations: Employees' perceptions of the influence on empowerment. *Journal of Applied Communication Research*, 23, 1–25.

Colón-Emeric, C. S., Ammarell, N., Bailey, B., Corazzini, K., Lekan-Rutledge, D., Piven, M. L., et al. (2006). Patterns of medical and nursing staff communication in nursing homes: Implications and insights from complexity science. *Qualitative Health Research*, 16, 173–88.

Comarow, A. (2003, July 28). Jessica's Story. *U.S. News and World Report*, 135, 51–4.

Conrad, P. (1988). Learning to doctor: reflections on recent accounts of the medical school years. *Journal of Health and Social Behavior*, 29, 323–32.

Cooper, L. A., Beach, M. C., Johnson, R. L., and Inui, T. (2006). Delving below the surface: Understanding how race and ethnicity influence relationships in health care. *Journal of General Internal Medicine*, 21, S21–S27.

Cox, T. (1994). *Multicultural organizations: Theory, research, and practice.* San Francisco: Berrett-Koehler Publishers.

Croasdale, M. (2006, April 24). Rewriting the hidden curriculum: Keeping empathy alive. *American Medical News*, 49, 9. Retrieved from http://www.ama-assn.org/amednews/2006/04/24/prsa0424.htm

Cross, T., Brazron, B., Dennis, K., and Isaacs, M. (1989). *Towards a culturally competent care* (Vol. 1). Washington DC: Georgetown University Child Development Center.

Davidhizar, R., and Dowd, S. (2001). How to get along with doctors and other health professionals. *Journal of Practical Nursing*, 51, 12–14.

de Castro, A. B., Agnew, J., and Fitzgerald, S. T. (2004). Emotional labor: Relevant theory for occupational health practice in post-industrial America. *American Association of Occupational Health Nursing Journal*, 52, 109–15.

Deetz, S. (2001). Conceptual foundations. In F. M. Jablin and L. L. Putnam (eds), *The new handbook of organizational communication: Advances in theory, research, and methods.* Thousand Oaks, CA: Sage, pp. 3–47.

DeLellis, A. J. (2006). Leadership for cross-cultural respect among health care personnel: An alternative approach. *Health Care Manager*, 25, 85–9.

DeSouza, R., and Dutta, M. J. (2008). Global and local networking for HIV/AIDS Prevention: The case of the Saathii E-forum. *Journal of Health Communication*, 13, 326–44.

DiPalma, C. (2004). Power at work: Navigating hierarchies, teamwork and webs. *Journal of Medical Humanities*, 25, 291–308.

DiSanza, J. R., and Bullis, C. (1999). "Everybody identifies with Smokey the Bear": Employee response to newsletter identification inducements at the U.S. Forest Service. *Management Communication Quarterly*, 12, 347–99.

Dorsey, J. L., and Berwick, D. M. (2008, February 27). Dirty words in healthcare. *Boston Globe*. Retrieved from http://www.boston. com/bostonglobe/editorial_opinion/oped/articles/2008/02/27/ dirty_words_in_healthcare

Dreachslin, J. L., Weech-Maldonado, R., and Dansky, K. H. (2004). Racial and ethnic diversity and organizational behavior: A focused research agenda for health services management. *Social Science and Medicine*, 59, 961–71.

Dukerich, J. M., Golden, B. R., and Shortell, S. M. (2002). Beauty is in the eye of the beholder: The impact of organizational identification, identity, and image on the cooperative behaviors of physicians. *Administrative Science Quarterly*, 47, 507–33.

Duncan, W. J., Ginter, P. M., Rucks, A. C., Wingate, M. S., and McCormick, L. C. (2007). Organizing emergency preparedness within United States public health departments. *Public Health*, 121, 241–50.

du Pre, A. (2005). *Communicating about health: Current issues and perspectives* (2nd ed.). New York: Mc-Graw Hill.

Dutta, M. J. (2008). *Communicating about health*. Cambridge, UK: Polity.

Dutton, J. E., Ashford, S. J., O'Neil, R. M., and Lawrence, K. A. (2001). Moves that matter: Issue selling and organizational change. *The Academy of Management Journal*, 44, 716–36.

Dysart-Gale, D. (2005). Communication models, professionalization, and the work of medical interpreters. *Health Communication*, 17, 91–103.

Dysart-Gale, D. (2007). Clinicians and medical interpreters: Negotiating culturally appropriate care for patients with limited English ability. *Family Community Health*, 30, 237–46.

Dzenowagis, J., Pleasant, A., and Kuruvilla, S. (2004). Bridging the digital divide: Lessons from the Health InterNetwork India. In P. Whitten and D. Cook (eds), *Understanding health communication technologies*. San Francisco: Jossey-Bass, pp. 337–46.

Edejer, T. T. (2000). Disseminating health information in developing countries: The role of the internet. *British Medical Journal*, 321, 797–800.

Edmondson, A. C. (2003). Speaking up in the operating room: How team leaders promote learning in interdisciplinary action teams. *Journal of Management Studies*, 40, 1419–52.

Eisenberg, E. M. (2006). *Strategic ambiguities: Essays on communication, organization, and identity*. Thousand Oaks, CA: Sage.

Eisenberg, E. M., Murphy, A. G., Sutcliffe, K., Wears, R., Schenkel, S., Perry, S. J., et al. (2005). Communication in emergency medicine:

Implications for patient safety. *Communication Monographs*, 72, 390–413.

Ellingson, L. L. (2003). Interdisciplinary health care teamwork in the clinic backstage. *Journal of Applied Communication Research*, 31, 93–117.

Ellingson, L. L. (2005). *Communicating in the clinic: Negotiating frontstage and backstage teamwork.* Cresskill, NJ: Hampton Press.

Ellingson, L. L. (2007). The performance of dialysis care: Routinization and adaptation on the floor. *Health Communication*, 22, 103–14.

Ellingson, L. L. (2008). Changing realities and entrenched norms in dialysis: A case study of power, knowledge, and communication in health-care delivery. In M. J. Dutta and H. M. Zoller (eds), *Emerging perspectives in health communication: Meaning, culture, and power.* New York: Routledge, pp. 293–312.

Ellis, B. H., and Miller, K. I. (1993). The role of assertiveness, personal control, and participation in the prediction of nurse burnout. *Journal of Applied Communication Research*, 21, 327–42.

Ellis, B. H., and Miller, K. I. (1994). Supportive communication among nurses: Effects on commitment, burnout, and retention. *Health Communication*, 6, 77–96.

Eng, T. R. (2001). *The eHealth landscape: A terrain map of emerging information and communication technologies in health and health care.* Princeton, NJ: The Robert Wood Johnson Foundation.

Engle, G. L. (1977). The need for a new medical model: A challenge for biomedicine. *Science*, 196, 129–36.

Epstein, R. M. (1999). Mindful practice. *JAMA*, 282, 833–9.

Epstein, R. M. (2003). Mindful practice in action (I): Technical competence, evidence-based medicine, and relationship-centered care. *Families, Systems, and Health*, 21, 1–9.

Epstein, R. M., Morse, D. S., Williams, G. C., leRoux, P., Suchman, A. L., and Quill, T. E. (2003). Clinical practice and the biopsychosocial approach. In R. M. Frankel, T. E. Quill and S. H. McDaniel (eds), *The biopsychosocial approach: Past, present, and future.* Rochester, NY: University of Rochester Press, pp. 33–66.

Epstein, R. M., and Street, R. L., Jr. (2007). Patient-centered communication in cancer care: Promoting healing and reducing suffering. Retrieved from http://outcomes.cancer.gov/areas/pcc/communication/monograph.html

Etheridge, S. A. (2007). Learning to think like a nurse: Stories from new nurse graduates. *Journal of Continuing Education in Nursing*, 38, 24–30.

ExploreHealthCareers.org (2009). Explore health careers. Retrieved from http://www.explorehealthcareers.org/en/Index.aspx

Eysenbach, G. (2008). Medicine 2.0: Social networking, collaboration, participation, apomediation, and openness. *Journal of Medical Internet Research*, 10. Retrieved from http://www.ncbi.nlm.nih.gov/pmc/articles/PMC2626430

Fahrenkopf, A. M., Sectish, T. C., Barger, L. K., Sharek, P. J., Lewin, D., Chiang, V. W., et al. (2008). Rates of medication errors among depressed and burnt out residents: Prospective cohort study. *British Medical Journal*, 335, 488–91.

Fewster-Thuente, L., and Velsor-Friedrich, B. (2008). Interdisciplinary collaboration for healthcare professionals. *Nursing Administration Quarterly*, 32, 40–8.

Figley, C. R. (1999). Compassion fatigue: Toward a new understanding of the costs of caring. In B. H. Stamm (ed.), *Secondary traumatic stress* (2nd ed.). Baltimore: Sidrian Press.

Foley, L., and Faircloth, C. A. (2003). Medicine as discursive resource: Legitimation in the work narratives of midwives. *Sociology of Health and Illness*, 25, 165–84.

Ford, L. A., and Ellis, B. H. (1998). A preliminary analysis of memorable messages and nonsupport messages received by nurses in acute care settings. *Health Communication*, 10, 37–63.

Foucault, M. (1973). *The birth of the clinic: An archeology of medical perception*. New York: Pantheon Books.

Foucault, M. (1980). *Power/knowledge: Selected interviews and other writings 1972–1977*. New York: Pantheon Books.

Fox, S. (2006, October). *Online health search 2006*. Washington DC: Pew Internet and American Life Project. Retrieved from http://www.pewinternet.org/Reports/2006/Online-Health-Search-2006.aspx

Fox, S., and Fallows, D. (2003). Internet health resources. Available from http://www.pewinternet.org

Frankel, A. S., Leonard, M. W., and Denham, C. R. (2006). Fair and just culture, team behavior, and leadership engagement: The tools to achieve high reliability. *Health Research and Educational Trust*, 41, 1690–1709.

Frankel, R. M., and Quill, T. (2005). Integrating biopsychosocial and relationship-centered care into mainstream medical practice: A challenge that continues to produce positive results. *Families, Systems, and Health*, 23, 413–21.

Freidson, E. (1975). *Doctoring together*. New York: Elsevier Scientific Publishing.

Freire, K., Davis, R., Umble, K., and Menkens, A. (2008). Creating public health teams that work. *Journal of Public Health Management and Practice*, 14, 76–9.

French J. R. P. Jr, and Raven, B. H. (1959). The bases of social power. In D. Cartwright (ed.), *Studies in social power*. Ann Arbor: University of Michigan Press, pp. 150–67.

Gawande, A. (2009). *The checklist manifesto*. New York: Metropolitan Books.

Geist, P., and Dreyer, J. (1993). The demise of dialogue: A critique of medical encounter ideology. *Western Journal of Communication*, 57, 233–46.

Geist, P., and Hardesty, M. (1992). *Negotiating the crisis: DRGs and the transformation of hospitals*. Mahwah, NJ: Lawrence Erlbaum Associates.

Geist-Martin, P., Ray, E. B., and Sharf, B. F. (2003). *Communicating health: Personal, cultural, and political complexities*. Belmont, CA: Wadsworth/Thomson Learning.

Gershon, R. R. M., Stone, P. W., Bakken, S., and Larson, E. (2004). Measurement of organizational culture and climate in healthcare. *Journal of Nursing Administration*, 34, 33–40.

Gittell, J. H. (2008). Relationships and resilience: Care provider responses to pressures from managed care. *Journal of Applied Behavioral Science*, 44, 25–47.

Goffman, E. (1959). *The presentation of self in everyday life*. Garden City, NY: Doubleday Anchor Books.

Goldberg, J. L. (2008). Humanism or professionalism? The white coat ceremony and medical education. *Academic Medicine*, 80, 715–22.

Goldsmith, S. B. (2005). *Principles of health care management: Compliance, consumerism, and accountability in the 21st Century*. Sudbury, MS: Jones and Barlett Publishers.

Graen, G. B. (1976). Role-making processes within complex organizations. In M. D. Dunnette (ed.), *Handbook of industrial and organizational psychology*. Chicago: Rand McNally, pp. 1201–45.

Graen, G. B., and Scandura, T. A. (1987). Toward a psychology of dyadic organizing. *Research in Organizational Behavior*, 9, 175–208.

Graham, S. L. (2009). Hospitalk: Politeness and hierarchical structures in interdisciplinary discharge rounds. *Journal of Politeness Research*, 5, 11–31.

Gresenz, C. R., Rogowski, J., and Escarce, J. J. (2007). Health care markets, the safety net, and utilization of care among the uninsured. *Health Research and Educational Trust*, 42 (1), 239–64.

Grumbach, K., and Bodenheimer, T. (2004). Can health care teams improve primary care practice? *JAMA*, 291, 1246–51.

Haas, J., and Shaffir, W. (1982). Taking on the role of doctor: A dramaturgical analysis of professionalization. *Symbolic Interaction*, 5, 187–203.

Hacker, J. S., and Marmor, T. R. (1999a). The misleading language of managed care. *Journal of Health Politics, Policy and Law*, 24, 1033–43.

Hacker, J. S., and Marmor, T. R. (1999b). How not to think about "managed care." *University of Michigan Journal of Law Reform*, 32, 661–84.

Haeuser, J., and Preston, J. (2006). Medical staff collaboration: Communication strategies that get results. *Healthcare Executive*, 21, 8–14.

Hafferty, F. W. (1988). Cadaver stories and the emotional socialization of medical students. *Journal of Health and Social Behavior*, 29, 344–56.

Hafferty, F. W. (1994). Beyond curriculum reform: Confronting medicine's hidden curriculum. *Academic Medicine*, 73, 403–7.

Hafferty, F. W., and Light, D. W. (1995). Professional dynamics and the changing nature of medical work. *Journal of Health and Social Behavior*, Extra issue, 132–53.

Halbesleben, J. R. B., and Rathert, C. (2008). Linking physician burnout and patient outcomes: Exploring the dyadic relationship between physicians and patients. *Health Care Review*, 33 (29), 29–39.

Harms, B. A., Heise, C. P., Gould, J. C., and Starling, J. R. (2005). A 25-year single institution analysis of health, practice, and fate of general surgeons. *Annals of Surgery*, 242, 520–29

Harris, L., Dresser, C., and Kreps, G. L. (2004). E-Health as dialogue: Communication and quality of cancer care. *AAII Fall Symposium*, FS-04–04, 50–7.

Harter, L. M., and Kirby, E. L. (2004). Socializing medical students in an era of managed care: The ideological significance of standardized and virtual patients. *Communication Studies*, 55, 48–67.

Harter, L. M., and Krone, K. J. (2001). Exploring the emergent identities of future physicians: Toward an understanding of the ideological socialization of osteopathic medical students. *Southern Journal of Communication*, 67, 66–83.

Hartmann, C. W., Meterko, M., Rosen, A. K., Zhao, S., Shokeen, P., Singer., S., et al. (2009). Relationship of hospital organizational culture to patient safety climate in the veterans health administration. *Medical Care Research and Review*, 66, 320–38.

Hayes, E. (2007). Embattled and embittered or empowered and evolving: Nurse practitioner attitudes toward managed care. *Journal of the American Academy of Nurse Practitioners, 19,* 143–51.

Hayhurst, A., Saylor, C., and Stuenkel, D. (2005). Work environmental factors and retention of nurses. *Nursing Care Quality, 20,* 283–8.

Health Resources and Services Administration (HRSA) (2006a). The registered nurse population: Findings from the March 2004 sample survey of registered nurses. Retrieved from ftp://ftp.hrsa.gov/bhpr/workforce/0306rnss.pdf

Health Resources and Services Administration (HRSA) (2006b). The rationale for diversity in the health professions: A review of the evidence. Retrieved from ftp://ftp.hrsa.gov/bhpr/workforce/diversity.pdf

Health Resources and Services Administration (HRSA) (2007, March). Burnout. *CareAction.* Retrieved from http://hab.hrsa.gov/publications/march2007/default.htm

Health Resources and Services Administration (HRSA) (2008a). The physician workforce: Projections and research into current issues affecting supply and demand. Retrieved from ftp://ftp.hrsa.gov/bhpr/workforce/physicianworkforce.pdf

Health Resources and Services Administration (HRSA) (2008b). The adequacy of pharmacist supply: 2004 to 2030. Retrieved from ftp://ftp.hrsa.gov/bhpr/workforce/pharmacy.pdf

Health Resources and Services Administration (HRSA) (2010). The registered nurse population: Initial findings from the 2008 national sample survey of registered nurses. Retrieved from http://bhpr.hrsa.gov/healthworkforce/rnsurvey/initialfindings2008.pdf

Helmreich, R. L., and Merritt, A. C. (2001). *Culture at work in aviation and medicine: National, organizational, and professional influences.* Hampshire, UK: Ashgate.

Hersey, P., and Blanchard, K. (1977). *Management of organizational behavior: Utilizing human resources* (3rd ed.). Englewood Cliffs, NJ: Prentice Hall.

Hillestad, R., Bigelow, J., Bower, A., Girosi, F., Meili, R., Scoville, R., et al. (2005). Can electronic medical record systems transform health care? Potential health benefits, savings, and costs. *Health Affairs, 24,* 1103–17.

Hirschmann, K. (1999). Blood, vomit, and communication: The days and nights of an intern on call. *Health Communication, 11,* 35–57.

Hochschild, A. R. (1983). *The managed heart: Commercialization of human feeling.* Berkeley, CA: University of California Press.

Hodges, H. F., Keeley, A. C., and Grier, E. C. (2005). Professional resilience, practice longevity, and Parse's theory for baccalaureate education. *Journal of Nursing Education, 44*, 548–54.

Hoff, T. J. (2000). Professional commitment among US physician executives in managed care. *Social Science and Medicine, 50*, 1433–44.

Hoff, T. J., and McCaffrey, D. P. (1996). Adapting, resisting, and negotiating: How physicians cope with organizational and economic change. *Work and Occupations, 23*, 165–89.

Houston, T. K., Sands, D. Z., Nash, B. R., and Ford, D. E. (2003). Experiences of physicians who frequently use e-mail with patients. *Health Communication, 15*, 515–25.

Hsieh, E. (2006a). Understanding medical interpreters: Reconceptualizing bilingual health communication. *Health Communication, 20*, 177–86.

Hsieh, E. (2006b). Conflict in how interpreters manage their roles in provider-patient interactions. *Social Science and Medicine, 62*, 721–30.

Hsieh, E. (2007). Interpreters as co-diagnosticians: Overlapping roles and services between providers and interpreters. *Social Science and Medicine, 64*, 924–37.

Hsieh, E. (2010). Provider-interpreter collaboration in bilingual health care: Competitions of control over interpreter-mediated interactions. *Patient Education and Counseling, 78*, 154–9.

Hughes, E. C. (1956). The making of a physician: A general statement of ideas and problems. *Human Organization, 14*, 21–5.

Huynen, M., Martens, P., and Hilderink, H. (2005). The health impacts of globalisation: A conceptual framework. *Globalization and Health, 1*. Retrieved from http://www.globalizationandhealth.com/content/1/1/14

Institute of Medicine (IOM) (2000). *To err is human: Building a safer health system.* Washington DC: National Academies Press.

Institute of Medicine (IOM) (2001). *Crossing the quality chasm: A new health system for the 21st century.* Washington, DC: National Academies Press.

Institute of Medicine (IOM) (2003a). *Who will keep the public healthy?: Educating public health professionals for the 21st century.* Washington DC: National Academies Press.

Institute of Medicine (IOM) (2003b). *Priority areas for national action: Transforming health care quality.* Washington DC: National Academies Press.

Institute of Medicine (IOM) (2004a). *In the nation's compelling interest: Ensuring diversity in the health-care workforce.* Washington DC: National Academies Press.

Institute of Medicine (IOM) (2004b). *Health literacy: A prescription to end confusion*. Washington DC: National Academies Press.

Institute of Medicine (IOM) (2006). *Hospital-based emergency medicine: At the breaking point*. Washington DC: National Academies Press.

Institute of Medicine (IOM) (2009). *America's uninsured crisis: Consequences for health and health care*. Washington, DC: National Academies Press.

Inui, T. (2003). *A flag in the wind: Educating for professionalism in medicine*. Washington DC: Association of American Medical Colleges.

Jablin, F. M. (1987). Organizational entry, assimilation, and exit. In F. M. Jablin, L. L. Putnam, K. H. Roberts and L. W. Porter (eds), *Handbook of organizational communication: An interdisciplinary perspective*. Newbury Park, CA: Sage, pp. 679–740.

Jablin, F. M. (2001). Organization entry, assimilation, and disengagement/exit. In F. M. Jablin and L. L. Putnam (eds), *The new handbook of organizational communication: Advances in theory, research, and methods*. Thousand Oaks, CA: Sage, pp. 732–818.

Jablin, F. M., and Miller, V. D. (1993). *Newcomer-supervisor role negotiation processes: A preliminary report of a longitudinal investigation*. Paper presented at the Speech Communication Association Annual Meeting, Miami, Fl.

Jablin, F. M., and Putnam, L. L. (2001). *The new handbook of organizational communication: Advances in theory, research, and methods*. Thousand Oaks, CA: Sage.

Jaskyte, K. (2005). The impact of organizational socialization tactics on role ambiguity and role conflict of newly hired social workers. *Administration in Social Work*, 29, 69–87.

Jaskyte, K., and Lee, M. (2009). Organizational commitment of social workers: An exploratory study. *Administration in Social Work*, 33, 227–41.

Jenkins, R., and Elliott, P. (2004). Stressors, burnout and social support: nurses in acute mental health settings. *Journal of Advanced Nursing*, 48, 622–31.

Jervis, L. L. (2002). Working in and around the "chain of command": Power relations among nursing staff in an urban nursing home. *Nursing Inquiry*, 9, 12–23.

Joint Commission on Accreditation of Healthcare Organizations (2005). Strategies to improve hand-off communication: Implementing a process to resolve strategies. *Joint Commission Perspectives on Patient Safety*, 5, 11.

Joint Commission on Accreditation of Healthcare Organizations (2008,

July 9). Behaviors that undermine a culture of safety. *Sentinel Event Alert*, 40. Retrieved from http://www.jointcommission.org/ SentinelEvents/SentinelEventAlert/sea_40.htm

Jonas, S., Goldsteen, R. L., and Goldsteen, K. (2007). *An introduction to the U.S. health care system* (6th ed.). New York: Springer Publishing.

Kahaleh, A., and Gaither, C. (2007). The effects of work setting on pharmacists' empowerment and organizational behaviors. *Research in Social and Administrative Pharmacy*, 3, 199–222.

Kahn, W. A. (1993). Caring for the caregivers: Patterns of organizational caregiving. *Administrative Science Quarterly*, 38, 539–63.

Kaiser Family Foundation (2009). Health care costs: a primer. Key information on health care costs and their impact. Retrieved from www.kff.org

Kaiser Permanente (2010, March 3). Kaiser Permanente complete electronic health record implementation. Retrieved from www.kp.org/newscenter

Kane, B., and Sands, D. Z. (1998). Guidelines for the clinical use of electronic mail with patients. *Journal of the American Medical Informatics Association*, 5, 104–11.

Kaplan, W. A. (2006). Can the ubiquitous power of mobile phones be used to improve health outcomes in developing countries? *Globalization and Health*, 2. Retrieved from http:www.globalizationandhealth.com/content/2/1/19

Katz, D., and Kahn, R. L. (1978). *The social psychology of organizations* (2nd ed.). New York: Wiley.

Katzenbach, J. R., and Smith, D. K. (1993). *The wisdom of teams: Creating the high-performance organization*. Boston: Harvard Business School Press.

Keeton, K., Fenner, D. E., Johnson, T. R., and Hayward, R. A. (2007). Predictors of physician career satisfaction, work-life balance, and burnout. *Obstetrics Gynecology*, 109, 949–55.

Keigher, S. M. (2000). Communication in the evolving world of case management. *Health and Social Work*, 25, 227–31.

Kelly, N. R., and Mathews, M. (2001). The transition to first position as nurse practitioner. *Journal of Nursing Education*, 40, 156–62.

Kennedy, B. R. (2005). Stress and burnout of nursing staff working with geriatric clients in long-term care. *Journal of Nursing Scholarship*, 37, 381–2.

Kennedy, H. P., and Lyndon, A. (2008). Tensions and teamwork in nursing and midwifery relationships. *Journal of Obstetric, Neonatal, and Gynecologic Nursing*, 37, 426–35.

Kennedy, T. J. T., and Lindgard, L. A. (2007). Questioning competence: A discourse analysis of attending physicians' use of questions to assess trainee competence. *Academic Medicine*, 82, S12–S15.

Kim, H., and Lee, S. Y. (2009). Supervisory communication, burnout, and turnover intention among social workers in health care settings. *Social Work in Health Care*, 48, 364–85.

King, R. (2009, April 7). How Kaiser Permanente went paperless. *BusinessWeek*. Retrieved from http://www.businessweek.com/technology/content/apr2009/tc2009047_562738.htm

Kreps, G. L., and Kunimoto, E. (1994). *Effective communication in multicultural health care settings*. Thousand Oaks, CA: Sage.

Kreuter, M., Farrell, D., Olevitch, L., and Brennen, L. (2000). *Tailoring health messages: Customizing communication with computer technology*. Mahwah, NJ: Lawrence Erlbaum Associates.

Kupperschmidt, B. R. (2006). Addressing multigenerational conflict: mutual respect and carefronting as strategy. *OJIN: The Online Journal of Issues in Nursing*, 11. Retrieved from www.nursingworld.org/ojin/topic30/tpc30_3.htm

Lacey, T. A., and Wright, B. (2009, November). Occupational employment projections to 2018. *Monthly Labor Review*, 82–123. Retrieved from http://www.bls.gov/opub/mlr/2009/11/art5full.pdf

Lammers, J. C., Barbour, J. B., and Duggan, A. P. (2003). Organizational forms of the provision of health care: An institutional perspective. In T. L. Thompson, A. Dorsey, K. I. Miller and R. Parrott (eds), *Handbook of health communication*. Mahwah, NJ: Lawrence Erlbaum Associates, pp. 319–46.

Lammers, J. C., and Duggan, A. P. (2002). Bringing the physician back in: Communication predictors of physicians' satisfaction with managed care. *Health Communication*, 14, 493–513.

Landry, B. J. L., Mahesh, S., and Hartman, S. J. (2005). The impact of the pervasive information age on healthcare organizations. *Journal of Health and Human Services Administration*, 27, 444–64.

Larson, G. S., and Pepper, G. L. (2003). Strategies for managing multiple organizational identifications: A case of competing identities. *Management Communication Quarterly*, 16, 528–57.

Laschinger, H. K. S., and Finegan, J. (2005). Empowering nurses for work engagement and health in hospital settings. *Journal of Nursing Administration*, 35, 439–49.

Layne, C. M., Hohenshil, T. H., and Singh, K. (2004). The relationship of occupational stress, psychological strain, and coping resources to the turnover intentions of rehabilitation counselors. *Rehabilitation Counseling Bulletin*, 48, 19–30.

Leach, L. S. (2005). Nurse executive transformational leadership and organizational commitment. *Journal of Nursing Administration*, 35, 228–37.

Ledlow, G. R., O'Hair, H. D., and Moore, S. (2003). Predictors of communication quality: The patient, provider, and nurse call center triad. *Health Communication*, 15, 431–55.

Lee, C. (2008). Does the internet displace health professionals? *Journal of Health Communication*, 13, 450–64.

Leicht, K. T., Fennell, M. L., and Witkowski, K. M. (1995). The effects of hospital characteristics and radical organizational change on the relative standing of health care professionals. *Journal of Health and Social Behavior*, 36, 151–67.

Levinson, W., Gorawara-Bhat, R., Duek, R., Egener, B., Kao, A., Kerr, C., et al. (1999). Resolving disagreements in the patient-physician relationship: Tools for improving communication in managed care. *JAMA*, 282, 1477–83.

Lewis, L. K. (1997). Users' individual communicative responses to intraorganizationally implemented innovations and other planned changes. *Management Communication Quarterly*, 10, 455–90.

Lewis, L. K. (2006). Employee perspectives on implementation communication as predictors of perceptions of success and resistance. *Western Journal of Communication*, 70, 23–46.

Lohr, K. M. (ed.). (1990). *Medicare: A strategy for quality assurance, vol. 1*. Washington DC: National Academies Press.

Longtermcareeducation.com (2007). Learn about the field. Retrieved from http://www.longtermcareeducation.com/learn_about_the_ field

Lowery, W., and Anderson, W. B. (2006). The impact of internet use on the public perception of physicians: A perspective from the sociology of physicians literature. *Health Communication*, 19, 125–31.

Lucas, H. (2008). Information and communications technology for future health systems in developing countries. *Social Science and Medicine*, 66, 2122–32.

Lupton, D. (1994). Toward the development of critical health communication praxis. *Health Communication*, 6, 55–67.

McCauley, K., and Irwin, R. S. (2006). Changing the work environment in ICUs to achieve patient-focused care: The time has come. *Chest*, 130, 1571–8.

McCue, J. D., and Beach, K. J. (1994). Communication barriers between attending physicians and residents. *Journal of General Internal Medicine*, 9, 158–61.

McGrail, K. A., Morse, D. S., Glessner, T., and Gardner, K. (2009). "What is found there:" Qualitative analysis of physician-nurse collaboration stories. *Journal of General Internal Medicine*, 24, 198–204.

McNeely, E. (2005). The consequences of job stress for nurses' health: Time for a check-up. *Nursing Outlook*, 53, 291–9.

Madden, M. (2006). Internet penetration and impact. Retrieved from http://www.pewinternet.org/PPF/r/182/report_display.asp

Mahar, M. (2006). *Money-driven medicine: The real reason healthcare costs so much.* New York: HarperCollins.

Maheu, M. M., Whitten, P., and Allen, A. (2001). *E-health, telehealth, and telemedicine: A guide to start-up and success.* San Francisco: Jossey-Bass.

Makary, M. A., Sexton, J. B., Freischlag, J. A., Holzmueller, C. G., Millman, E. A., Rowen, L., et al. (2006). Operating room teamwork among physicians and nurses: Teamwork in the eye of the beholder. *Journal of the American College of Surgeons*, 202, 746–52.

Management for Sciences for Health (n.d.). Culturally competent organizations. Retrieved from http//erc.msh.org

Management Sciences for Health (n.d.). The provider's guide to quality and culture: Culturally competent organizations. Retrieved from http://erc.msh.org/mainpage.cfm?file=9.1.htmandmodule=providera ndlanguage=English

Manion, J. (2005). *From management to leadership: Practical health care leaders* (2nd ed.). San Francisco: Jossey-Bass.

Manion, J., Lorimer, W., and Leander, W. J. (1996). *Team-based health care organizations: Blueprint for success.* Gaithersburg, MD: Aspen Publishers.

Manojlovich, M. (2007). Power and empowerment in nursing: Looking backward to inform the future. *Online Journal of Issues in Nursing*, 12. Retrieved from www.nursingworld.org/MainMenuCategories/ ANAMarketplace/ANAPeriodicals/OJIN/TableofContents/ Volume122007/No1Jan07/LookingBackwardtoInformtheFuture. aspx

Martin, W. F., and Keogh, T. J. (2004). Managing medical groups: 21st century challenges and the impact of physician leadership styles. *Journal of Medical Practice Management*, 20, 102–6.

Maslach, C., and Jackson, S. E. (1981). The measurement of experienced burnout. *Journal of Occupational Behavior*, 2, 99–113.

Maslach, C., and Leiter, M. P. (1997). *The truth about burnout: How organizations cause personal stress and what to do about it.* San Francisco: Jossey-Bass.

Matusitz, J., and Breen, G. (2007). Telemedicine: Its effects on health communication. *Health Communication,* 21, 73–83.

Matveev, A. V., and Nelson, P. E. (2004). Cross cultural communication competence and multicultural team performance. *International Journal of Cross Cultural Management,* 4, 253–70.

Mayer, G. G., and Villaire, M. (2007). *Health literacy in primary care: A clinician's guide.* New York: Springer Publishing Company.

Mechanic, D. (2001). The managed care backlash: Perceptions and rhetoric in health care policy and the potential for health care reform. *Milbank Quarterly,* 79, 35–54.

Mechanic, D. (2003). Physician discontent: Challenges and opportunities. *JAMA,* 290, 941–6.

Mechanic, D. (2008). Rethinking medical professionalism: The role of information technology and practice innovations. *Milbank Quarterly,* 86, 327–58.

Medved, C. E., Morrison, K., Dearing, J. W., Larson, S. E., Cline, G., and Brummens, B. H. J. M. (2001). Tensions in community health improvement initiatives: Communication and collaboration in a managed care environment. *Journal of Applied Communication Research,* 29, 137–52.

Meiners, E. B., and Miller, V. D. (2004). The effect of formality and relational tone on supervisor/subordinate negotiation episodes. *Western Journal of Communication,* 68, 302–21.

Meltzer, L. S., and Huckabay, L. M. (2004). Critical care nurses' perceptions of futile care and its effect on burnout. *American Journal of Critical Care,* 13, 202–8.

Menaker, R., and Bahn, R. S. (2008). How perceived physician leadership behavior affects physician satisfaction. *Mayo Clinic Proceedings,* 83, 983–8.

Meterko, M., Mohr, D. C., and Young, G. J. (2004). Teamwork culture and patient satisfaction in hospitals. *Medical Care,* 42, 492–8.

Michie, S., Miles, J., and Weinman, J. (2003). Patient-centeredness in chronic illness: What is it and does it matter? *Patient Education and Counseling,* 51, 197–206.

Miller, K. I. (2003). Organizational issues. In T. L. Thompson, A. Dorsey, K. I. Miller and R. Parrott (eds), *Handbook of health communication.* Mahwah, NJ: Lawrence Erlbaum Associates, pp. 315–17.

Miller, K. I. (2009). *Organizational communication: Approaches and processes* (5th ed.). Boston: Wadsworth Cengage Learning.

Miller, K. I., and Considine, J. R. (2009). Communication in the helping professions. *Handbook of applied communication research*. New York: Routledge, pp. 405–28.

Miller, K. I., Ellis, B. H., Zook, E. G., and Lyles, J. (1990). An integrated model of communication, stress, and burnout in the workplace. *Communication Research*, 17, 300–26.

Miller, K. I., Joseph, L., and Apker, J. (2000). Strategic ambiguity in the role development process. *Journal of Applied Communication Research*, 28, 193–214.

Miller, K. I., and Monge, P. R. (1985). Social information and employee anxiety about organizational change. *Human Communication Research*, 11, 365–86.

Miller, K. I., and Ryan, D. J. (2001). Communication in the age of managed care: Introduction to the special issue. *Journal of Applied Communication Research*, 29, 91–6.

Miller, K. I., Stiff, J., and Ellis, B. H. (1988). Communication and empathy as precursors to burnout among human service workers. *Communication Monographs*, 55, 250–65.

Miller, V. D., and Jablin, F. M. (1991). Information seeking during organizational entry: Influences, tactics, and a model of the process. *Academy of Management Review*, 16, 92–120.

Miller, V. D., Jablin, F. M., Casey, M. K., Lamphear-Van Horn, M., and Ethington, C. (1996). The maternity leave as a role negotiation process. *Journal of Managerial Issues*, 8, 286–309.

Mishler, E. G. (1984). *The discourse of medicine: Dialectics of medical interviews*. Norwood, NJ: Ablex.

Modaff, D. P., DeWine, S., and Butler, J. (2008). *Organizational communication: Foundations, challenges and misunderstandings* (2nd ed.). Boston: Pearson Education, Inc.

Montaño, D. (2009, July 20). Promoting health in the community: Special team works to make sure immigrants, minorities get care. *Milwaukee Journal Sentinel*, E1.

Montgomery, B. M., and Baxter, L. A. (1998). Dialogism and relational dialectics. In B. M. Montgomery and L. A. Baxter (eds), *Dialectical approaches to studying personal relationships*. Mahwah, NJ: Elrbaum, pp. 155–83.

Moore, S. D., and Thurston, J. (2007). Cultural competence and barriers to the delivery of healthcare. In K. B. Wright and S. D. Moore (eds), *Applied Health Communication*, New York: Hampton Press, pp. 105–24.

Morath, J. M., and Turnbull, J. E. (2005). *To do no harm: Ensuring patient safety in health organizations*. San Francisco: Jossey-Bass.

Morgan, J. M., and Krone, K. J. (2001). Bending the rules of "professional" display: emotional improvisation in caregiver performances. *Journal of Applied Behavioral Studies*, 39, 317–40.

Mumby, D. K. (1987). The political function of narrative in organizations. *Communication Monographs*, 54, 113–27.

Mun, S. K., and Turner, J. W. (1999). Telemedicine: Emerging e-machine. *Annual Review of Biomedical Engineering*, 1, 589–610.

Murphy, A. G., Eisenberg, E. M., Wears, R., and Perry, S. J. (2008). Contested streams of action: Power and deference in emergency medicine. In H. M. Zoller and M. J. Dutta (eds), *Emerging perspectives in health communication: meaning, culture, and power*. New York: Routledge, pp. 275–92.

Murphy, J. (2008). Globalization: Implications for information professionals. *Health Information and Library Journal*, 25, 62–8.

Myerson, D. E. (2000). If emotions were honoured: A cultural analysis. In S. Fineman (ed.), *Emotion in organizations* (2nd ed.). London: Sage, pp. 167–83.

National Association of Social Workers (n.d.). Code of ethics. Retrieved from http://www.naswdc.org/pubs/code/code.asp

National Association of Social Workers (n.d.). This could be you: The many faces of social work. Retrieved from http://www.youtube.com/watch?v=77UGDj48oHsandfeature=pyvandad=6129264812andkw=social%20work

National Center for Health Statistics (2008). *Health*. Retrieved from http://www.cdc.gov/nchs/data/hus/hus08.pdf

Neuhauser, L., and Kreps, G. L. (2003). Rethinking communication in the E-health era. *Journal of Health Psychology*, 8, 7–23.

Newton, B. W., Barber, L., Clardy, J., Cleveland, E., and O'Sullivan, P. (2008). Is there hardening of the heart during medical school? *Academic Medicine*, 83, 244–9.

Nicholson, N. (1984). A theory of work role transitions. *Administrative Science Quarterly*, 29, 172–91.

Niemeier, J. P., Burnett, D. M., and Whitaker, D. A. (2003). Cultural communication in the multidisciplinary rehabilitation setting: Are we falling short of meeting needs? *Archives of Physical Medicine and Rehabilitation*, 84, 1240–5.

Norbut, M. (2006, July 3). Imaging gatekeepers: Another thing to slow down doctors. *American Medical News*. Retrieved from amednews.com

Northouse, P. G. (2007). *Leadership theory and practice* (4th ed.). Thousand Oaks, CA: Sage.

Nosse, L. J., and Sagiv, L. (2005). Theory-based study of the basic values of 565 physical therapists. *Physical Therapy*, 85, 834–50.

O'Connell, P. (2004, April). How doctors manage managed care. *BusinessWeek*. Retrieved from http://www.msnbc.msn.com/id/4798087

Odwazny, R., Hasler, S., Abrams, R., and McNutt, R. (2005). Organizational and cultural changes for providing safe patient care. *Quality Management in Health Care*, 14, 132–43.

Office of Disease Prevention and Health Promotion (2003). Communicating health: Priorities and strategies for progress. Retrieved from http://odphp.osophs.dhhs.gov/projects/HealthComm

Office of Disease Prevention and Health Promotion (n.d.). Fact sheet: Health literacy basics. Retrieved from http://www.health.gov/communication/literacy/quickguide/factsbasic.htm

Office of Minority Health (2005). What is cultural competency? Retrieved from http://minorityhealth.hhs.gov/templates/browse.aspx?lvl=2andlvlid=11

Old MD Girl. (2009, December 9). How I learned to stop asking questions during medical school. Retrieved from http://oldmdgirl.blogspot.com

Papa, M. J., Daniels, T. D., and Spiker, B. K. (2008). *Organizational communication: Perspectives and trends*. Thousand Oaks, CA: Sage.

Park, K.-O., Wilson, M. G., and Lee, M. S. (2004). Effects of social support at work on depression and organizational productivity. *American Journal of Health Behavior*, 28, 444–55.

Parker, L. E., Kirchner, J. E., Bonner, L. M., Fickel, J. J., Ritchie, M. J., Simons, C. E., et al. (2009). Creating a quality-improvement dialogue: Utilizing knowledge from frontline staff, managers, and experts to foster health care quality improvement. *Qualitative Health Research*, 19, 229–42.

Parker, R. M., and Gazmararian, J. A. (2003). Health literacy: Essential for health communication. *Journal of Health Communication*, 8, 116–18.

Parker, R. M., Ratzan, S. C., and Lurie, N. (2003). Health literacy: A policy challenge for advancing high-quality health care. *Health Affairs*, 22, 147.

Parker, V. A. (2002). Connecting relational work and workgroup context in caregiving organizations. *Journal of Applied Behavioral Science*, 38, 276–97.

Parker-Oliver, D., Bronstein, L. R., and Kurzejeski, L. (2005). Examining variables related to successful collaboration on the hospice team. *Health and Social Work*, 30, 279–86.

Parrott, L., and Madoc-Jones, I. (2008). Reclaiming information and communication technologies for empowering social work practice. *Journal of Social Work*, 8, 181–97.

Pecukonis, E., Doyle, O., and Bliss, D. L. (2008). Reducing barriers to interprofessional training: Promoting interprofessional cultural competence. *Journal of Interprofessional Care*, 22, 417–28.

Perloff, R. M., Bonder, B., Ray, G. B., Ray, E. B., and Siminoff, L. A. (2006). Doctor-patient communication, cultural competence, and minority health: Theoretical and empirical perspectives. *American Behavioral Scientist*, 49, 835–52.

Pfefferle, S. G., and Weinberg, D. B. (2008). Certified nurse assistants making meaning of direct care. *Qualitative Health Research*, 18, 952–61.

Pillsbury, B., and Mayer, D. (2005). Women Connect! Strengthening communications to meet sexual and reproductive health challenges *Journal of Health Communication*, 10, 361–71.

Plsek, P. (2003, January). *Complexity and the adoption of innovation in health care*. Paper presented at the Accelerating Quality Improvement in Health Care Strategies to Speed the Diffusion of Evidence-Based Innovations Conference, Washington DC.

Pluyter-Wenting, E. S. P. (2002). Communication among health care professionals. In J. Mantas and A. Hasman (eds), *Textbook in health informatics: A nursing perspective*. Amsterdam: IOS Press, pp. 440–9.

Poole, M. S., and Real, K. (2003). Groups and teams in health care: Communication and effectiveness. In T. L. Thompson, A. Dorsey, K. I. Miller and R. Parrott (eds), *Handbook of health communication*. Mahwah, NJ: Lawrence Erlbaum Associates, pp. 369–402.

Poole, M. S., and van de Ven, A. H. (2004). Theories of organizational change and innovation process. In M. S. Poole and A. H. van de Ven (eds), *Handbook of organizational change and innovation*. Oxford: Oxford University Press, pp. 374–98.

Porter-O'Grady, T. (2010). Leadership for innovation: From knowledge creation to transforming health care. In T. Porter-O'Grady and K. Malloch (eds), *Innovation leadership: Creating the landscape of health care*. Sudbury, MA: Jones and Bartlett Publishers, pp. 1–28.

Porter-O'Grady, T., and Wilson, C. K. (1998). *The healthcare teambook*. St. Louis: Mosby.

Pratt, M. G., and Rafaeli, A. (1997). Organizational dress as a symbol of multilayered social identities. *Academy of Management Journal*, 40, 862–98.

Pratt, M. G., Rockmann, K. W., and Kauffman, J. B. (2006). Constructing professional identity: The role of work and identity learning cycles in the customization of identity among medical residents. *Academy of Management Journal*, 49, 235–62.

Preston, P. (2005). The power image: Strategies for acting and being powerful. *Journal of Healthcare Management*, 50, 222–5.

Propp, K. M., Apker, J., Wendy, S. Z. F., Wallace, N., Serbenski, M., and Hofmeister, N. (2010). Meeting the complex needs of the health care team: Identification of nurse team communication practices perceived to enhance patient outcomes. *Qualitative Health Research*, 20, 15–28.

Putnam, L., and Poole, M. S. (1987). Conflict and negotiation. In F. Jablin, L. Putnam, K. Roberts and L. Porter (eds), *Handbook of organizational communication*. Newbury Park, CA: Sage, pp. 549–99.

Rada, R. E., and Johnson-Leong, C. (2004). Stress, burnout, anxiety, and depression among dentists. *Journal of the American Dental Association*, 135, 788–94.

Radcliffe, C., and Lester, H. (2003). Perceived stress during undergraduate medical training: A qualitative study. *Medical Education*, 37, 32–8.

Raup, G. H. (2008). The impact of ED nurse manager leadership style on staff nurse turnover and patient satisfaction in academic health center hospitals. *Journal of Emergency Nursing*, 34, 403–9.

Ray, E. B. (1993). When the links become chains: Considering dysfunctions of supportive communication in the workplace. *Communication Monographs*, 60, 106–11.

Ray, E. B., and Donohew, L. (1990). Introduction: Systems perspectives on health communication. In E. B. Ray and L. Donohew (eds), *Communication and health: Systems and applications*. Hillsdale, NJ: Lawrence Erlbaum Associates, pp. 3–8.

Ray, E. B., and Miller, K. I. (1990). Communication in health organizations. In E. B. Ray and L. Donohew (eds), *Communication and health: Systems and applications*. Hillsdale, NJ: Lawrence Erlbaum Associates, pp. 92–107.

Ray, E. B., and Miller, K. I. (1994). Social support, home/work stress and burnout: Who can help? *Journal of Applied Behavioral Studies*, 30, 357–73.

Real, K., Bramson, R., and Poole, M. S. (2009). The symbolic and material nature of physician identity: Implications for physician-patient communication. *Health Communication*, 24, 575–87.

Reese, D. J., and Sontag, M. (2001). Successful interprofessional collaboration on the hospice team. *Health and Social Work*, 26, 167–74.

Rein, L. (2009, July 21). Hospitals tally their avoidable mistakes. *Washington Post*, HE01.

Rice, R. E. (2001). The internet and health communication: A framework of experiences. In R. E. Rice and J. E. Katz (eds), *The internet and health communication: Experiences and expectations.* Thousand Oaks, CA: Sage, pp. 5–46.

Rider, E. A., and Keefer, C. H. (2006). Communication skills competencies: definitions and a teaching toolbox. *Medical Education, 40,* 624–29.

Robbins, B., and Davidhizar, R. (2007). Transformational leadership in health care today. *The Health Care Manager, 26,* 234–9.

Roberts, V., and Perryman, M. M. (2007). Creating a culture for health care quality and safety. *The Health Care Manager, 26,* 155–8.

Rogers, A. E., Hwang, W.-T., Scott, L. D., Aiken, L. H., and Dinges, D. F. (2004). The working hours of hospital staff nurses and patient safety. *Health Affairs, 23,* 202–12.

Rosen, J., Mittal, V., Degenholz, H., Castle, N., Mulsant, B., Hulland, S., et al. (2006). Ability, incentives, and management feedback: Organizational change to reduce pressure ulcers in a nursing home. *Journal of the American Medical Directors Association, 7,* 141–6.

Rosenberg, E., Richard, C., Lussier, M., and Abdool, S. N. (2006). Intercultural communication competence in family medicine: Lessons from the field. *Patient Education and Counseling, 61,* 236–45.

Rosenstein, A. H. (2002). Nurse-physician relationships: Impact on nurse satisfaction and retention. *American Journal of Nursing, 102,* 26–34.

Rosenstein, A. H., and O'Daniel, M. (2005). Disruptive and clinical perceptions of behavior outcomes: Nurses and physicians. *Nursing Management, 36,* 18–29.

Roter, D. L., and Hall, J. A. (2006). *Doctors talking with patients/patients talking with doctors: Improving communication in medical visits* (2nd ed.). Westport, CT: Praeger.

Roter, D. L., Stewart, M., Putnam, S. M., Mack, L., Jr., Stiles, W., and Inui, T. S. (1997). Communication patterns of primary physicians. *JAMA, 277* (4), 350–6.

Rowitz, L. (2006). *Public health for the 21st century: The prepared leader.* Sudbury, MA: Jones and Bartlett.

Rudd, R. E., Comings, J. P., and Hyde, J. N. (2003). Leave no one behind: Improving health and risk communication through attention to literacy. *Journal of Health Communication, 8,* 104–15.

Rudd, R. E., Kaphingst, K., Colton, T., Gregoire, J., and Hyde, J. (2004).

Rewriting public health information in plain language. *Journal of Health Communication*, 9, 195–206.

Rundall, T. G., Davies, H. T. O., and Hodges, C. (2004). Doctor-manager relationships in the United States and the United Kingdom. *Journal of Healthcare Management*, 49, 251–70.

Runde, C. E., and Flanagan, T. A. (2008). *Building conflict competent teams*. San Francisco: Jossey-Bass.

Safran, D. G., Miller, W., and Beckman, H. (2006). Organizational dimensions of relationship-centered care. *Journal of General Internal Medicine*, 21, S9–S15.

Sanchez, R., and Malveaux, S. (2009, August 12). President Obama hands out Presidential Medal of Freedom. *CNN Newsroom*. Retrieved from http://www.lexisnexis.com.libproxy.library.wmich.edu/us/lnacademic/search/newssubmitForm.do

Sarangi, S. (2004). Editorial: Towards a communicative mentality in medical and healthcare practice. *Communication and Medicine*, 1, 1–11.

Satellife (n.d.). ICT for health: Empowering health workers to save lives. Retrieved from http://www.satellife.org

Scalise, D. (2006). Patient satisfaction and the new consumer. *Hospital and Health Networks*, 80, 57–61.

Schapira, L., Vargas, E., Hidalgo, R., Brier, M., Sanchez, L., Horbrecker, K., et al. (2008). Lost in translation: Integrating medical interpreters into the multidisciplinary team. *The Oncologist*, 13, 586–92.

Scheibel, D. (1996). Appropriating bodies: Organ(izing) ideology and cultural practice in medical school. *Journal of Applied Communication Research*, 24, 310–31.

Schein, E. H. (2004). *Organizational culture and leadership* (3rd ed.). San Francisco: Jossey-Bass.

Scott, C. R. (1997). Identification with multiple targets in a geographically dispersed organization. *Management Communication Quarterly*, 10, 491–522.

Scott, C. R., Corman, S. R., and Cheney, G. (1998). Development of a structurational model of identification in the organization. *Communication Theory*, 8, 298–336.

Scott-Cawiezell, J., Jones, K., Moore, L., and Vojir, C. (2005). Nursing home culture: A critical component in sustained improvement. *Journal of Nursing Care Quality*, 20, 341–8.

Scott-Findlay, S., and Estabrooks, C. A. (2006). Mapping the organizational culture research in nursing: A literature review. *Journal of Advanced Nursing*, 56, 498–513.

Shi, L., and Singh, D. A. (2000). *Delivering health care in America: A systems approach.* Gaithersburg, MD: Aspen.

Shirey, M. R. (2006). Stress and coping in nurse managers: Two decades of research. *Nursing Economics, 24,* 193–203; 211.

Shortell, S. M., Jones, R. H., Rademaker, A. W., Gillies, R. R., Dranove, D. S., Hughes, E. F. X., et al. (2000). Assessing the impact of total quality management and organizational culture on multiple outcomes of care for coronary artery bypass graft surgery patients. *Medical Care, 38,* 207–17.

Silversin, J., and Kornacki, M. J. (2003). Implementing change: From ideas to reality. *Family Practice Management, 10,* 57–62.

Smedley, B. D., Stith, A. Y., and Nelson, A. R. (eds). (2003). *Unequal treatment: Confronting racial and ethnic disparities in health care.* Washington DC: National Academies Press.

Smith, A. C., and Kleinman, S. (1989). Managing emotions in medical school: Students' contacts with the living and the dead. *Social Psychology Quarterly, 52,* 56–69.

Smith, M. R. (2007, December 15). Brain surgery errors rack up at prestigious R.I. hospital. *The Virginian-Pilot Edition,* A4.

Smith, R. D. (2006). Responding to global infectious disease outbreaks: Lessons from SARS on the role of risk perception, communication, and management. *Social Science and Medicine, 63,* 3113–23.

Solet, D. J., Norvell, J. M., Rutan, G. H., and Frankel, R. M. (2005). Lost in translation: Challenges and opportunities in physician-to-physician communication during patient handoffs. *Academic Medicine, 80,* 1094–9.

Spiegel, A. (2009, October 12). How the modern patient drives up health costs. *Morning Edition* Retrieved from http://www.npr.org/templates/story/story.php?storyId=113664923

Starr, P. (2004). Social transformation twenty years on. *Journal of Health Politics, Policy and Law, 29,* 1005–19.

Steiger, B. (2006). Survey results: doctors say morale is hurting. *Physician Executive, 32,* 6–15.

Stetler, C. B., McQueen, L., Demakis, J., and Mittman, B. S. (2008). An organizational framework and strategic implementation for system-level change to enhance research-based practice: QUERI Series. *Implementation Science.* Retrieved from http://www.implementationscience.com/content/3/1/30. doi:10.1186/1748-5908-3-30

Stogdill, R. M. (1948). Personal factors associated with leadership: A survey of the literature. *Journal of Psychology, 25,* 35–71.

Stogdill, R. M. (1974). *Handbook of leadership: A survey of theory and research*. New York: Free Press.

Suggs, L. S. (2006). A 10-year retrospective of research in new technologies for health communication. *Journal of Health Communication*, 11, 61–74.

Sultz, H. A., and Young, K. M. (2009). *Health Care USA: Understanding its organization and delivery* (6th ed.). Sudbury, MA: Jones and Bartlett Publishers.

Susan G. Komen for the Cure (2009, August 12). Ambassador Nancy G. Brinker receives Presidential Medal of Freedom. Retrieved from http://ww5.komen.org/KomenNewsArticle.aspx?id=6442451015

Susan G. Komen for the Cure (2008, February 8). Nancy G. Brinker delivers an inspiring message at the 2008 Affiliate Leadership Conference. Retrieved from http://ww5.komen.org/news/komenvideos.html

Taris, T. W. (2006). Is there a relationship between burnout and objective performance? A critical review of 16 studies. *Work and Stress*, 20, 316–34.

Taylor, S. L., and Lurie, N. (2004). The role of culturally competent communication in reducing ethnic and racial healthcare disparities. *American Journal of Managed Care*, 10, SP1–SP4.

Thompson, B. W. (2005). The transformative effect of handheld computers on nursing practice. *Nursing Administration Quarterly*, 4, 308–14.

Thomson, S. (2007). Nurse-physician collaboration: Comparison of attitudes of nurses and physicians in the medical-surgical patient care setting. *MEDSURG Nursing*, 16, 87–104.

Timmerman, C. E. (2003). Media selection during the implementation of planned organizational change: A predictive framework based on implementation approach and phase. *Management Communication Quarterly*, 16, 301–40.

Tracy, S. J., Myers, K. K., and Scott, C. W. (2006). Cracking jokes and crafting selves: Sensemaking and identity management among human service workers. *Communication Monographs*, 73, 283–308.

Turner, J. W. (2003). Telemedicine: Expanding health care into virtual environments. In T. L. Thompson, A. Dorsey, K. I. Miller, and R. Parrott (eds), *Handbook of health communication*. Mahwah, NJ: Lawrence Erlbaum Associates, pp. 515–36.

Ulrey, K. L., and Amason, P. (2001). Intercultural communication between patients and health care providers: An exploration of intercultural communication effectiveness, cultural sensitivity, stress, and anxiety. *Health Communication*, 13, 449–63.

University of Michigan Center for Health Communication Research (2008–2009). The Michigan tailoring system. Retrieved from http://chcr.umich.edu/mts/index.php

University of Michigan Health System Program for Multicultural Health (n.d.). Cultural competency: Approaches for cross-cultural relationships. Retrieved from http://www.med.umich.edu/multicultural/ccp/approaches.htm#clinicians

U.S. Census Bureau (2008, August 14). An older and more diverse nation by midcentury. Retrieved from http://www.census.gov/Press-Release/www/releases/archives/population/012496.html

U.S. News and World Report (2009, May 26). Healthcare costs rising for average family of four. Retrieved from http://www.usnews.com/articles/opinion/2009/05/26/healthcare-costs-rising-for-average-family-of-four.html

Valdes-Pierce, C. (2004). New kid on the block: Mentoring and networking as survival strategies for novice NPs. *Advance for Nurse Practitioners*, 12, 45–7.

van de Ven, A. H., and Poole, M. S. (1995). Explaining development and change in organizations. *The Academy of Management Review*, 20, 510–40.

Van Eaton, E. G., Horvath, K. D., Lober, W. B., Rossini, A., and Pellegrini, C. A. (2005). A randomized, controlled trial evaluating the impact of a computerized rounding and sign-out system on continuity of care and resident work hours. *Journal of American College of Surgeons*, 200, 538–45.

Van Maanen, J., and Schein, E. H. (1979). Toward a theory of organizational socialization. In B. M. Staw (ed.), *Research in organizational behavior*, Vol. 1. Greenwich, CT: JAI Press, pp. 209–64.

Vina, E. R., Rhew, D. C., Weingarten, S. R., Weingarten, J. B., and Chang, J. T. (2009). Relationship between organizational factors and performance among pay-for-performance hospitals. *Journal of General Internal Medicine*, 24, 833–40.

von Bertalanffy, L. (1968). *General systems theory*. New York: Braziller.

Wade, D. T., and Halligan, P. W. (2004). Do biomedical models of illness make for good healthcare systems? *British Medical Journal*, 329, 1398–1401.

Waitzkin, H. (1979). Medicine, superstructure and micropolitics. *Social Science and Medicine*, 13, 601–9.

Waitzkin, H. (1991). *The politics of medical encounters: How patients and doctors deal with social problems*. New Haven: Yale University Press.

Wechsler, M. (2008, May). Bringing communication together. *Healthcare Informatics*, 56–8.

Weick, K. E. (1979). *The social psychology of organizing* (2nd ed.). Reading. MA: Addison-Wesley.

Weiner, M., and Biondich, P. (2006). The influence of information technology on patient-physician relationships. *Journal of General Internal Medicine*, 21, S35–S39.

West, C. P., Huschka, M. M., Novotney, P. J., Sloan, J. A., Kolars, J. C., Habermann, T. M., et al. (2006). Association of perceived medical errors with resident distress and empathy: A prospective longitudinal study. *JAMA*, 296, 1071–8.

West, M., Borrill, C., Dawson, J., Brodbeck, F., Shapiro, D., and Haward, B. (2003). Leadership clarity and team innovation in health care. *Leadership Quarterly*, 14, 393–410.

Whatispublichealth.org (n.d.). Pursue a career in public health. Retrieved from www.whatispublichealth.org/careers/careers.html

Wheaton, B. (1985). Models of stress – buffering functions of coping resources. *Journal of Health and Social Behavior*, 26, 352–64.

Whitten, P., Sypher, B. D., and Patterson, J. D. (2000). Transcending the technology of telemedicine: An analysis of telemedicine in North Carolina. *Health Communication*, 12, 109–35.

Wilkstrom, A. C., Cederborg, A. C., and Johanson, M. (2007). Meaning of technology in an intensive care unit: An interview study. *Intensive and Critical Care Nursing*, 23, 187–97.

Wolff, M., Young, S., Beck, B., and Maurana, C. A. (2004). Leadership in a public housing community. *Journal of Health Communication*, 9, 119–26.

Woodside, J. R., Miller, M. N., Flyod, M. R., McGowen, K. R., and Pfortmiller, D. T. (2008). Observations on burnout in family medicine and psychiatry residents. *Academic Psychiatry*, 32, 13–19.

World Health Organization (WHO) (2006). World health report 2006: Working together for health. Retrieved from http://www.who.int/whr/2006/en

Wright, K. B., Sparks, L., and O'Hair, H. D. (2008). *Health communication in the 21st century*. Malden, MA: Blackwell Publishing.

Xirasagar, S., Samuels, M. E., and Stoskopf, C. H. (2005). Physician leadership styles and effectiveness: An empirical study. *Medical Care Research and Review*, 62, 720–40.

Yun, S., Faraj, S., Xiao, Y., and Sims, H. P. (2003). Team leadership and coordination in trauma resuscitation. In M. M. Beyerlein, D. A.

Johnson and S. T. Beyerlein (eds), *Team-based organizing*. Oxford, UK: Elsevier Science, pp. 189–214.

Zager, L. R., and Walker, E. C. (2005). One vision, one voice transforming caregiving in nursing. *Orthopaedic Nursing*, 24, 130–3.

Zorn, T. E., and Gregory, K. W. (2005). Learning the ropes together: Assimilation and friendship development among first-year male medical students. *Health Communication*, 17, 211–31.

Index